Engulfed

Engulfed

The Death of
Paramount Pictures
and the Birth of
Corporate Hollywood

BERNARD F. DICK

THE UNIVERSITY PRESS OF KENTUCKY

Publication of this volume was made possible in part by a grant
from the National Endowment for the Humanities.

Editorial and Sales Offices: The University Press of Kentucky
663 South Limestone Street, Lexington, Kentucky 40508–4008

05 04 03 02 01   5 4 3 2 1

Library of Congress Cataloging-in-Publication Data

Dick, Bernard F.
  Engulfed: the death of Paramount Pictures and the birth of
  corporate Hollywood / Bernard F. Dick.
       p. cm.
    Includes bibliographical references and index.
    ISBN 0-8131-2202-3 (cloth : acid-free paper)
    1. Paramount Pictures Corporation–History. 2. Title.
PN1999.P3 D53 2001
384'.8'06579494   00012276

This book is printed on acid-free recycled paper meeting
the requirements of the American National Standard
for Permanence in Paper for Printed Library Materials.

Manufactured in the United States of America.

Contents

Photo insert follows page 118

For Katherine

Preface

In Mel Brooks's *Silent Movie* (1977), Sid Caesar nearly has a heart attack when he learns that a megaconglomerate called "Engulf and Devour" has designs on his little studio. Insiders would have associated "Engulf and Devour" with Gulf + Western, the corporate octopus that entangled Paramount Pictures in 1966 and added one more tentacle to the creature that Charles Bluhdorn, "the mad Austrian," had constructed out of auto replacement parts in the 1950s. By the time *Silent Movie* was released, Gulf + Western had acquired other appendages such as sugar, beef, fruit, metals, natural gas, paper, and cigars. Why, then, not a movie studio, especially since Paramount was in jeopardy, having become a gerontocracy where the average age of the board members was seventy and its president, Adolph Zukor, was pushing ninety?

Once Paramount was one of Hollywood's most venerable studios. It was the studio that made *Wings* (1929), the first Academy Award winner for Best Picture. In the 1920s, it was the studio of Cecil B. DeMille, who combined sex, sand, America, and God in a formula that paid off at the box office; it was the home of matinee idols (Ricardo Cortez, Rudolph Valentino, Ronald Colman) and love goddesses (Gloria Swanson, vamp Nita Naldi, and the "It Girl," Clara Bow). In the 1930s, it was Mae West's reduction of the double entendre to a level where only one meaning was possible that led to the enforcement of the Production Code. During the Golden Age of Radio, Paramount provided the faces that went with the voices coming over the air by featuring such radio personalities as Jack Benny, Fred Allen, George Burns and Gracie Allen, and Bob Hope in the "Big Broadcast" movies of the 1930s.

The 1940s were the decade of Preston Sturges's screwball comedies, the Bing Crosby–Bob Hope–Dorothy Lamour "Road" series, Paramount's film noir debut with Billy Wilder's *Double Indemnity* (1944), and an atypical foray into social realism with Wilder's *The Lost Weekend* (1945). At the end of the decade, Dean Martin and Jerry Lewis joined the Paramount family, as did Elvis Presley in the mid-fifties.

As the 1950s were coming to an end, so was the studio system. One by one, the studios fell to conglomerates, starting with Universal in 1962. Four years later, it was Paramount's turn.

Engulfed is not intended as a history of Paramount Pictures; a complete history would have to be in two volumes: volume 1, the studio; volume 2, the subsidiary. However, it is impossible to write about the death of a studio without first describing its birth. Thus, I have devoted the first chapter to an account of Paramount's formation in an attempt to show how the studio evolved and how it became identified with a particular kind of film—comedy with an operettalike quality, frequently interspersed with musical numbers, so that the result was not musical comedy but comedy with music. To see Paramount in its glory days is to see a true studio in operation; to see it as the sun was about to set on the star-spangled mountain that was Paramount's proud logo is to see a studio about to expire.

I am privileged to have been the first to use the George Weltner Collection at the University of Wyoming's American Heritage Center. I have worked with archival materials in the past, but this collection of the memos and letters of George Weltner, Paramount's last president before the Gulf + Western takeover, is the most revealing I have ever seen. Weltner may not have known it, but he was documenting the end of a studio as well as the end of an era. Since the collection is not accessible to many readers, I have cited specific memos I thought were especially pertinent. Biographical information, unless otherwise indicated, derives from the incredibly complete files of the Center for Motion Picture Study (CMPS) in Los Angeles.

Unlike Blanche du Bois, I have never depended on the kindness of strangers, only of friends. I have also been fortunate to be able to draw on the knowledge, and in some cases, patience, of others: Kristine Krueger of the National Film Information Service (NFIS); the entire CMPS staff, especially Barbara Hall and Sandra Archer; my wife and partner in research, Dr. Katherine M. Restaino; Fairleigh Dickinson University reference librarians Judy Katz and Laila Rogers; and Peter Bart, editor-in-chief of *Variety*; also Bill Mechanic; Martin Nocente; Dr. James Pegolotti; Henry Seggerman; the late "Buddy" Silberman; American Heritage Center archivist Matt Sprinkle; and, finally, Dr. Jack Weltner, who had the foresight to make the fruit of his father's experience available to others.

1

Mountain Glory

It is a truism to call the American motion picture industry the creation of Central and Eastern European immigrants and their sons. For the most part, the statement is correct, but it fails to acknowledge the contributions of Nebraska-born Darryl F. Zanuck, the creative force behind Twentieth Century–Fox, and the quartet that founded United Artists: Charlie Chaplin, Mary Pickford, D.W. Griffith, and Douglas Fairbanks, who hailed, respectively, from England, Canada, Kentucky, and Colorado. It might be more accurate to call Hollywood the creation of former glove cutters, store managers, fish peddlers, jewelers, junk dealers, furriers, vaudeville performers, arcade owners, and pulp writers.

There was a time when there were no departments of cinema studies where students could specialize in any of the fields comprising the art of moviemaking. At the turn of the century, movies were the equivalent of internet service providers—first, with the East Coast as Silicon Valley, then the West, and now anywhere. Others provided the technology; the entrepreneurs provided the vision and money. *Carpe diem* was the philosophy, even of those whose knowledge of Latin was limited to Roman numerals. But if they knew Latin, they might have amended the phrase to read, *Carpe rem:* Seize the thing at hand, or, more prosaically, "Go for it."

And that is what Adolph Zukor did, not knowing when he emigrated from Hungary in 1888 that he was destined to found a company that would undergo a number of permutations until it became a studio whose name resonates throughout film history: Paramount Pictures.

Adolph Zukor was born on 7 January 1873 in Risce, a village in Hungary's wine-growing district.[1] Like so many future studio heads, Zukor came from origins that almost discouraged greatness. His father, Jacob, was a storekeeper; his mother, Hannah, a rabbi's daughter. Jacob Zukor died from blood poisoning a year after Adolph was born. Although Hannah remarried, she never recovered from her first husband's death. Her own occurred seven years after his. Adolph was then eight.

Although Adolph had siblings and relatives who rallied when he decided to emigrate to America in 1888, he grew up thinking of himself as an orphan. That was certainly how he was treated. During his apprenticeship to a storekeeper, Adolph read dime novels that mythicized the American West and encouraged rags-to-riches thinking. At fifteen, he took a hard look at himself. He would never be a scholar like his brother Arthur. And in Risce, what future was there for a five-foot, four-inch, hundred–pound clerk except to follow in his father's footsteps and perhaps experience a similar fate?

Adolph was determined to emigrate. The problem was his age. As a minor and, legally, an orphan, he persuaded his uncle to intercede for him with the Orphans Bureau so that he could draw on his parents' estate to pay for his passage. With the consent of the Orphans Bureau, the fifteen-year-old Adolph left Risce in autumn 1888 with forty dollars in American currency sewn into the lining of his vest.

When Adolph arrived in New York, he was fit only for apprenticing. First, it was for an upholsterer at two dollars a week. Realizing he was too slight of build for such work, Adolph switched to fur, where apprentices were getting four dollars a week. When his friend, fellow-Hungarian Max Shosberg, decided to leave New York for Chicago, where the fur business was just starting up, Adolph, then nineteen, also headed west— not so much because he was interested in building up the Chicago fur trade as he was in attending the 1893 World's Columbian Exhibition there.

If Adolph Zukor's entry into the film business had been told Hollywood-style, it would have started with a close-up of a wide-eyed youth plunking down his nickel to enter Eadweard Muybridge's Zoopraxographical Hall at the exhibition. There he would have seen a host of moving images, including racehorses galloping along the track. The young man would have found the projection primitive: the pictures were mounted on a rotating disc, while another disc—this one with slots—revolved in the opposite direction. Regardless, he would have experienced an epiphany: MOVING PICTURES! But the truth is that the "jerky pictures of animal movements"[2] left young Zukor unimpressed. Even if Edison's more sophisticated kinetoscope had been ready in time for the exhibition, it is hard to imagine Zukor's being any more taken with Edison's peep show than he was with Muybridge's racehorses.

It was not until 1904 that Zukor realized the potential of film—and then he considered it only an investment. In the meantime, Zukor had to work at the only trade he knew. After tracking down Shosberg, Zukor became his partner in the Novelty Fur Company, which was never as successful as Zukor claimed in his autobiography. Eager to remain in the fur trade but not in the foundering Novelty Fur Company, Zukor sought out another furrier and compatriot, Morris Kohn. Zukor's meeting with Kohn was doubly significant: Kohn was planning to switch from selling furs to manufacturing them and needed someone like Zukor who was conscious of fashion trends, having witnessed the rise and fall of the fur cloak. It was also through Kohn that Zukor met Lottie Kaufmann, the daughter of Kohn's brother-in-law, who became Mrs. Adolph Zukor in 1897.

Zukor joined Kohn and Company, which had become successful enough for Zukor to be sent back east in 1900 to set up a New York branch at East Twelfth Street, on the fringe of the entertainment district. By 1904 it was hard to remain impervious to the new medium, however crude it may have appeared. "Moving pictures" were being shown in bars, amusement park arcades, kinetoscope parlors, music halls, and converted storefronts that would become known as nickelodeons. Even Zukor had to admit that he was taken with the wildly popular *May Irwin Kiss* (1896) in which two stage actors, May Irwin and John C. Rice, recreated a scene from a play in which they were appearing and actually kissed on camera! Despite their singular unattractiveness, the couple made film history. What mattered was that intimacy had been visualized.

In 1904, Zukor's cousin, Max Goldstein, offered Zukor and Kohn the opportunity to invest in a penny arcade that would include, along with other attractions, peep shows. Zukor was now ready to consider, if not embrace, the new medium. And so Zukor and Kohn became investors in the Automatic One-Cent Vaudeville, which was located in the heart of New York's "Broadway" on East Fourteenth Street and featured rows of various film-viewing machines as well as phonographs for those who preferred sound to image.[3]

Zukor had seen the future. The nickelodeon had become the first movie theater, and Zukor had no intention of being excluded from the newest form of exhibition. His years in the fur trade had made him conscious of style. And like exhibitors, who considered their theaters movie palaces rather than "picture shows," with a fountain or a goldfish pool in the lobby and a starlit sky for a ceiling, Zukor decided to upgrade the One-Cent Vaudeville by renovating the second story, creating a second theater called the Crystal Hall, appropriately named for its glass staircase and fake iridescent waterfall.

In 1905, when Zukor decided to open another arcade in Pittsburgh, his choice of city was not arbitrary. Pittsburgh was thriving, and workers in the steel mills were making the kind of wages that allowed them to spend money on entertainment.[4] For Pittsburgh, Zukor wanted a class act: an elegantly appointed venue with uniformed ushers. The man who once fretted over furs had now turned his fastidiousness to film.

If the early careers of the moguls not only seemed to resemble biopics but also to replicate their structure, with time compressed through frequent dissolves and cuts, it is because they progressed at a speed to which only film could do justice: CUT FROM Zukor in fur trade (1903) to ZUKOR in the nickelodeon business (1904); DISSOLVE TO Zukor, in 1910, now an exhibitor with a nickelodeon chain, about to join forces with another ex-furrier, Marcus Loew, who had his own chain of theaters that, like Zukor's, featured vaudeville as well as movies. The two merged their circuits to form Loew's Consolidated Enterprises, the forerunner of Loew's Inc., which became the parent company of MGM.

Although Zukor was treasurer of Loew's Consolidated, he did not remain with the company very long. He had become a showman, but his shows were limited to the one-reelers in his nickelodeons. Zukor wanted a showpiece, not a reel of film that ran ten minutes. Since Zukor's initial exposure to exhibition had been in New York's theater district, he appreciated the aura a stage celebrity could bring to film. When he had the opportunity to buy the rights to the French-made *Queen Elizabeth (Les Amours de la Reine Elisabeth* [1912]), starring Sarah Bernhardt, he sold his shares in Loew's Consolidated for thirty-five thousand dollars to finance the purchase. Since *Queen Elizabeth* had already scored a major success abroad, it seemed a foregone conclusion that a film starring the "divine Sarah," whose only concession to mortality was her love affairs, would do equally well in the States. Zukor, however, was taking no chances. First, *Queen Elizabeth* was longer than most films of the time; although it was advertised as a four-reeler, it was a three-reeler and thus not really a feature, since it ran under an hour.[5] Second, Bernhardt had become such a cult figure, known from her world tours and famous for her eccentricities (including sleeping in a coffin, although that seems to have been a piece of self-mythologizing), that audiences would be doubly gratified if they could see her in person. Booking vaudeville performers had made Zukor sensitive to the public's desire to see its idols in the flesh. Thus Bernhardt received, in addition to a percentage of the gross, $350 a day for personal appearances. And since, at the time, Bernhardt was the world's best-known actress, *Queen Elizabeth's* American premiere would have to be in a legitimate theater. Zukor had become friendly with stage producer Daniel Frohman, who owned the venerable Lyceum Theatre, which still stands on West Forty-fifth Street, east of Broadway. The Lyceum was available for the premiere, and so was Daniel Frohman, who expected some recognition for his largesse. And so, when *Queen Elizabeth* opened on 12 July 1912, the first words audiences saw on the screen were not the title but "Daniel Frohman Presents."

The success of *Queen Elizabeth* convinced Zukor that there was a market for movies with stage celebrities, despite their stylized acting, which, if anything, only highlighted the enormous difference between playing to the camera and playing to an audience. Still, the next-best thing to hearing Bernhardt declaim was seeing her gesticulate, and audiences were satisfied with the broad, sweeping gestures, perhaps imagining the eloquence that would have accompanied them on the stage.

Zukor was now ready to enter production—not alone, since he lacked the contacts, but with attorney Elek John Ludvigh, a fellow Hungarian whom he knew from Loew's Consolidated; Edwin S. Porter, the famous director of *The Great Train Robbery* (1903); Al Lichtman, the brilliant publicist who had handled the road show engagements of *Queen Elizabeth,* insisting it be shown not in nickelodeons but in legitimate theaters; and Daniel Frohman. Since Zukor was interested only in famous players in, if possible, famous plays, Famous Players in Famous Plays (later known as just the Famous Players Film Company) became the name of the newest arrival on the filmmaking scene, headquartered on West Twenty-sixth Street.

Zukor was fortunate that Famous Players was founded at a time when the power of the Motion Picture Patents Company (MPPCo)—a trust comprising ten film companies that pooled their patents on cameras and projectors, making it difficult, but not impossible, for non-MPPCo producers to function—was coming to an end.[6] In fact, in the same year that Famous Players was founded, the Justice Department declared that MPPCo was in violation of the 1890 Sherman Antitrust Act, although MPPCo was not dissolved until 1915. Since Zukor refused to limit his films to ten- to twelve-minute one-reelers in accordance with MPPCo requirements, he was forced to operate as an independent. Still, Zukor needed cameras, which, in 1912, meant MPPCo equipment that could only be licensed to MPPCo members. Supposedly, it was Frohman who interceded for Zukor. Edison, whose litigious nature and obsession with patent infringement was partly responsible for the formation of MPPCo, was apparently in the giving vein the afternoon that Frohman paid him a visit. At any rate, Frohman won Edison over.[7] Perhaps it was because Edison, who also wooed stage talent to perform before his camera, sensed a kindred spirit in Zukor; perhaps it was Edison's realization that MPPCo's days were numbered; but more likely it was Frohman's powers of persuasion. At any rate, Zukor was allowed to use the Edison cameras.

Famous Players made every effort to live up to its name. There was James O'Neill, the father of—arguably—America's greatest playwright, Eugene O'Neill, reprising the vehicle that made him famous (and that also prevented his moving on to more challenging roles), *The Count of Monte Cristo;* Mrs. Fiske in *Tess of the d'Urbervilles;* John Barrymore in *An American Citizen;* Lily Langtry in *His Neighbor's Wife.* But the most famous player as far as the public was concerned was Mary Pickford, who, although she made been making pictures since 1909, became a screen star when Zukor hired her in 1914 at five hundred dollars a week to repeat her starring role in David Belasco's production of *A Good Little Devil* (1914), in which she was appearing in New York.[8] Zukor had scored a coup, but after he saw *A Good Little Devil* he realized that, despite Pickford's performance, the film was not good enough for her Famous Players debut. He kept *Devil* on the shelf for almost a year, releasing instead films that showed his star to better advantage: *In the Bishop's Carriage* (1913), *Caprice* (1913), and *Hearts Adrift* (1914), so that the public's interest in Pickford would grow incrementally. He need not have worried about *Devil.* Pickford was now "America's sweetheart," thanks to B.P. Schulberg, the publicist and later general manager of Paramount's West Coast studio, who coined the sobriquet that became as much a part of Pickford's image as "the Big Bambino" was of Babe Ruth's.

Zukor was not the only one interested in featuring famous players in movies. San Franciscan Jesse L. Lasky originally planned on being known as the world's greatest cornetist until he experienced an attack of gold fever and set out for the Klondike.[9] When he failed to strike it rich, he returned to the family home in California, where his widowed mother and his sister Blanche were living, to discover that in his absence Blanche had also become an accomplished cornetist. To support their mother, Jesse and Blanche put together a vaudeville act, "The Singing Laskys," which eventually led to Jesse's becoming an agent for vaudevillians.

A perennial go-getter, Jesse then decided upon a career in the theater. He envisioned an operetta set in California's mission country. Seeking a librettist, Lasky contacted playwright William DeMille, who claimed he was preoccupied with his own work. DeMille's mother, Beatrice, a theatrical agent, suggested that Lasky try her other son, Cecil, who was initially cool to the idea but finally conceded. The musical, *California* (1910), proved moderately successful. That same year, Blanche decided to marry. She had been courted by a glove salesman—a Polish immigrant who had taken the name of Samuel Goldfish and would soon call himself Sam Goldwyn. She agreed to marry Goldfish not out of love but because she was tired of working in vaudeville. As Goldwyn's biographer noted, "It was a marriage of inconvenience, in trouble from the start."[10]

At the time, however, Blanche's marriage to Goldwyn was as serendipitous as Jesse's collaboration with Cecil DeMille, soon to be known worldwide as Cecil B. DeMille, the producer-director who later proved that sex and religion are not strange bedfellows.

Just as Blanche had wearied of vaudeville, so had Cecil of the theater, once he realized he could never compete with his brother. Cecil yearned for "a stimulating and colorful change of scene."[11] After he saw *Queen Elizabeth,* he had found that change of scene.

Even though his marriage to Blanche ended in divorce in 1916, it was providential that Sam Goldwyn became Jesse Lasky's brother-in-law, for it was Goldwyn who first became a convert to the new medium after seeing *Bronco Billy's Adventures* (1911), which also convinced him that the real money was not to be made in the theater but in the movies. Once Goldwyn learned he would never be a partner in the Elite Glove Company, where he was sales manager, he encouraged his brother-in-law to enter the movie business, from which both of them could profit—Goldwyn more so than Lasky, as it happened. Goldwyn even came up with the name of the company: the Jesse L. Lasky Feature Play Company, with Lasky as president, DeMille as director-general, and Goldwyn himself as treasurer and general manager.

Like Zukor, Lasky was interested in a stage star for his first film. DeMille suggested Dustin Farnum, who had appeared in the successful 1901 revival of Edwin Milton Royle's *The Squaw Man* and was eventually persuaded to appear in the film version. The problem was the setting: the

Old West. The ideal place to shoot *The Squaw Man* was across the Hudson in Fort Lee, New Jersey, which then looked like a western town with its dusty roads and winding trails along the palisades. But since the Feature Play Company was not a member of MPPCo, which was still thrashing about like a dinosaur refusing to face extinction, the only alternative was to shoot it somewhere in the Southwest out of the reach of the MPPCo regulators, who had a habit of suddenly appearing on the sets of non-members and destroying their cameras.

Thus, DeMille set out for Flagstaff, Arizona, in December 1913. When Flagstaff proved unsatisfactory, DeMille moved on to Los Angeles, which he knew was becoming increasingly popular with independent filmmakers. Yet DeMille needed more than a natural setting; he needed a studio, or what would pass for one. The telegram he sent to Lasky is now part of film history: "FLAGSTAFF NO GOOD FOR OUR PURPOSE. HAVE PROCEEDED TO CALIFORNIA. WANT AUTHORITY TO RENT A BARN IN PLACE CALLED HOLLYWOOD FOR SEV-ENTY-FIVE DOLLARS A MONTH. CECIL."[12] The barn, which was on the corner of Selma and Vine, is also part of film history. Now known as the Lasky Barn, it is a tourist attraction at the Hollywood Heritage Museum on Highland Avenue, just across from the Hollywood Bowl.

Zukor was not surprised at the success of *The Squaw Man* (1914), a six-reeler and therefore a true feature—the first, in fact, to be shot in Hollywood. He could also not help but sense a similarity between Feature Play and Famous Players, which went beyond their sound-alike names. Feature Play was on a roll. The Selma Avenue barn was not enough, and soon Lasky was renting acreage from Selma to Sunset and Vine, and from Vine to El Centro. Goldwyn took over distribution, selling the films on the states' rights market; Lasky signed up the stars and bought the proper-ties; and DeMille produced and directed. These were head-spinning times that could best be captured on the screen, where time is elastic and years go by in a montage of headlines and calendar pages. In the case of Feature Play, only rapid cutting could achieve the speed with which the company took off. In 1914, William DeMille came on board to organize a story department, and soon Feature Play began to resemble a true studio, with a research department and even a story department with classes in sce-nario writing.

Shortly after *The Squaw Man* premiered, Zukor wired congratula-tions to Lasky, not knowing that the accolades should have been shared by DeMille and his uncredited codirector, Oscar Apfel, who had worked in both theater and film and taught DeMille the difference between them. Around the same time, Zukor also decided to do something about the way his films were being distributed.

W. W. (William Wadsworth) Hodkinson was a former Utah exhibitor who had become an expert on film exchanges while working for MPPCo's distribution arm, General Film Company, which he revolutionized by offering exhibitors, accustomed to paying a flat fee for a one-day program, better films that might cost more but could be run for more than a day. When Hodkinson's views proved too progressive for General Film, he set out to form his own distribution company, assuming that MPPCo would soon recede into history. However, in 1912, Hodkinson was really planning another conglomerate, which, although not as tyrannical as MPPCo, would still try to bring states' rights producers together under one aegis "for the purpose of bringing order, method and system to raise the industry out of its early nickelodeon state."[13]

Since Hodkinson had founded the Progressive film exchanges on the West Coast, he thought "Progressive Pictures Corporation" would be a distinctive name for his new company, particularly since he considered himself a progressive when it came to distribution. When his attorney informed him that he could not use "progressive" again, Hodkinson began leafing through the "P's" in a New York telephone directory in search of something similar. A listing for a Paramount apartment house provided the inspiration for both the name and the logo.[14] "Paramount" conjured up an image of Pike's Peak, which Hodkinson had seen at the turn of the century when he was working as a telegrapher in Pueblo, Colorado. Hodkinson immediately started sketching a mountain, which was later adorned with a circlet of stars. And although Paramount underwent the usual changes of owners and personnel over the years, the logo has remained intact.

At first, Zukor was interested in having Hodkinson distribute Famous Players's product, but he disliked the name "Paramount," doubting that exhibitors would know what it meant. Jesse Lasky felt similarly, insisting that "Paramount" sounded "like a brand of cheese or woolen mittens."[15] Hodkinson was so eager to get as many independents as possible to join the company that he began studying trademarks of other companies—not necessarily those of studios but of any business that had come up with a self-promoting logo. When Hodkinson realized that all the mountain needed was some embellishment, he procured the services of a lithographer, who crowned the mountain with a halo of stars. Zukor and

Lasky had no argument with the new logo, nor did two other short-lived companies that also joined Paramount Pictures Corporation: Howard Bosworth's Pallas Pictures and the Oliver Morosco Photoplay Company, both of which also aspired to Hodkinson's goal of "highest class movies." In May 1914, the trades, unable to figure out how Paramount would differ from MPPCo except that it would be composed of independents, referred to the new company by a variety of names, including "alliance," "combine," "collective," and, more to the point, "distributing agency." However, Paramount Pictures Corporation would be a special kind of distributing agency: it would only distribute features.

Hodkinson devised a distribution plan, the precursor of the once-common 65/35 arrangement, in which a producer would be advanced a certain amount—say, thirty-five thousand dollars—per film, with Paramount getting 35 percent of the gross and the producer 65 percent after the advance had been recouped. According to Hodkinson, "everyone in the industry thought that it would be impossible to distribute for 35%; but under my program . . . the exhibitor became commited [sic] to a longer run, higher admission price and [was] required to give 4 weeks notice of cancellation of his contract. . . ."[16]

Hodkinson also favored block booking. Zukor was not present at Paramount's first annual convention on September 14 at Chicago's LaSalle Hotel. According to Hodkinson, Zukor behaved "like Achilles, sulking in his tent."[17] Zukor knew he could make Paramount into a true corporation—specifically, a studio, but, as yet, he lacked the means to do so. Had Zukor been in attendance, he would have heard general sales manager Frank D. Sniffen pushing for "Request Days," during which exhibitors could book the latest releases, not individually but as part of a package, or even rebook a block of films that had proved successful.[18] Once Zukor moved into exhibition, he became an advocate of block booking. Obviously, he did not need a sales manager to tell him that package deals made more sense than individual rentals.

Inevitably, Hodkinson and Zukor would clash. Zukor may have claimed he resented the thirty-five-thousand-dollar cap on production, but it was really Hodkinson whom he resented and his concept that "Paramount" came before the companies that comprised it. Nor was Zukor consoled at the thought that Famous Players's films made up half of Paramount's releases. With Zukor, it was all or nothing. Zukor wanted more than a "distributing agency"; he wanted a studio with a theater chain as well. Zukor started buying up as much stock as he could, including that of Hiram Abrams, one of the states' rights distributors whom Hodkinson had courted when he formed Paramount Pictures Corporation in 1914 (and who was now on the board of directors). In a well-orchestrated putsch at the 13 July 1916 annual meeting, Hodkinson, expecting to be reelected president, found himself unseated by Abrams, who won by a single vote. In accepting the presidency, Abrams, who in the past had twice voted for Hodkinson, announced: "On behalf of Adolph Zukor, who has purchased my shares in Paramount, I call this meeting to order."[19]

On 19 July, within a week of the deposing of Hodkinson, Famous Players and the Jesse Lasky Feature Play Company merged to form Famous Players–Lasky with Zukor as president and Lasky as vice president in charge of production. There was no room for Goldwyn, whom Zukor had grown to distrust, having sensed that Goldwyn was more interested in moviemaking than in managing the company. Lasky concurred, since Goldwyn was no longer family after his divorce from Blanche.

For a while, Famous Players–Lasky operated as a holding company for its subsidiaries, but on 29 December 1917, consolidation occurred as the subsidiaries (Famous Players, Feature Play, Oliver Morosco Photoplay, Bosworth, Cardinal, Paramount Pictures Corporation, Artcraft, and George M. Cohan Film Corporation) were brought into the fold of Famous Players–Lasky.

Consolidation was not enough for Zukor. He then conceived the idea of combining production, distribution, and exhibition under one aegis: Paramount Pictures Corporation. In this instance, Zukor was motivated as much by necessity as by corporate greed. Famous Players–Lasky was still held to a twenty-five–year contract with Paramount Pictures Corporation; however, the company was losing money because story costs were rising and stars were demanding higher salaries.[20] By early 1917, Zukor had negotiated enough stock transfers and had bought up enough stock from the exchange members to acquire Paramount, thus uniting, for the moment, production and distribution. He had assumed that Hiram Abrams understood that his title of president was an honorific; when Abrams behaved as if it were not, Zukor had him removed. Supposedly, Zukor invited Hodkinson to lunch, during which he proposed that Hodkinson return to the presidency.[21] It was not so much a matter of letting bygones be bygones as it was of expediency. Zukor presumed Hodkinson shared his vision of a vertically integrated company; he also knew that Hodkinson had made significant innovations in distribution policies, not only with the 65/35 percentage arrangement but also with his idea of first-run features in first-run houses. "I told him I would consider [the presidency]. He then assured me that I was under no obligation to my associates who had deposed me, so I could return with no consideration for them. Again I demurred and then he laid his cards on the table. He told me of his meeting with powerful financial interests who were willing to go in with him in his obsession, which I had long been aware, of combining all functions of the industry in one organization, production, distribution, and exhibition—to be headed by him!"[22]

Zukor had overestimated Hodkinson, who, at heart, was a distributor with a couple of production companies that functioned like spokes in his corporate umbrella. Exhibition was a business unto itself, and not one that Hodkinson was interested in exploring. To Hodkinson, theaters were like display windows that he decorated for the owners. Thus, when Hodkinson agreed to take on the presidency without necessarily committing himself to vertical integration, Zukor was no longer interested.

Zukor's relationship with Lasky was more collegial, since it was based on the division-of-labor principle: Lasky tended to production, while Zukor compiled a shopping list—not of potential films, but theaters. Again, necessity partly explains Zukor's foray into exhibition, although he probably would have done the same even if Famous Players–Lasky had been thriving. Zukor entered exhibition "not . . . primarily . . . for the sake of the revenue which [theaters] would produce but rather as a means of insuring a market for his films."[23]

Zukor was facing a boycott from the First National Exhibitions Circuit, which in 1919 controlled some 596 theaters through various franchise and subfranchise arrangements.[24] Famous Players–Lasky had various distribution policies such as "program distribution," in which an exhibitor books a single evening's entertainment; "stars series," in which an exhibitor signs up for a given number of films a year featuring a particular star; and "selective booking," in which a film is sold on its own merits.[25] However, the company tended to favor block booking, or the package arrangement, in which the exhibitor would agree to purchase a block of films, often sight unseen—a method Hodkinson favored and probably would have implemented at Paramount had he not been deposed.

In addition to Zukor's block-booking and blind-bidding policies, theater owners were also irked by his rentals, especially of Mary Pickford films, which were distributed through Artcraft, a division of Paramount that was often perceived as a new studio. Since Zukor insisted he was making only quality films, exhibitors balked at paying more for a quality Artcraft than for a similar one from another subsidiary (e.g., Oliver Morosco Photoplay, Bosworth, George M. Cohan Film Corporation) within Famous Players–Lasky.

Desperately needing its own theaters, Famous Players went on a buying binge in 1919–20, acquiring a controlling interest in New York's Rialto, Rivoli, and Criterion and a half interest in Grauman's Theater in Los Angeles. But Zukor's greatest coup occurred in 1926 when he gained control of the Balaban-Katz chain.

In 1915 Barney Balaban had been in the movie business for seven years. A grain merchant's son, the Chicago-born Balaban went straight from high school to the Western Cold Storage Company, never thinking that his knowledge of refrigeration would come in handy if he ever changed jobs, as he did in 1908 when he and his four brothers decided to move into exhibition. Balaban considered a theater to be a space able to accommodate any form of entertainment; if a legitimate theater could have a balcony, why not a movie theater? And so, when Balaban's first theater, Chicago's Kedzie, opened in 1913, audiences had a choice of sitting upstairs or downstairs.

Playing the piano in Carl Laemmle's White Front Theatre in Chicago in 1906 convinced Sam Katz to get a theater of his own. But one theater was not enough; impressed with Balaban's ingenuity, Katz became his partner. Together, they built a number of prestige theaters, the first being Chicago's Central Park Theatre, which opened in 1917 and sported another Balaban innovation: air conditioning or, more likely, air cooling. Soon, they had a circuit consisting of forty-five theaters in Chicago alone and sixty-eight throughout Illinois. In 1923, the men consolidated their theater operations under the banner of the Balaban & Katz Corporation—a venture that did not escape the attention of Zukor, who three years later managed to buy Balaban & Katz.

By drawing Balaban & Katz out of First National's orbit and into his own, Zukor succeeded in destroying his rival. He also succeeded (temporarily, at least) in complying with the Federal Trade Commission's order to sever production from exhibition—that is, either make movies or exhibit them. The FTC feared that Zukor's theater-buying mania was leading to a monopoly, as indeed it was. Zukor therefore folded the theaters into a separate operation, the Publix Theatre Corporation, headed by Sam Katz.[26] Publix, then, was just a subsidiary of Paramount–Famous-Lasky, the new corporate name.

Zukor projected a Janus-faced image. To the competition, he was a predator; to the FTC, a potential monopolist. Zukor tried to temper his warlord image with occasional acts of beneficence, which, naturally, were recorded in the press. In June 1922, Zukor announced the formation of a Paramount Stock Company school, where students would be trained in the various branches of moviemaking. Inspired perhaps by DeMille's decision to begin work on *The Ten Commandments* (1923), Zukor had Jesse Lasky formulate Paramount's own decalogue for the stock company members. The first commandment was really an agreement to observe the other nine, which expected students to adopt a proper health regimen; achieve a passing grade of seventy-five in all classes; refrain from displays of temperament; accept neither gifts nor gratuities; refuse no role, however small; avoid bad companions; strive for self-improvement; and behave properly in public.[27] Zukor noted that "attendance at church" would be encouraged, but, given the heterogeneous makeup of the student body, it would not be enforced. Zukor's choice of "church" rather than "place of worship" may have been an attempt to downplay his Jewish origins, which was characteristic of the other Jewish studio chiefs, as well as to curry favor with churchgoers.

President Harding's secretary of labor, James L. Davis, congratulated Zukor on the Paramount stock company, hoping that actors with such high moral standards would help "clean up the movies." Zukor's timing could not have been better. On 2 February 1922, Paramount director William Desmond Taylor was murdered in his Los Angeles mansion. One of the suspects was Paramount star Mary Miles Minter. The Taylor murder, which is still unsolved, followed on the heels of the death of wannabe movie star Virginia Rappe, who died on 10 September 1921 of a ruptured bladder during some wild sex with the endearing, corpulent, and sexually unthreatening (at least on the screen) silent clown, "Fatty" Arbuckle. Arbuckle and his entourage, which included Rappe, descended upon San Francisco's Hotel St. Francis for a Labor Day weekend that consisted exclusively of sex and bootleg liquor. At some point on 5 September, Arbuckle's weight was literally too much for Rappe to bear. Arbuckle was obviously less graceful in person than he was on the screen. The official cause of Rappe's death was peritonitis resulting from a ruptured bladder that may have been caused not so much by Arbuckle's sexual aggressiveness as by his perverse sense of foreplay, which may have involved a sliver of ice or a champagne bottle. The fact that Arbuckle was acquitted after a third trial (the first two having resulted in hung juries) did not appease an outraged public that found one of its idols had feet of clay. Nor did it console Paramount, which had three Arbuckle films in release that few moviegoers wanted to see.

These and other scandals convinced the public that Hollywood needed monitoring, and who was Zukor to deny it? The reason a studio forms a stock company is not to create role models but to nurture talent. Still, it would not hurt, especially in 1922, to play Moses and issue a set of mandates for the stars of tomorrow, who probably found them as phony as Paramount did. Anyone who would entitle his autobiography *The Public Is Never Wrong* would hardly buck the tide, especially when it's coming in on the right. Thus, Zukor was one of the first to support the installation of Will Hays, President Harding's former postmaster general (and an elder of the Presbyterian church), as head of the Motion Picture Producers and Distributors of America (MPPDA), the industry's attempt at self-censorship to prevent state and possible federal intervention.

In 1922, Zukor had other problems. DeMille had become intractable and would leave Paramount two years later, although he would return in the early 1930s with his own production unit. Meanwhile, Zukor had to live up to his ads: "If it's a Paramount picture, it's the best show in town." Besides advertising in the trades, Paramount also used the popular *Saturday Evening Post* to promote itself and "the world's greatest array of talent." This was not hype; it was fact. By 1929, Mary Pickford, Lillian Gish, Gloria Swanson, Rudolph Valentino, John Barrymore, Conrad Nagel, William Boyd, Pola Negri, Ronald Colman, Wallace Beery, William Powell, Clara Bow, W.C. Fields, and Gary Cooper had been part of that array—as had such directors as D.W. Griffith, DeMille, William Wellman, Erich von Stroheim, and Ernst Lubitsch.

Still, Zukor needed a production head, especially after DeMille's departure. Paramount never had production chiefs on the order of MGM's Irving Thalberg or Warner Bros.' Hal B. Wallis. Rather, there was a succession of studio heads or vice presidents in charge of production. A few had vision, but most were lucky enough to have writers, art directors, directors, producers, and director-producers to create the Paramount signature that others could replicate.

DeMille would never return as "director general," a title that fell into such disuse that it was soon discarded. His replacement was Benjamin Percival Schulberg. Connecticut-born B.P. Schulberg was, essentially, a well-educated journalist for hire, whose search for assignments brought him to E.S. Porter's Rex Pictures, where he doubled as head of the scenario department and resident publicist. When Porter joined Famous Players in 1912 as production chief, Schulberg came along, doing pretty much the same as he had done at Rex: finding suitable screen stories and promoting their film versions.

When Zukor forced Hiram Abrams out of Famous Players–Lasky, Schulberg left, too, partly out of loyalty to Abrams, or so it seemed at the time, but more likely because he regarded Abrams as his ticket to something better than being Zukor's factotum. Schulberg insisted he had given Abrams the inspiration for a distribution company controlled solely by the artists themselves—in other words, United Artists, of which Abrams became general manager.

Schulberg, however, had no role in the new company; in 1920, he took out a suit against Abrams that was eventually settled out of court.[28] However, neither Schulberg's defection nor his lawsuit affected Zukor, who apparently thought enough of the "smart young fellow"[29] he had once hired as publicity director to bring him back as DeMille's replacement in 1925, with the title of general manager—"director general" having acquired too many authoritarian overtones.

Knowing he was not a filmmaker, Schulberg hired directors such as William Wellman, Lubitsch, Josef von Sternberg, and Rouben Mamoulian, who could—and did—provide Paramount with films that rank among the cinema's finest: Wellman's *Wings* (1927), the first motion picture to win an Oscar for Best Picture; Von Sternberg's *Underworld* and the eight films he made with Marlene Dietrich; Lubitsch's *The Love Parade* (1929) and *Monte Carlo* (1930); and Mamoulian's *Applause* (1932), *Dr. Jekyll and Mr. Hyde* (1932), *Love Me Tonight* (1932), and *Song of Songs* (1933). Schulberg also realized he needed a producer—someone who would not merely bring films in on budget but who could also function as a quasi production head. He thought the problem was solved when he hired David Selznick, fresh from MGM where his abrasiveness had alienated Irving Thalberg, who seemed unable to distinguish between a loudmouth and a gadfly. Selznick was the latter—although he could be loud, particularly when he did not get his way. Despite Selznick's less-than-winning ways, Schulberg brought him on board in 1927.

One would like to think Selznick was hired because Schulberg sensed his future greatness. That greatness, however, never manifested itself at Paramount, where Selznick produced ten films, none of which could even compare with *Gone with the Wind* (1939), much less with *Rebecca* (1940), *Suspicion* (1941), *Spellbound* (1945), and *Notorious* (1946), for which

Selznick was fortunate enough to have the services of Alfred Hitchcock. Of the films he made at Famous Players–Lasky, perhaps two—*The Man I Love* and *Chinatown Nights* (both 1929)—might be considered historically important, not so much for Selznick's participation as for that of the director, William Wellman.[30]

Selznick never thought of Paramount, or any studio, as his home. By 1935, he had his own, Selznick International; no longer would he have to defend his inspirations to the uninspired. Paramount then underwent a series of production heads, the turnover having more to do with the economy than with creativity.

Selznick's Paramount tenure, however brief, occurred during the decade when "ruthless Zukor" was hell-bent on vertical integration. Zukor may not have known the meaning of the term, but he knew how to swallow up theater chains and extend his realm. Throughout the 1920s, it seemed that Paramount was emulating its logo, except that the mountain had yet to culminate in a peak. The studio was really growing in tiers, like Dante's Mount Purgatory. In 1920, Paramount—or, to be more precise, Famous Players–Lasky—opened a studio in Astoria, Queens, that made it possible for actors working in New York to drive across the Queensboro Bridge or take the elevated to Astoria and be back before curtain time.[31] It made little difference that the Astoria facility looked more like a railroad terminal than a movie studio. What mattered was product. Between 1920 and 1927, 127 silent films were made at Astoria, with such stars as Gloria Swanson, Rudolph Valentino, and W.C. Fields.[32]

Shortly before Famous Players–Lasky launched the Astoria facility, Zukor and Lasky opened one in London in a former power station. One of the studio's first employees was twenty-one–year-old Alfred Hitchcock, who was hired—part-time, at first—to design the title cards on which various kinds of text (e.g., credits, dialogue, commentary) were printed and then inserted into the film, appearing in the form of intertitles.

During the 1920s, Famous Players–Lasky's profits rose from $5.2 million at the beginning of the decade to $15.5 million at the end. The increase was due to several factors: the popularity of Rudolph Valentino, Gloria Swanson, Nancy Carroll, Clara Bow, and Ruth Chatterton; the success of *The Sheik* (1921), *Blood and Sand* (1922), *The Ten Commandments* (1923), *The Covered Wagon* (1923), *Beau Geste* (1926), and *Wings* (1927); and, in no small part, the growth of Publix, which, by the end of the 1920s, consisted of over a thousand theaters. [33]

Exhibition, however important, was only one aspect of the company, renamed Paramount–Famous–Lasky in 1927. The previous year, Lasky, deciding that the barn on Selma and Vine had outlived its usefulness and could never be expanded into a real studio, set his sights on a twenty-three-acre property in West Hollywood. There would now be two studios, one on each coast. Naturally, there was rivalry between them, resulting in the temporary closing of the Astoria facility, which reopened at the beginning of the sound era when more space was needed. Astoria's contributions to the sound era include *The Letter* (1929) with Jeanne Eagels; the Marx Brothers' first two films, *The Cocoanuts* (1929) and *Animal Crackers* (1930); Rouben Mamoulian's *Applause* (1929); George Cukor's *The Royal Family of Broadway* (1930); and *Tarnished Lady* (1931), Tallulah Bankhead's film debut.

In 1926, Zukor not only wanted a presence on the West Coast other than the old Vine Street barn; he also wanted one on Broadway, but not at the 110 West Fortieth Street site, which Zukor considered Paramount–Famous–Lasky's temporary location. Ever since he began eating at Shanley's restaurant on Broadway and Forty-third Street, Zukor had envisioned a Times Square location for his company that, structurally, would resemble the mountain logo: a skyscraper, at the base of which would be a theater that would qualify as a palazzo, if not a movie palace. The Paramount building at 1501 Broadway between Forty-third and Forty-fourth Streets rose like a pyramid to a height of thirty-nine stories. At the base was Publix's crown jewel, the four-thousand-seat Paramount Theater, which opened on 19 November 1926. The theater was conceived as an opera house for moviegoers who had never been inside an opera house but expected it to conform to their image of one. The staircase was indeed operatic; so were the crystal chandeliers and the marble trimming in the lobby.

The theater, as well as the studio, survived the Great Depression, although for a while it seemed that the studio was either destined for a takeover or the Hollywood ash heap.

Zukor's acquisitiveness seemed to know no bounds. In 1929, Zukor discovered radio or, rather, its potential for film. Fascinated by the new medium—which he thought could be a good marketing tool, with radio personalities promoting movies on the air and appearing in some of them as well—Zukor authorized a stock swap that would give Paramount a half interest in the Columbia Broadcasting System (CBS). No doubt Zukor was influenced by the birth of the industry's newest studio, RKO Radio Pictures, in 1928. RKO was the inspiration of David Sarnoff, the chairman of the Radio Corporation of America (RCA), which was the parent of the NBC network. Sarnoff envisioned a company that would eventually house, under one roof, film, radio, live entertainment, and even television, then in its embryonic form. The fact that RKO's logo was a radio transmitter atop a globe was an indication that, to Sarnoff, the union of sight and sound went beyond the mere audiovisual.

Neither "General" Sarnoff nor Adolph Zukor achieved his dream. Sarnoff's was impossible, given RKO's high executive turnover rate and its inability to project an image that would have distinguished its product from that of other studios. Zukor's was thwarted by the Great Depression, which affected Paramount–Famous–Lasky adversely because of its vast theater holdings. The theaters that were part of Publix had been purchased partly through stock that could be redeemed at the fixed price of eighty dollars a share. Therefore, even though the stock plummeted to fifty dollars a share after the market crashed, the original price still had to be honored.[34]

To make matters worse, friction arose between Sidney Kent, the general sales manager of Paramount–Famous–Lasky, and Sam Katz, the president of Publix. Kent's commitment was to the studio; Katz's, to Publix. To Katz, Paramount–Famous–Lasky was little more than a feeder for the theater empire over which he presided. It was the familiar distribution-exhibition agon, with Kent (distribution) claiming that Katz (exhibition) was not paying the same price for Paramount films that he was for those of other companies; and Katz replying that he had to make rental fees as attractive as possible, especially for theaters that turned up their nose at Paramount's less desirable releases. When Lasky discovered that Kent's sales staff had no intention of foisting unwanted films on the theaters, Lasky intervened and played peacemaker. In an effort to resolve the distribution-exhibition conflict and project an image of unity, Lasky removed his name from the corporate title, which then became Paramount-Publix.

The name change was purely cosmetic. Paramount-Publix's profits fell from $18 million in 1930 to $6 million in 1931. Katz persuaded his friend from Chicago, taxicab tycoon John Daniel Hertz, to take over Paramount-Publix. Hertz decentralized the theater chain, thereby making it possible for the exhibitors to have greater autonomy. Hertz's bio reads like a page out of Zukor's; one could easily imagine Hertz's embarking on a career path that paralleled Zukor's except that, for Hertz, movies were an afterthought. Hertz was born in an Eastern European village north of Budapest in what is now the Slovak Republic. He was a mere child when his parents emigrated and settled in Chicago, where, at age eleven, Hertz decided he had enough education and was ready to make his way in the world. First, it was amateur boxing, then sports writing. When Hertz started selling cars, he figured out that he could make more money operating a fleet of taxicabs. And so, the Yellow Cab Manufacturing Company was born in 1915, followed a decade later by another innovation: the car rental service, the Hertz Drive-Ur-SELF Corporation. By the time Balaban approached him to rescue Paramount, Hertz, then in his early fifties, had retired and was spending his days breeding racehorses.

In November 1931, Katz, learning that Zukor had no intention of selling the company, persuaded Hertz to chair the finance committee. Hertz knew only one way to get a company to shape up: cut salaries and slash budgets. Seeing no reason why Paramount should be involved in radio, he sold Paramount's half-interest in CBS back to the network. Kent and Lasky saw the writing on the wall. Kent departed for Fox, where he became president; Lasky joined him later. Although Lasky could probably have stayed on, he had become so despondent over his sister's death from pneumonia that he welcomed the opportunity to go elsewhere. Paramount-Publix continued to hemorrhage from the fixed-price stock redemption arrangement with the theaters, the expenses incurred from converting the studio and its theaters to sound, and the falloff in movie attendance as the ranks of America's unemployed increased.

There were no profits in 1932, but a $121 million deficit. It is often alleged that Mae West, who came to Paramount in 1932, brought the studio out of the red. While it is true that her first films (*She Done Him Wrong and I'm No Angel*) did extremely well, no actor has ever saved a studio from bankruptcy. Similarly, Mae's double entendres alone did not bring about the enforcement of the Production Code in 1934. Hollywood's discovery of upwardly mobile gangsters like Rico (*Little Caesar* [1930]), Tommy Powers (*The Public Enemy* [1931]), and Tony Camonte (*Scarface* [1932]) generated a surge of self-righteousness in moviegoers who may have identified with the antiheroes, particularly if they themselves were out of work, but felt that hoods and bootleggers were hardly role models for the young (who may have identified with them even more than some of their elders).

Forced to declare bankruptcy in 1933, Paramount-Publix was saved from becoming a historical curiosity, or a case study in loose cannons like

Kent and Katz, by the installation of a board of directors consisting of bankers, lawyers, realtors—in general, Wall Street types, most of whom knew nothing about movies but enough about business to turn Paramount-Publix around.[35] When Paramount-Publix was renamed Paramount Pictures Corporation in 1935, the board thought it best to make Zukor chairman, thereby reducing his role in the affairs of the studio. Believing that movie industry types like Zukor and Lasky could not run a corporation, the board persuaded John Otterson to assume the presidency. Otterson, a former naval lieutenant, had been president of Electric Research Products Inc. (ERPI), a subsidiary of AT&T that held patents on vital electrical equipment needed for the making of sound pictures. That—and the fact that ERPI had established a division devoted to the making of educational films for schoolroom use—was the extent of Otterson's connection with film. Another unfortunate choice was Emmanuel "Manny" Cohen, a graduate of the City College of New York and a former political writer whose film background had been exclusively in newsreels. Originally hired to replace Schulberg, Cohen was so overwhelmed by the chaotic conditions at the studio that he evidenced it in his gruff manner and highhandedness.

At least Otterson knew that someone with a moviemaking background should be heading production. Although DeMille had returned to Paramount in 1932 and had given the studio one of its biggest hits of 1933, *The Sign of the Cross* (1932), he had not grown mellower in the intervening years. If Manny Cohen found it difficult to deal with DeMille, Otterson would have found it impossible. Since Cohen himself was no less troublesome, Otterson replaced him in 1935 with Ernst Lubitsch, who, he thought, would apply his fabled touch to production. But the Lubitsch touch, which had been applied so well to romantic comedy where innuendo reigned supreme and fadeouts were a cue for off-screen lovemaking, was art, not policy. Lubitsch lasted a year, leaving Paramount for good after *Bluebeard's Eighth Wife* (1938). Otterson departed even earlier—in 1936 after barely a year in the job. Otterson's replacement at least knew the kind of longevity associated with Golden Age Hollywood: like Columbia's Harry Cohn and MGM's Louis Mayer, Barney Balaban remained in the job for three decades.

If, during the 1930s, Paramount was able to make such classics as *Morocco* (1930), *Dr. Jekyll and Mr. Hyde* (1932), *Trouble in Paradise* (1932), *She Done Him Wrong* (1933), *The Trail of the Lonesome Pine* (1936), *Easy Living* (1937), and *Midnight* (1939) even while undergoing receivership and a round of stopgap saviors, the reason is its producer-directors and writers. Paramount's ads proclaimed, "Through These Gates Come the Best Shows in Town!" This was not false advertising; the shows were being produced and/or directed by DeMille, Lubitsch, Mamoulian, Fritz Lang, Leo McCarey, Frank Lloyd, Henry Hathaway, Wesley Ruggles, Mitchell Leisen, and William Wellman; and written by Billy Wilder and Charles Brackett, Preston Sturges, Claude Binyon, and Samson Raphaelson.

If Balaban could entice such talent to the studio, a production head would be superfluous. Yet Balaban knew he needed one, if for no other reason, to find vehicles for the contract talent. Balaban thought he had found one in William LeBaron, a New York University graduate who aspired to be a playwright—and had a few shows on Broadway—until he discovered there was more money to be made in movies. LeBaron's association with Paramount did not begin in Hollywood but in New York at the Astoria studio, where he had been an associate producer in the 1920s. Because he felt comfortable with theater people, LeBaron enjoyed the ambience of Astoria, where stage actors both worked and were screen-tested. With the advent of sound, LeBaron exited Astoria for Paramount's Hollywood studio. Now a full-fledged producer known for his respect for talent, LeBaron endeared himself to such Paramount stars as Mae West and Bing Crosby as well as to an emigré writer from Germany by the name of Billy Wilder. For LeBaron, it was an easy transition from Paramount producer to Paramount production head.

LeBaron was particularly attracted to the comedy (or drama)-with-music movie that had become Paramount's specialty. In 1934, while still a producer, LeBaron envisioned a movie version of Mascagni's opera, *Cavalleria Rusticana,* to be called "Chivalry"; he had gone so far as to enlist the aid of another New York University alumnus, composer Deems Taylor, with whom LeBaron had collaborated on several of the NYU senior shows.

Although "Chivalry" never materialized, LeBaron had not given up on opera. The enormous success of Columbia's *One Night of Love* (1934), with Metropolitan Opera soprano Grace Moore, convinced LeBaron that there was an audience for opera—not the few who would turn out for a movie version of *Cavalleria Rusticana,* but the average filmgoer who could accept opera within the context of a movie with an uncomplicated plot embellished with arias and duets. LeBaron thought he had found Paramount's answer to Grace Moore in another Met diva, mezzo soprano Gladys Swarthout. Swarthout may have been a favorite of Met audiences but was not with moviegoers, as it turned out. The Paramount musicals in which she appeared—*Rose of the Rancho* (1936), *Give Us This Night* (1936), *Champagne Waltz* (1937), and *Romance in the Dark* (1938)—suffered from hokey plots and uncharismatic leading men. Swarthout's failure in Hollywood was typical of the fate of the movie mezzo; Rise Stevens, another gifted mezzo and the finest Carmen of her generation, also failed to register with film audiences. Sopranos—e.g., Moore, Jeanette MacDonald, Deanna Durbin, Ann Blyth, Susanna Foster, Kathryn Grayson—did much better in Hollywood, perhaps because their high notes and bright sounds were more in keeping with what moviegoers considered "operatic." LeBaron fared much better with Mae West. He was responsible for her film debut in *Night after Night* (1932), which was followed by the more memorable *She Done Him Wrong* and *I'm No Angel* (both 1933).

In 1936, LeBaron seemed to meet all the requirements for production head. What he had not counted on was Y. (for Young) Frank Freeman's becoming vice president of studio operations two years later. Freeman was no different from the myriads who stumbled into the movies—some developing into real filmmakers and others, like himself, into a succession of executive positions with a different title at each stage. To Freeman, there was not that much difference between operating a cotton mill, managing a theater, or running a studio.

Freeman, a Georgia native and Georgia Tech alumnus, was essentially a businessman or, to be more specific, a man for whom business was the one constant in a world of variables. The nature of the business could vary, and did, during Freeman's career; but the nature of business did not. Freeman was in the service of business, rather like a knight in the service of the lady. When Freeman left Georgia Tech in 1910 with a degree in electrical engineering, he had planned to enter the burgeoning field of telephone operations. However, his father's death forced him to alter his plans and take over the family business, which happened to be cotton. Freeman's marriage to Margaret Harris, whose father owned a theater, brought about another career change as Freeman moved out of cotton and into exhibition—a career change that led to Paramount where, in 1935, Freeman became vice president of theater operations; and in 1938, vice president of the studio, a position he held for the next twenty years.

With LeBaron's departure in 1938, it was replacement time again. Balaban chose George Gard DeSylva, known professionally as B.G. "Buddy" DeSylva, the songwriter and Broadway producer who also coauthored the books of several musicals, including *Good News* and Cole Porter's *DuBarry Was a Lady* and *Panama Hattie*.

By the time DeSylva came on board, the Paramount signature had been forged, the product of many hands. While all the studios made the same kinds of films, each developed a specialty. MGM was known for family fare and elaborate musicals; Universal, for horror films; Warner Bros., for crime movies and melodramas; Fox, for literary adaptations. Paramount's forte became comedy: there were campus capers during the 1930s (*College Humor* [1933], *She Loves Me Not* [1934], *College Holiday* [1935], *College Swing* [1938], *Campus Confessions* [1938], *Million Dollar Legs* [1939], *$1,000 Dollars a Touchdown* [1939]); Mae West quadrupling double entendres; the globe-trotting trio of Bob Hope, Bing Crosby, and Dorothy Lamour in the DeSylva-inspired "Road" movies; Betty Hutton, "The Blonde Bombshell," converting her body into a pogo stick; and Jerry Lewis crossing his eyes until they seemed to converge at his nose.

Comedy—sophisticated, topical, farcical, and musical—was Paramount's forte. During radio's Golden Age, Paramount provided the faces that went with the voices, introducing radio personalities such as Bing Crosby, Jack Benny, Fred Allen, and George Burns and Gracie Allen—always, of course, in comedies, specifically comedies with music. Actually, the form of the Paramount comedy had been established earlier by Lubitsch, famed for his feather-light touch. The form was operetta—with or without music. Operetta appropriates the conventions of opera—deception, disguise, discovery—and softens them, lightening them musically and inverting them dramatically. An error in love is not a cue for the tenor to denounce the soprano, but to mask his disillusionment by putting on a macho front. Thus the crushed Danilo announces in *The Merry Widow*, with masculine bravado, that he will go to Maxim's to nurse his unrequited love; Alfredo in *La Traviata*, on the other hand, thinking Violetta has returned to her old ways, pelts her publicly with banknotes.

Operetta, particularly the Viennese kind, is ripe with adulterous situations. Johann Strauss's *Die Fledermaus*, one of the world's most popular operettas, numbers among its main characters a bored housewife who is sleeping with an Italian tenor; her husband, who seduces young girls by dangling a pocket watch in front of their eyes; her maid, who is not beyond turning a few tricks on the side; and a dissolute prince whose parties are places of assignation. But in the world of operetta, one does not speak of adultery, only flirtation; or of sluts, only soubrettes.

The Lubitsch Touch had a civilizing effect on Paramount comedy, for it was Lubitsch who transformed the sexual merry-go-round into an elegant carousel. Lubitsch gave audiences something better than sex: sex transfigured, sex as a game played with only one rule: decorum. No fleshy bodies intertwined, no messy vestiges of passion, and always a perfectly made bed the next morning. It is also a game that is never resolved; while it seems that the players make love, we do not even see the usual cinematic metaphors for lovemaking: rain pelting the windowpanes or a fire flaring up in the hearth and then turning to embers. Rather, we see men loosening their neckties or women kicking off their shoes and wiggling their toes, as they do in *One Night with You* (1932).

"Did they or didn't they?" we ask in a Lubitsch film. They did—and they didn't. In *Trouble in Paradise* (1932), Lubitsch closes the bedroom door on Herbert Marshall and Kay Francis in a moment of passion. Conclusion: They did. In the next scene, they awaken in their respective rooms. Conclusion: They didn't. Lubitsch was even able to parody his own touch. In *One Night with You*, Maurice Chevalier and Jeanette MacDonald play a married couple who still enjoy acting like lovers. As they retire to their bedroom, the camera accompanies them to the door. Suddenly, Chevalier emerges and speaks directly to the audience. "I know what you're thinking," he begins, and then goes on to remind them that he and MacDonald are married. That said, he returns to the bedroom.

The Lubitsch Touch was so much a part of Paramount comedy that it operated in films Lubitsch did not direct. In *Desire* (1936), produced by Lubitsch but directed by Frank Borzage, Marlene Dietrich and Gary Cooper pledge their love and presumably consummate it off camera. When John Halliday awakens each of them the next morning, they are in separate rooms. Yet each thinks he or she is being awakened by the other. They did—and they didn't. Regardless, they did it *beautifully*. At breakfast the next morning, Cooper is wearing a white cashmere sweater so spotless that it seems to dispel any thought of sex. However, Cooper is so famished that he asks to eat Marlene's eggs. Only Lubitsch could make soft-boiled eggs sexy.

Not all of Paramount's contract talent could play the Lubitsch game: Hope, Crosby, Lamour, Mary Carlisle, Cass Dailey, Virginia Dale, and Betty Hutton were too down-to-earth for artifice. Just as every art has its higher and lower forms, the lower form of Paramount operetta was Paramount comedy with music, as opposed to musical comedy. If Paramount opted for comedies interspersed with music, rather than musical comedies, the reason was that the studio had stars under contract, many of whom came from radio or vaudeville and could do light comedy as well as sing—but within a plot that would make few demands on their acting. Except for

Crosby, none of Paramount's musical performers (e.g., Lamour, Mary Carlisle, Shirley Ross, Betty Hutton, Joan Caulfield, Olga San Juan) ranked with MGM's Judy Garland, Gene Kelly, Frank Sinatra, and Esther Williams. They could, however, enliven a script that, without music, would be forgettable. Even Elvis Presley's Paramount movies (e.g., *Loving You* [1957], *King Creole* [1959], *G.I. Blues* [1960], *Blue Hawaii* [1961]) were comedies, or dramas, with music and a format loose enough to accommodate a couple of songs without derailing the plot.

Not all comedy at Paramount was musical, however; a good deal of it was verbal, especially the films of Mitchell Leisen, Preston Sturges, and Billy Wilder. Significantly, all three received the support and encouragement first of LeBaron and then DeSylva, who saw them as the natural heirs to the studio's comedic tradition, which each would perpetuate in his own way: Leisen, by mingling the sophisticated and the baroque; Sturges, by merging satire with humanism; and Wilder, by casting a cynical eye on whatever passed before it, sometimes winking, sometimes staring.

Leisen began his career by designing costumes for DeMille's films; when he turned director in 1933, he continued the Paramount practice of showing deception, disguise, and infidelity through a lens brightly, applying the Lubitsch hand, if not the touch, to fairy tales like *Easy Living* (1937), in which Jean Arthur becomes Cinderella when a sable coat literally descends on her as she is riding up Fifth Avenue in a double-decker bus; and in *Midnight* (1939), in which Claudette Colbert, a good-natured gold digger, acquires John Barrymore as a fairy godfather.

Leisen, who could design sets as well as clothes, perpetuated the DeMille glitter as well as the Lubitsch Touch; to the Touch, Leisen added the DeMille opulence, creating the Paramount baroque. While Josef von Sternberg favored fishnet and gauze, and DeMille sunken baths and plumes, Leisen turned to swirling blue smoke, mink dresses, and embossed goblets on brocade tablecloths.

Leisen also inherited Marlene Dietrich, whose films show how a star is created and her image perpetuated. It was von Sternberg who persuaded Paramount to bring Dietrich to America. With her first American film, *Morocco* (1930), she became the quintessence of Paramount—and the quintessence of von Sternberg, who often boasted that Dietrich was nothing more than the incarnation of his vision of woman. Von Sternberg's vision of woman was also Paramount's.

Visually, Paramount was known for the "white look," partly the creation of art director Hans Dreier, who, from 1927 to 1951, helped create the studio's visual style.[36] Bedrooms looked like shrines; walls and staircases gleamed like burnished ivory. The studio seemed to revel in whiteness, from satin sheets to that indisputable touch of class, the white telephone.

In a Dietrich film, lighting was everything. It was as if sunlight had been winnowed into an unbroken stream of white, flecked with liquid silver and then allowed to flow around the contours of the body, glazing the face with a mask of ivory that absorbed even time itself. Paramount's women were women in white whose luminosity blended perfectly with Dreier's white decor.

Leisen's first film with Dietrich was *The Lady Is Willing* (1942), in which Dietrich was all Paramount shimmer in wedding-cake white. However, *The Lady Is Willing* was not made at Paramount but at Columbia on Gower Street. Geographically, Marathon Street was not that far from Gower, but, aesthetically, the distance was enormous. Paramount was one of the Big Five, but Columbia was still on Poverty Row. Yet the Paramount style survived relocation, remaining intact. The formula, once perfected and packaged, was ready for export.

Leisen's second picture with Dietrich was *Golden Earrings* (1947), in which he transformed the star into a swarthy gypsy with beauty-parlor ringlets, not unlike the look DeMille had created for Paulette Goddard in *Northwest Mounted Police* (1940), in which she played the untamed Louvette, a role originally intended for Dietrich. From *Golden Earrings,* one can see how Dietrich might have looked had she appeared in the DeMille outdoor epic. To the question, "How much of Leisen is Leisen?" one can only answer that Leisen was heir to a tradition that was being created at Paramount when he arrived there. Having served as either art or set director for sixteen DeMille productions between 1924 and 1933, and as costume designer for many others, Leisen was as much a product of the studio as he was a reflection of the films with which he was involved. That he developed a personal style is as much a tribute to Paramount as it is to himself.

Like other studios, Paramount believed in continuity, which is generally achieved by building up a repertory company of contract players, tailoring the script to the star (and not vice versa), seeking replacements that would be replicas of the originals, and remaking earlier films that had proved successful or had a surefire formula. Paramount relied on some of these methods, although it did not remake its hits as often as Warner Bros. and Fox did. The basis for continuity at Paramount was its policy of graduation from the ranks, guaranteeing a cross-fertilization of talent that, in turn, gave the films a distinctive character. Just as Leisen worked for DeMille before becoming a director, Wilder coauthored the screenplays of three Leisen films—*Midnight; Arise, My Love* (1940); and *Hold Back the Dawn* (1941)—before directing his first film, *The Major and the Minor* (1942). Similarly, Preston Sturges wrote the screenplays for Leisen's *Easy Living* (1937) and *Remember the Day* (1940) before he turned director with *The Great McGinty* (1940).

While Sturges's films may seem, on the surface, to be atypical of Paramount, his blend of parody and satire, the self-conscious and the self-reflexive, were in keeping with studio tradition. In *Monte Carlo* (1930), Lubitsch parodied the conventions of operetta by having the characters attend one that mirrored their own lives. Sometimes art not only imitates life, but unreality mimics reality. In *Monte Carlo,* the operetta turns in upon itself, uniting the mirror and the spectator, the illusion and the reality, into a single universe where the conventions of the stage prevail as actual modes of behavior—a universe where life is lived as theater.

In *Sullivan's Travels* (1942), Sturges also tried to combine two worlds: the world of the Warner Bros. social consciousness film and the world of the Paramount comedy. In a bizarre way, the grim realities of the one become the comic conventions of the other. In the other, Joel McCrea portrays movie director John L. Sullivan, who sets out to make a serious film about the Great Depression, *O Brother, Where Art Thou?* Sullivan, however, is a director at Paramount, not at Warner's. Thus he is ill-equipped to handle such a serious theme. At first Sullivan balked when the studio heads asked him to make "Ants in Your Pants of 1939," a jibe at Leisen's 1937 and 1938 *Big Broadcast* movies. After trying to experience poverty firsthand so that he could make a Depression classic, Sullivan realizes that one does not make a Warner Bros. movie on the Paramount lot. Chastened, Sullivan recants, becoming Paramount's spokesperson at the end when he admits: "There's a lot to be said for making people laugh. . . . It isn't much but it's better than nothing in this cockeyed caravan." That Sturges could both accept and reject reality was due, in part, to a dilemma he was never able to resolve: the desire to produce high art versus the need for popular success.

Billy Wilder did not share Sturges's dilemma. Wilder understood Paramount better than either Leisen or Sturges. While Leisen saw Paramount in terms of films about masquerading in haute couture, and Sturges as a laboratory in which he could work out a theory of comedy acceptable to intellectuals and the masses, Wilder saw the studio as the alma mater of von Sternberg and Lubitsch, with himself as a graduating senior soon to become a faithful alumnus. Wilder knew there was a Paramount tradition. When Wilder was making *A Foreign Affair* (1948), set in postwar Berlin, he cast Marlene Dietrich as a nightclub singer performing in a cellar café similar to the one in which she had performed in *The Blue Angel* (1930); he commissioned Friedrich Hollander, who had written the songs for *The Blue Angel,* to compose three new ones for Dietrich; finally, he offered the actress a chance to humanize—but not discard— her *Blue Angel* image by playing a born survivor in a divided city where it is no longer a matter of sleeping with the enemy but with the occupiers, too. In *A Foreign Affair,* Wilder came up with his own version of the Lubitsch Touch by creating a dichotomy between person and persona. Personally, Dietrich loathed Nazism and interrupted her film career to entertain the men and women of the armed forces during World War II—something Dietrich the icon would never have done for fear of shattering her image.[37] Wilder gave Dietrich the opportunity to keep her persona intact by playing the ex-mistress of a high-ranking Nazi—a role completely at odds with the public's image of Dietrich, the Hollywood star in battle fatigues who proudly referred to herself as a soldier.

Wilder did the reverse in *Sunset Boulevard* (1950), in which he made the life of silent star Norma Desmond (Gloria Swanson) conform to the image a 1950s moviegoer might have of a silent star like Swanson. The Lubitsch Touch works in two ways, and Wilder knew them both: the conceit can become the reality; or the reality, the conceit. *Sunset Boulevard* was not only a Paramount film; it was also a film about Paramount that even showed moviegoers the Paramount lot, including the famous gate. All the principals had a Paramount connection in both the film and real life: Norma was a former Paramount star, as was Swanson; Max von Mayerling (Erich von Stroheim), Norma's butler and former husband, was once a major director at Paramount, unlike von Stroheim, whose megalomania, disregard for budgets, and obsession with detail eventually made him persona non grata at Paramount, and elsewhere, after his one and only Paramount feature, *The Wedding March* (1928); Joe Gillis, the down-on-his-luck writer, desperate for Paramount to option his script, was played by William Holden, who had been at the studio since 1938; and Nancy Olson, a more recent contract player, was Betty Schaeffer, the Paramount story analyst. The casting of von Stroheim as Swanson's one-time director is even more ironic when one realizes that von Stroheim directed Swanson in *Queen Kelly* (1928), a scene from which appears in *Sunset Boulevard.*

The studio itself figures so prominently in *Sunset Boulevard* that we see the back lot on three different occasions, including one in which DeMille is shooting another of his biblical epics. The lot is real to those who work there; however, Norma has not worked there since the coming of sound.

For Norma, Paramount is an illusion; to Joe and Betty, a reality. The confusion between illusion and reality forms the crux of the film. But comedy is based on exactly such confusion. Because Norma Desmond and Gloria Swanson seem to live by the same conventions, the confusion is doubled; so is the comic potential. One might object to calling *Sunset Boulevard* a comedy; after all, it is about a silent star who refuses to believe that her day is over, plans a comeback as Salome, cajoles a screenwriter into helping her fashion a script, shoots him, goes mad, and in a state of sweet delirium, descends the staircase of her Beverly Hills mansion, thinking she is on a Paramount soundstage playing Salome under DeMille's direction, although it is really Max/von Stroheim behind the camera.

Still, *Sunset Boulevard* has some wonderfully comic moments, the best being Swanson's elongating her eyes into cow goddess slits as she replies to William Holden's comment that she used to be "big": "I am big. It's the pictures that got small." If the film elicits occasional laughter (and Wilder once envisioned it as a comedy, with Mae West as Norma), it is because there is a thin line between the comic and the gothic. Both derive from the incongruous, with the gothic sometimes veering into the extreme and becoming the ludicrous. It is ludicrous that Norma is planning a comeback at Paramount when the studio system is on the verge of ending. However, the very fact that Paramount made *Sunset Boulevard* is a reflection of its sense of identity, its sense of humor, and, even more, its sense of its own history.

Even when Wilder ventured into film noir with *Double Indemnity,* he darkened the Lubitsch touch, as one might expect in a film in which a married woman, Phyllis Dietrichson (Barbara Stanwyck), conspires with a smarmy insurance agent, Walter Neff (Fred MacMurray), to kill her oafish husband. There is something grimly humorous about the way Phyllis entraps Walter—first engaging him in "can you top this?" dialogue in which she gets the last word; then becoming his accomplice, lover, ex-lover, and would-be murderer. Walter undergoes the same stages of their relationship except that he has no qualms about killing Phyllis; when he presses his revolver against her heart, saying "Bye, Baby," it is the long goodbye.

There was no reason why Wilder, who coauthored the script with

Raymond Chandler, should have changed the wife's name from Phyllis Nirdlinger, as it was in James Cain's novel, to Phyllis Dietrichson, unless he expected the knowledgeable to make a connection between the character and femme fatale epitomized by Marlene Dietrich in *The Blue Angel*. Nor would Wilder have had Stanwyck don a blonde wig and make her first appearance draped in a white bath towel unless he was trying to perpetuate the Paramount white look in a different context. Wilder even has the couple commit adultery in the Lubitsch tradition. As the camera tracks back from Phyllis and Walter, seated together on a sofa, Walter's voice-over answers the "Did they or didn't they?" question. "We just sat there," Walter is heard saying matter-of-factly. They probably did, until Wilder called "Cut!" Then the imagination took over, as it generally did in such films.

That so many Paramount films of the 1940s echoed each other was a reflection of the studio's unabashed self-promotion. Paramount sang the song of the self, and its famous Spanish-style gate was often featured in its films and newsreels. In the prologue to *Hold Back the Dawn* (1941), Charles Boyer sneaks onto the Paramount lot, where Mitchell Leisen is shooting *I Wanted Wings* (1941). Boyer offers to sell his story to Leisen, who, despite a busy schedule, lights a cigarette and listens. In other words, a Paramount director (Leisen), in the midst of shooting a Paramount film (*I Wanted Wings*), hears the tale of a fictional character (a Romanian immigrant played by Boyer), which provides the impetus for another Paramount film, *Hold Back the Dawn,* released four months after *Wings*.

Star-Spangled Rhythm (1942) was an excuse for showcasing the Paramount pantheon (e.g., Bing Crosby, Bob Hope, Dorothy Lamour, Veronica Lake, and even DeMille and Sturges) in a film celebrating both the war effort and the studio. A Paramount security guard has deceived his son, a recent Navy enlistee, into thinking he is a movie executive; when the son turns up at the Paramount gate hoping his father will use his influence to put on a variety show for his buddies, the gatekeeper's attempt to play producer is an opportunity for Paramount to host a studio tour, presenting its actors as people rather than stars.

In *Duffy's Tavern* (1945), many of the same Paramount stars who entertained the Navy in *Star-Spangled Rhythm* rallied to prevent the closing of a bar known to radio audiences from the NBC series of the same name. In *Variety Girl* (1947), an unknown becomes a star thanks to Paramount's altruistic actors, especially Bing Crosby, who had graduated from priest (*Going My Way* [1944], *The Bells of St. Mary's* [1945]) to deus ex machina.

The "Road" movies with Bing Crosby, Bob Hope, and Dorothy Lamour were shamelessly self-referential. "You know, I've the strangest feeling we've been through this before," Lamour muses at the end of *Road to Morocco* (1942). She was right: *Morocco* was the third in the series. At the end of the film, as the trio gaze at the New York skyline, Hope says, "Three years and three pictures! We've been waiting to get back." In the Road movies, nothing was sacred, including Paramount. In the *Road to Morocco* title song, Hope and Crosby sing: "We have no doubts or fears/ Paramount will protect us/'cause we're signed for five more years."

Road to Utopia (1945) offers the ultimate in self-parody when the Paramount logo, the star-spangled mountain, appears like the aurora borealis over the Alaskan snowscape. Hope sees the mountain and says, "Look at all that bread and butter." Crosby replies, "Bread and butter? You're losing your grip. That's a mountain." Hope answers, "It may be a mountain to you, but it's bread and butter to me."

Paramount's ability to see itself with a double vision that mirrored the studio as well as its films is basically a technique deriving from the oldest source of comedy: the incongruous. For nothing is more incongruous than an echo, which is both a reflection and a reduction of the self—and often a reduction of the self to the absurd, to a single reverberating note. Paramount took a chance with self-parody; unless it is tongue-in-cheek, self—parody can become self-denigration. But it was all in the spirit of good-natured fun, which, the studio hoped, would translate into good box office.

In *Variety Girl,* when Olga San Juan barges onto a soundstage where DeMille is shooting a film, it is really a Paramount star creating havoc on a Paramount set. The victim of the gag and the perpetrator are the same: Paramount Pictures. Like Gypsy Rose Lee, who boasted that she laughed at herself before others had a chance to, Paramount got a head start on the parodists by kidding itself first. There was no need for critics to call attention to the gleeful disregard for verisimilitude in *Road to Morocco.* A camel does it by staring into the camera and saying, "This is the screwiest movie I ever saw!"

When a heart ailment caused DeSylva to relinquish the production reins in 1944, the studio was not thrown into a state of turmoil. The Paramount product had taken on such a distinctive character—especially in comedy, DeSylva's forte—that it only needed someone to continue the tradition, at least until the winds of change blew in a different direction. The popularity of Paramount's stars; hit movies such as *Reap the Wild*

Wind (1942), *For Whom the Bell Tolls* (1943), and *Holiday Inn* (1942), which introduced the immortal "White Christmas," and the seven-category Oscar winner, *Going My Way* (1944), which grossed $6 million domestically—all contributed to Paramount's $17.95 million net profit in 1945. Revenues nearly tripled the following year, making Paramount the most profitable studio in Hollywood.[38]

Thus, there was no need to replace DeSylva with someone who had production experience. Instead, Henry Ginsberg was upped from general manager to executive producer. Ginsberg, who had served as general manager for Hal Roach's and David Selznick's companies, came to Paramount in 1940, where his mandate was to reorganize the various units within the studio, strengthening those (e.g., the talent, publicity, and story departments) that needed it and fine-tuning others.

In July 1944, when Ginsberg took over production, Paramount had enough producers (e.g., Arthur Hornblow, Fred Kohlmar, Paul Jones) and producer-directors (DeMille, Sturges, Wilder, Leisen, Mark Sandrich, and Leo McCarey) to require only the most basic kind of supervision: budgetary. Ginsberg, who believed he was creative in his own (i.e., managerial) way, left fame to the moviemakers: "I was more or less an administrator and executive of a creative type but not thrown into the category of producers in the sense of having my name on the screen."[39]

There were also independent producers on the lot. Every studio turned out its quota of B movies in the 1940s; many of Paramount's were released under the Pine-Thomas banner. Sharing the same first name, William, Pine and Thomas became known as the "Dollar Bills" because of the high-grossing power of their low-budget films, which could cost anywhere from $86,000 (*Power Dive* [1941], the team's first production, shot in ten days) to $1 million (*El Paso* [1949]). Pine and Thomas were both college graduates (Columbia and the University of Southern California, respectively) who found themselves working as associate producers at Paramount in the late 1930s. Knowing that Paramount needed inexpensively made product with lesser-known but popular actors (e.g., Richard Arlen, Chester Morris, Jean Parker, Nancy Kelly), Pine and Thomas persuaded the studio to finance and distribute their films, for which they would receive a supervision fee and a percentage of the gross once the costs had been recouped. By the time Pine and Thomas left Paramount in the mid-1950s, they had given the studio sixty films.

In March 1943, Hal B. Wallis—an executive producer at Warner Bros. whose list of credits was legendary then and awesome today (e.g., *I*

Am a Fugitive from a Chain Gang [1932], *Captain Blood* [1935], *Marked Woman* [1937], *Dark Victory* [1939], *High Sierra* [1941], *Casablanca* [1942])—made no secret of the fact that he was looking for a studio where he and attorney Joseph Hazen could set up their own production company. Wallis had been content at Warner Bros., particularly after Jack Warner agreed to a production deal allowing him to make four pictures a year of his own choice, to be financed by the studio, with Wallis receiving a percentage of the profits. At first, Warner honored the arrangement, and Wallis reciprocated with *Casablanca* (1942), *Now, Voyager* (1942), *Watch on the Rhine* (1943), and *Air Force* (1943). However, on Academy Awards night, 2 March 1944, as soon as Sidney Franklin announced that *Casablanca* had won the Oscar for Best Picture, Wallis rose from his seat and began walking up the aisle of Grauman's Chinese Theatre, when Jack Warner darted past him, rushing onto the stage to claim an award for a film in whose production he had played no role.[40]

Although other studios extended the welcome mat to Wallis, he chose Paramount and by 1944 had an office on the Marathon Street lot. Wallis could never hope to duplicate his Warner Bros. record at Paramount; he would never produce another *Casablanca,* much less a *Gold Diggers of 1933* or *Yankee Doodle Dandy* (1942). The times had changed, the creative climate was different, and the talent pool had been refilled. Gone were the days when Wallis had such stars as Humphrey Bogart, Errol Flynn, Bette Davis, Edward G. Robinson, Paul Muni, James Cagney, Olivia DeHavilland, Ida Lupino, and even Ronald Reagan at his disposal. He was able to stage a reunion of three of the old Warner gang—Paul Henreid, Peter Lorre, and Claude Rains—in *Rope of Sand* (1949). But, for the most part, Wallis relied on Paramount contract players (e.g., Ann Richards, Wendell Corey, Diana Lynn, Mona Freeman) and freelancers such as Loretta Young, Barbara Stanwyck, Joseph Cotten, Joan Fontaine, and Burt Lancaster. Always the starmaker, Wallis was on the lookout for newcomers, hoping a few of them might make it. Several did; some enjoyed their brief gaudy hour (Lizabeth Scott, Corinne Calvet), and two became icons: Kirk Douglas and Charlton Heston.

Arguably, Wallis's greatest discovery was the team of Dean Martin and Jerry Lewis, whom Wallis first saw at the Copacabana in New York and, despite his indifference to nightclub performers, signed for their first film, *My Friend Irma* (1949), based on the popular radio show. There was nothing odd about Wallis's belief that a team consisting of a straight man and a top banana in the form of a laid-back singer and a zany could make it in the movies. Wallis was now at Paramount, home of the "Road" movies, whose success was due primarily to the pairing of Bing Crosby and Bob Hope, with Dorothy Lamour as an added attraction. However, in the case of Martin and Lewis, who were film novices, there was the matter of finding a script to suit their personalities, not their acting ability, which was as yet unknown. After a few disastrous screentests, Wallis realized what was wrong: Martin and Lewis were not experienced enough to play characters. They would therefore have to play types: Lewis, the stooge; and Martin, the amorous crooner.[41] Martin would sing a few songs, and Lewis would do shtick. In one of the funniest moments in *Irma*, Lewis stalks about like the Frankenstein monster with his fingers curled into claws from squeezing too many oranges. Eventually, Lewis came into his own, but that was only after he parted company with Martin in 1956. During his fifteen-year relationship with Wallis, Lewis was not so much a thorn as a lance in the producer's side. As Lewis's ego grew "as tall as the Empire State Building,"[42] his demands became more outrageous, including throwing temper tantrums in a four-star Paris hotel when room service could not oblige him with a salami sandwich at 2:00 A.M. When Lewis began directing his own films in 1960, Wallis refrained from criticism: "There is no need to comment on their quality," he wrote in his autobiography.[43]

While Elvis Presley cannot be called a Wallis discovery, it was Wallis who first saw Elvis's potential as a movie star. Elvis's discoverer was Col. Tom Parker, who also functioned as his manager and regarded Elvis as his protégé. In April 1956, Parker agreed to allow Elvis to appear in three pictures at fifteen thousand dollars per picture.[44] Wallis had purchased the rights to N. Richard Nash's play, *The Rainmaker*, as a vehicle for Burt Lancaster and Katharine Hepburn. Elvis tested for the supporting role of Hepburn's younger brother, which was eventually played by Earl Holliman. The character was a hayseed, and Elvis would have been laughable in such a part. Ironically, Elvis would have been perfect for the title character—a fast-talking, preacher-like con man, but he would have needed a much younger costar than Hepburn.

Although Parker was Elvis's manager, he was represented by the William Morris Agency, which balked at Elvis's having to remain idle until Wallis found the right vehicle for him. Thus, Elvis's film debut occurred at Fox, where he was loaned out for *Love Me Tender* (1957), which not only made Elvis a star but also gave him a hit single with his recording of the title song. The outside picture deal with Fox was also a triumph for Colonel Parker, who used it as an opportunity to get Elvis more money (one hundred thousand instead of fifteen thousand dollars) and himself screen credit as technical advisor.[45]

Elvis's Paramount films, beginning with *Loving You* (1957), were in the Paramount tradition of comedy or, in some cases, drama enlivened by a few musical numbers. However, Elvis did not work exclusively for Wallis. Once Parker understood how lucrative loanouts were, he insisted that Wallis negotiate with him on a yearly basis. Elvis never became the screen icon on the order of Errol Flynn that Wallis envisioned. Actually, Elvis did his best acting not in his Paramount films but in MGM's *Jailhouse Rock* (1957) and Fox's *Flaming Star* (1960) and *Wild in the Country* (1961).

Wallis may have been a starmaker, as the title of his autobiography proclaims. However, the films he produced for Paramount—except perhaps for *Come Back, Little Sheba* (1952), *The Rose Tattoo* (1955), and *True Grit* (1969)—cannot compare with his Warner Bros. legacy. While some of Wallis's Paramount films won Oscars in various categories, none ever received an Academy Award for Best Picture, as did *Casablanca*.

When Wallis's first two Paramount films, *The Affairs of Susan* and *Love Letters* (both 1945), went into release, the studio was in the black. Profits had soared from $15.4 million in 1945 to $39.2 million in 1946; by the end of the decade, however, they had plummeted to $3.3 million. Television is usually billed as the heavy in "Who Killed the Movies?" scenarios, but in 1947 television's shadow was not adumbrating Hollywood. The shadows falling over the industry were cast by much larger bodies.

First, there was the House Committee on UnAmerican Activities (HUAC), which had been looking for a cause to garner publicity for its shameless snooping into people's lives. HUAC found one in the anti-Communist paranoia that gripped the nation following the end of World War II when the former Soviet Union, America's ally during the conflict, brought an iron curtain down on Eastern Europe. Deciding that the screen had been, and still might be, a conduit for Communist propaganda, HUAC moved in for the kill. In September 1947 a climate of anger, panic, and defiance prevailed in Hollywood as forty-three members of the industry—actors, producers, and writers—were subpoenaed to appear before the committee the following month to testify about the alleged Communist subversion of the movie industry. Today, "Hollywood Communist" is an oxymoron, but in 1947 it was a charge that could either get one blacklisted or imprisoned.

Of the subpoenaed, nineteen expressed their opposition to HUAC, calling the investigation unconstitutional. Eleven of the nineteen were called; the eleventh was German playwright Bertolt Brecht, who was only peripherally associated with the movies. After swearing he was not a Communist, Brecht left the stand and, later, the country. The remaining ten, who invoked their First Amendment rights, became known as the Hollywood Ten and received prison sentences ranging from six months to a year, although no one served his full term. Still, the damage had been done. Over two hundred lives were affected by the blacklist—and an indeterminate number by the greylist—that came in the wake of the hearings.[46] Writers resorted to pseudonyms and fronts; actors and directors deemed unemployable by the studios found themselves barred from television as well, with no other choice but to work in Europe or in the theater. "The time of the toad," as Dalton Trumbo christened the era of hysteria and informing, was not Hollywood's finest hour. The industry that had rallied during World War II, when stars enlisted in the armed forces, sold war bonds, and entertained GIs, had caved in to a publicity-hungry committee that targeted Hollywood, knowing that, if it had picked on academics or other less newsworthy types, there would not have been much of an audience.

Nineteen forty-seven was not a good year for Hollywood. Britain, eager to revive its own film industry and at the same time prevent Hollywood movies from dominating British screens, imposed a 75 percent tax on all revenues derived from foreign (meaning, for all practical purposes, American) films shown in the United Kingdom. And, as if that were not enough, American actors working in Britain would be paid in dollars, not pounds.

What HUAC and Britain left undone, the Justice Department completed. Since 1938, the Justice Department had been looking for a way to dissolve the hegemony of the five leading studios (Paramount, RKO, Warner Bros., MGM, and Fox), also known as the "Big Five," which, along with the "Little Three" (Columbia, Universal, and United Artists), produced 65 to 70 percent of the films shown in first-run theaters throughout the country. The argument that the studios were competing for the same audience—faithful moviegoers who preferred a major release in a first-run theater to a "B" flick in a side street venue but could settle for the latter, if necessary—had no effect on the Justice Department, which was hellbent on breaking up what it perceived as a monopoly, with the Big Five not only producing and distributing their films but also funneling them into their own theaters.[47] While it is true that the Five operated

their own theater chains, they could never have used them to exhibit
their own films exclusively. For one thing, no studio ever produced enough
films annually to restrict its theaters to its own releases; for another, audiences wanted variety. Nineteen-forties moviegoers could distinguish between studios; they knew that a Universal horror movie was not on a par
with a Paramount drama, even if they were on a double bill. And if, in
1945, Universal's *House of Dracula* was shown in one theater, and
Paramount's *The Lost Weekend* in another, the movie fan would see both;
the horror enthusiast, *Dracula;* and the serious-minded type, *Weekend.* Yet
the same moviegoers who put *The Lost Weekend* on their "must see" list
would also have found time that year for Warner Bros.' *Confidential Agent,*
Fox's *Fallen Angel,* and MGM's *Adventure*—but probably not for *House of
Dracula.*

The antitrust suit that the Justice Department brought against the
studios did not exclude the Little Three, even though they had no theater
chains. Columbia, United Artists, and Universal were accused of favoring
the Big Five's theaters over those of independent exhibitors.[48] Yet they
too were bound by the Supreme Court's 1948 decision (often referred to
as the Paramount decision because Paramount had the largest number of
theaters), which, in addition to requiring studios with theater circuits to
sever production from exhibition (becoming, in effect, production-distribution companies), also banned such practices as block booking (renting films en bloc rather than individually) and fixing admission prices.

Paramount and RKO were the first to sign the consent decrees.
Even Paramount's stockholders knew divestiture was inevitable and voted
60 to 1 for it. Paramount's theater chain consisted of some 1,450 theaters,
although that figure is misleading because Paramount had interests in
others, ranging from 25 to 33 percent.[49] Paramount, however, was not
exactly left theaterless—a concession for its having agreed to divestiture
so soon after the decision. On 3 March 1949, the New York District
Court approved a restructuring plan, according to which Paramount would
be split into two companies, production-distribution and theater operations, with a five-year ban on stock ownership in both companies by any
one individual. Paramount could retain up to 650 theaters that would
become part of United Paramount Theaters Inc., a separately owned and
operated chain with a board of directors made up mostly of members without
any previous Paramount connection. The flagship theater at 1501 Broadway was a special case: Paramount was given five years to dispose of it.

The blacklist silenced voices, banished faces, and caused premature deaths; the Justice Department privatized exhibition—but only until movies ceased being a mass medium, and the studios became subsidiaries of conglomerates, which could acquire interests in such enterprises as music and book publishing, cable and network television, hotel chains, insurance companies, national park concessions, soft drink bottling, sports clubs, and—why not?—theater circuits. A violation of the Sherman Act in one year is a triumph for laissez faire in another.

In 1949, the question was not whether the Big Five should be allowed to keep their theaters as much as it was whether there would be anything to draw audiences to the theaters if they kept them. Granted that the studios were dealt a blow by the Paramount decision, they still had to face the fact that the moviegoers of the 1930s and 1940s were aging, developing other interests, fretting about inflation, watching their screen idols grow old with them, wondering whether they should invest in a twelve-and-one-half–inch Motorola television set or wait until a sixteen–inch screen was available, and, finally, questioning whether movies were worth the price of admission, which seemed to have doubled overnight.

The price was worth it. Although Paramount always produced its share of quality films, it now had to aim for excellence. Between 1949 and 1955, Paramount was nominated every year for Best Picture, winning in 1952 for *The Greatest Show on Earth*. Best Actress Oscars went to Olivia de Havilland for *The Heiress* (1949), Shirley Booth for *Come Back, Little Sheba* (1952), Grace Kelly for *The Country Girl* (1954), and Anna Magnani for *The Rose Tattoo* (1955). William Holden was named Best Actor for *Stalag 17* in 1953, the same year *Shane* won for Best Color Cinematography. Although Billy Wilder was nominated for his direction of *Sunset Boulevard* and *Stalag 17,* it was George Stevens who received the Best Director Oscar for *A Place in the Sun* (1951). The Oscar winners in the writing categories were *Sunset Boulevard* (Story and Screenplay), *A Place in the Sun* (Screenplay), *The Greatest Show on Earth* (Story), *Roman Holiday* (Story), and *The Country Girl* (Screenplay). Financially, the studio was not hurting. After hitting a low of $3.3 million in 1949, revenues rose slowly, reaching $9.4 million in 1958.

Still, Paramount had changed dramatically in the 1950s. The contract talent of the previous decade had dwindled to a handful: William Holden, Hope and Crosby, Nancy Olson, Corinne Calvet, a less bouncy Betty Hutton, and a few others. Except for Martin and Lewis, Elvis, and Audrey Hepburn (Paramount's only bonafide new star of the 1950s), the studio did not seem intent on grooming new talent, relying instead on loanouts (Elizabeth Taylor in *Elephant Walk* [1954] and Kim Novak in *Vertigo* [1958]) and freelancers (e.g., Rosalind Russell, Deborah Kerr, James Stewart, Joan Fontaine, Fredric March) for one- or two-picture deals. The clearest sign that the studio era was ending was the preponderance of stars, formerly associated with competitors (Warner Bros.' regulars Jane Wyman, James Cagney, Humphrey Bogart; MGM family members Kathryn Grayson, June Allyson, Spencer Tracy, Clark Gable, and Lana Turner), who were now appearing—not always memorably—in Paramount films.

The accolades that Paramount received during the first half of the decade were offset by the less-than-distinguished releases of the late 1950s. Yet Paramount remained indifferent; in fact, even in the early 1950s, the studio seemed less interested in the recognition *The Heiress, Sunset Boulevard,* and *A Place in the Sun* received than it was in touting Hal Wallis's latest production.

Studio-distributed independent productions seemed to be the wave of the future. On 5 July 1950, Henry Ginsberg, who had been at Paramount since 1940, resigned as production head. On the same day, Hal Wallis signed a new contract with Paramount, giving him $19.5 million for thirteen pictures. Although Ginsberg's departure was amicable, W.R. Wilkerson in his *Hollywood Reporter* column (7 July 1950) implied that it was precipitated by Ginsberg's realization that Balaban was planning to turn the studio into a base for independent production companies such as Wallis's and William Perlberg and George Seaton's—a move that would eventually reduce Paramount to a distributor of other people's product. Yet the entire industry was heading in that direction, as in-house productions became increasingly rare until, by the 1970s, they were virtually nonexistent.

Balaban had another agenda. In 1937, Balaban became conscious of television, which, he believed, could be the ideal complement to film. In 1937, "television" was not a new coinage. There had been experimental telecasting as early as 1928. With the future in mind, Paramount acquired a 26 percent interest (i.e., all of the class B stock) in the Allen B. DuMont Laboratories, the television set and picture tube manufacturer, raising its investment to 50 percent the following year.[50] Shortly thereafter, Paramount acquired experimental station W6XYZ (later renamed KTLA) and formed Paramount Television Productions for operating the station and testing contract talent for possible television appearances. At first, the programming on W6XYZ was minimal; the station was only on the air

Thursdays from 8:00 to 9:00 P.M. Still, the few who had a set could tune in to see Bob Hope hosting the station's premiere in 1941, and Alan Ladd and Veronica Lake being interviewed on the set of *This Gun for Hire* (1942). Little did Hope realize when he was welcoming viewers to the new station that a decade later he would be starring in *The Bob Hope Show* on NBC and that, with his yearly television specials, he would become one of the most familiar faces on the tube.

Paramount, like other studios, would eventually move into television production, providing the networks with such series as *Cheers, Family Ties, Webster, Star Trek, Frazier,* and *JAG*. However, in the 1940s, Paramount viewed television as another form of exhibition. Paul Raibourn, a Columbia University graduate with a B.S. in electrical engineering—and former treasurer and director of the DuMont Laboratories who had been at the studio in various capacities (mostly technical) since 1920—was the moving force behind Paramount's early venture into television. The fact that Raibourn was elevated to president of Paramount Television Productions in 1950 was a clear indication of the studio's desire to stake its claim in the new, and eventually competitive, medium. Raibourn saw the future, and in 1948 it was—so he believed—theater television: variety shows and sporting events transmitted live in movie theaters, the equivalent of the live stage shows that were frequently part of the bill at many of Paramount's theaters.[51] As history has shown, theater television's appeal was short-lived, and the studios had to resort to other gimmicks: 3–D and various forms of widescreen technology (CinemaScope, Warnerscope, VistaVision) to attract audiences.

Film and television are separate and unequal, as Hollywood discovered the hard way. Paramount's mistake was imagining theater television could replace the thrill of seeing pop stars like Frank Sinatra and Peggy Lee in person, along with a movie. Soon, Sinatra and Lee were appearing live—on the Ed Sullivan Show on Sunday nights, courtesy of CBS-TV, not Paramount or any other studio.

Raibourn also erred in placing too much confidence in DuMont's attempt to create a network that would be on a par with CBS and NBC. That distinction fell to ABC, which became the third network, while DuMont had to settle for fourth. In 1951, ABC merged with United Paramount Theaters, the residue of Paramount's theater chain after the consent decrees, leaving DuMont with a large number of stations but few committed viewers. By 1955, DuMont quietly exited television broadcasting; four years later, Metromedia bought Paramount's DuMont shares.

Even Metromedia faded away, the victim of a 1985 leveraged buyout that left Fox's new owner, Rupert Murdoch, in control of Metromedia's stations. Paramount's flirtation with television amounted to little, proving only that the two media would have to coexist and that, while films could be shown on television, audiences were not willing to pay movie admission prices for small-screen entertainment in alien venues.

Paramount, however, had other problems in the 1950s. Don Hartman, who replaced Ginsburg in 1951 with the title of executive producer, had the right resumé for production chief. He had been a stage actor and had turned to screenwriting; together with Frank Butler, he had written the scripts for the first three "Road" movies: *Road to Singapore* (1940), *Road to Zanzibar* (1941), and *Road to Morocco* (1942). He had also served as associate producer of several Danny Kaye films for Goldwyn. Hartman even dabbled in directing. Although he never was a house director like Mitchell Leisen or Billy Wilder, Columbia hired him for the Ginger Rogers movie *It Had to be You* (1947); RKO, for the Cary Grant–Betsy Drake comedy, *Every Girl Should be Married* (1948), and the Robert Mitchum–Janet Leigh yuletide romance, *Holiday Affair* (1949); and MGM, for the musical *Mr. Imperium* (1950) with Lana Turner and Ezio Pinza.

Since Paramount's revenues dropped from $6.6 million in 1950 to $5.5 in 1951, Hartman, who had never been involved in big-budget productions, instituted a policy in 1952 calling for careful story selection to eliminate extensive rewrites, shorter scripts to generate more ninety–minute movies, fewer sets to save money, and fewer camera setups to save time.

Retrenchment need not presage the end of quality. However, whatever quality was achieved in the 1950–55 period was due primarily to Hal Wallis; writer-director George Seaton, who was nominated for an Oscar for his direction and screenplay of *The Country Girl* (1954), winning for screenplay; and producer-directors Billy Wilder, George Stevens, William Wyler, and Alfred Hitchcock, a Paramount newcomer whose agent, Lew Wasserman, negotiated a multipicture contract for the director, whose first Paramount film was the classic *Rear Window* (1954). However, from the mid-fifties to the end of the decade, little quality was in evidence. Wilder, Stevens, and Wyler had all departed by 1955; Wallis seemed to have given up on art in favor of Martin and Lewis and Elvis; Hitchcock, who gave Paramount the then-underrated and now-canonized *Vertigo* (1958), became so disillusioned with the studio that he moved over to Universal in 1961; and Seaton left after making *The Counterfeit Traitor* (1962), another film unappreciated in its time.

In 1953, Hartman's contract was extended for five years; however, he abruptly left the studio in early 1956. The usual explanation, the desire to go into independent production, was given as the reason, although Hartman's health may also have been a factor. Two years later, he died of a heart attack at the age of fifty-seven.

Paramount was cutting costs however it could. In 1955, Balaban decided that foreign and domestic distribution—previously separate divisions, each with its own head—should be consolidated under someone whose expertise was in foreign sales, which were capable of generating higher revenues than domestic (generally, 60 percent higher). There was only one person qualified for the job: George Weltner, one of the few Paramount executives—if not the only one—who was widely respected both at the studio and within the industry. When Weltner accepted the job, he had no idea that ten years later he would be Paramount's president or, more accurately, the last president of Paramount Pictures Corporation.

2

Mountain Gloom

When George Weltner joined Paramount in 1922, a little more than a month after graduating from Columbia University, he probably never expected to spend his entire career there.[1] Growing up in Chicago, he had witnessed the nickelodeon era and the rise of the movie palace but never thought he would be part of an industry that produced the kind of entertainment he had enjoyed in his youth. At twenty-one, Weltner considered himself an engineer, not a potential film executive, much less a filmmaker. With a B.S. in chemical engineering, Weltner had no dearth of job offers upon graduation. If he chose Paramount, his decision was based partly on his parents' connection with Adolph Zukor. Sigmund and Ernestine Weltner, who were both born in Budapest, became part of New York's Hungarian community, through which they came to know Zukor. If Zukor was instrumental in Weltner's coming to Paramount, it was characteristic of his willingness to help compatriots. Zukor even returned to Hungary after World War I to provide financial assistance to Risce, his birthplace; finding a job for a landsman's son was a far easier matter.

The job also appealed to Weltner, since it would allow him to make use of his chemical engineering degree. And so, on 22 July 1922, Weltner reported for work at Paramount's film laboratory in Astoria in northwestern Queens, across the street from the studio that had opened in 1920 and was where such Paramount films as *Monsieur Beaucaire* (1924) with Rudolph Valentino; the Gloria Swanson vehicles *A Society Scandal* (1924), *Manhandled* (1924), and *The Wages of Virtue* (1924); and *The Cocoanuts* (1929) with the Marx Brothers were shot. Weltner was not the type to be awed by the sight of Valentino, Swanson, W.C. Fields, Jeanne Eagels, Helen Morgan, or the other stars who came to work at Astoria. To the young Weltner, it was just an eighteen-dollars–a-week entry-level position that would either lead to something better or someplace else. Yet the experience of working in the lab soon made Weltner appreciate the complex nature of moviemaking; it also prepared him for the field he would soon enter.

It was virtually impossible to work in an environment in which films are printed and made ready for release without becoming aware of the logistics involved in shipping those prints to the theaters, particularly theaters abroad. In addition to learning how films were processed, Weltner was receiving his first lessons in distribution.

Distribution, especially foreign, fascinated Weltner. That fascination led to an assignment two years later in Argentina, marking the beginning of a career that made him a globe-trotter and sent him to Paramount exchanges throughout the world. Weltner swiftly moved up the ranks. By 1934 he was assistant to the head of Paramount International; ten years later he was president of Paramount International. In 1955, he took over domestic distribution as well, becoming director of both domestic and foreign sales.

Weltner's distribution background was not the only reason for his appointment; he had also assisted Eric Johnston, the head of the Motion Picture Association of America, in his efforts to revive the international market, which had been seriously affected by World War II, during which the Hollywood product was absent from the screens of Axis-controlled countries.

Weltner's appointment confirmed the significance of the international market in a changing Hollywood. By 1956, television was clearly a mass medium, as evidenced by the common sight of former movie houses converted into food markets and drugstores; the dramatic drop-off in attendance at theaters—from 90 million in 1946 to almost half that number ten years later; and the burgeoning of drive-ins (from two thousand in 1950 to more than four thousand in 1956, which made moviegoing more affordable, especially to amorous couples who were not particular about what they saw and families who were not particular about where they saw it.[2] Weltner knew the industry had changed; until he became distribution chief and Barney Balaban's troubleshooter, he did not know how much.

Weltner's ability to maintain a low profile and work quietly behind the scenes also proved desirable in an industry dominated by ego, hype, and spin. Now in his early fifties, Weltner was quickly moving into a position that would soon require his presiding over the end of Paramount Pictures as a freestanding company. But at the time he could not have known that; what he knew was that he would be based in New York. He would miss the home in Woodmere, Long Island, where he lived with his wife, Bertha, and son, Jack; he would also miss the weekends he spent fishing with Jack and relaxing on his boat. Although he and his family lived in an apartment on Central Park South during the week, weekends found them in their new home on idyllic Katydid Lane in Stamford, Connecticut, where the Weltners moved in 1954. Stamford was an easy commute from New York either by car or by train on the New Haven line (now Metro North). Although the opportunities for boating were not what they were on Long Island, Weltner still had a boat—smaller, of course—for those weekends when he could put aside the problems of an industry in disarray. His new lifestyle did not mean that his traveling days were over, only less frequent.

Balaban planned to introduce Weltner to production gradually—never with the intention of grooming him for production head (for which Weltner would have been unsuited); rather, Balaban expected Weltner to become knowledgeable about scripts, budgets, and the independent producers whose films dominated Paramount's releases and with whom he would eventually have to deal.

Weltner was a quick study; he sensed that there was no reason to disturb the Hal Wallis–Paramount relationship even though the Wallis production of *About Mrs. Leslie* (1954), despite the presence of Shirley Booth, was not another *Come Back, Little Sheba* (1952). Weltner had never encountered someone like Wallis, who determined the release dates for his films. Although Weltner favored an October release for *The Rose Tattoo* (1955), Wallis preferred December, and December it was—the same month Paramount had reserved for *The Desperate Hours* (1955). Nor was Weltner keen on Wallis's decision to make the latest Dean Martin and Jerry Lewis romp, *Artists and Models* (1955), the studio's New Year's attraction. A compromise was reached: it became a holiday release. Actually, the release date made no difference in terms of box office: *Artists and Models* was a financial flop.

Dealing with Wallis was Weltner's introduction to a changing Hollywood—a Hollywood at twilight with a few more years of hazy sunshine before the dawning of a new day. Wallis was Weltner's baptism by fire, which is what Balaban intended. Weltner rose to the challenge once he realized that producers were driven by a combination of ego and lucre that made them alternately vulnerable and intimidating. But knowledge is one thing; action is another.

On the strength of Rosalind Russell's spectacular performance in her first (and only) Broadway musical, Leonard Bernstein's *Wonderful Town* (1953), her producer-husband, Fred Brisson, put together a project for Paramount that resulted in an abysmal movie—*The Girl Rush* (1955), designed to capitalize on his wife's newly revealed musical comedy skills. What Russell revealed in *Wonderful Town* was woefully absent from *The Girl Rush*; still, Brisson bypassed Weltner and arranged screenings for the Legion of Decency (Russell was a devout Catholic) before the Paramount sales staff had a chance to view the film and determine how to market it. Weltner "somewhat chided"[3] Russell, insisting that the studio be furnished with a print so the sales staff could mount a campaign. Yet the fact that Brisson and Russell treated Paramount as if it were a factory outlet indicates the extent to which the studio was dependent on outside product; and the fact that Weltner "*somewhat* chided" Russell suggests that he was awed by her reputation and/or Brisson's recent success as producer of the Broadway hits *The Pajama Game* (1954) and *Damn Yankees* (1955).

While it is tempting to blame Russell and her husband for exploiting a studio that had seen better days, Russell certainly could recall a time when a star could dictate her own terms. When she was at Columbia in the 1940s, she discovered Harry Cohn had a shelf full of expensive French perfumes in his office that he would offer ambitious starlets willing to join him on the casting couch. Knowing Russell's standing among the Hollywood Catholics, Cohn never propositioned her. But Russell wanted some Arpège for agreeing to star in one picture a year. Russell got her perfume.[4] This may have been the only time Harry Cohn had to give something away that had been intended for services rendered. And although Paramount in the 1950s was not what Columbia—or any studio—had been a decade earlier, the star power mentality still prevailed—doubly, in Russell's case, given her rave reviews for *Wonderful Town*. Thus Paramount had little choice but to accommodate her and Brisson, despite the inferiority of the film. That Russell does not even mention *The Girl Rush* in her autobiography indicates that she and the public shared the same feelings about a film that should never have been made.

Before Balaban anointed Weltner, he wanted a complete reorganization of the domestic and foreign branches, which previously had operated more or less independently. This was a challenge for Weltner, whose background had been in foreign distribution. He did the obvious, given Paramount's consistently low profits that may have kept the company in the black but did not augur well for the future. Weltner began streamlining operations; he transferred personnel, eliminated assistant division managers along with their secretaries and numbers crunchers, overhauled the booking division by reducing the number of clerks and replacing them with bookers who were given greater authority, and authorized promising members of the sales staff to negotiate deals with exhibitors instead of merely presenting them with a percentage plan.

In Weltner, Balaban had found someone who could take the heat; he had also found an indefatigable worker. What Weltner found was a staff polarized by a long-standing problem that would make Paramount ripe for a takeover in the next decade: age disparity that first caused tension, then factionalism, between the old guard clinging tenaciously to jobs for which they were no longer suited and their replacements waiting impatiently in the wings for vacancies that only death or retirement seemed to create.

Aging executives were one thing: in 1955, Balaban was sixty-eight; Zukor, ninety. Compared to them, Weltner, at fifty-four, was a kid. But Weltner also had to contend with Edward Kelly O'Shea, vice president of Paramount Film Distributing, who, in 1955, was fifty-nine. O'Shea, who had spent most of his career in sales at MGM, had demoralized the younger divisional managers and other sales executives by failing to address what Weltner considered Paramount Distributing's chief problem: sales personnel who were not only less aggressive than their counterparts abroad but also representative of the malaise that characterized the studio as a whole: "Our bookers are weak. They consist of . . . either very old-timers who have been with us twenty or thirty years, and new kids who have little background or outstanding qualities for this all-important job."[5] Salary was one reason for the apathy of the new hires, but another was their inexperience in pushing hard-to-sell films, of which there were several in 1955: *The Girl Rush*; *My Three Angels* and *The Desperate Hours* (both with Humphrey Bogart, who had fared better the previous year in *Sabrina*); *Mambo*; *Run for Cover*; *Conquest of Space*; and *Hell's Island*.

Because O'Shea's lethargy (which may have been health-related, since he died in February 1958) affected the entire division, the sales staff was sent armed with insufficient or inaccurate statistics, often intentionally, to give exhibitors the impression that some films were playing better than they actually were. Clearly, O'Shea regarded Weltner as an outsider whose bailiwick was international distribution. Weltner saw O'Shea as someone who would have to be retired if Paramount Distributing was ever to be extricated from the morass in which it was mired. The irregularities that Weltner discovered caused him to do considerable revamping, which, unfortunately, came too late for the studio to accomplish what it might have a decade earlier. Weltner might have thought it was too late, also, but he forged ahead with his reforms as if World War II had just ended and the consent decrees had never occurred.

Weltner had to confront the various arrangements the divisional managers and their sales staff made with exhibitors. While there was never a standard percentage deal for exhibitors, 60/40 was common, as was 90/10, with ninety cents out of every dollar going to the distributor for the first week after the exhibitor had deducted the operating expenses (the "nut"), with a graduated percentage decrease during subsequent weeks as the distributor's share was reduced by 10 percent until a 35 percent minimum was reached.[6]

There were also films that were licensed for a flat fee as well as those for which the exhibitor had to guarantee a high percentage of the first week's gross or accept a 90/10 arrangement, which at least guaranteed exhibitors 10 percent of the gross, regardless of the nut. While all the studios used flexible formulas and had their share of exhibitors who were delinquent or exaggerated their overhead, Paramount's problems were so widespread that the company had become a textbook case of distribution in disorder. Estimates were always prepared for each film, but an estimate is precisely that: an approximation of the anticipated profits. The branch managers were then expected to correlate the estimates with the revenues generated. This policy, Weltner discovered to his annoyance, was widely ignored. Conversely, films were frequently overestimated, and when they failed to live up to the studio's expectations, the discrepancies were listed as "billing errors." Some films were even sold without contracts because there was no time to issue them!

While negotiation was standard practice between distributor and exhibitor, Paramount's sales staff had been striking percentage deals that favored the exhibitor, causing the accountants to revise the books to make the home office look good. Paramount had been operating on the policy of granting credit to exhibitors who could not meet the terms of their contracts because the films failed to generate the anticipated revenues. As opposed to the exhibitor, whose concern is his or her venue, the distributor must service a vast number of theater owners and cannot get around immediately to the delinquents. Thus time was on the side of exhibitors who claimed the house nut was higher than it actually was and expected the distributor to take what were often inflated operating expenses into consideration. Actually, Paramount's policy worked to the exhibitors' advantage, allowing them to pile up credits and making it impossible for the studio to come up with accurate statistics. What really disturbed Weltner was that, between 1 February and 1 September 1955, four films—*White Christmas, The Country Girl, The Bridges at Toko-Ri* (all 1954), and *Strategic Air Command* (1955)—were sold in such a way as to cost Paramount more than $2 million in credits, while taking in only $1.5 million during the same period.

Realizing that exhibitors cannot be denied credits, especially in the mid-1950s, Weltner inaugurated a policy that was midway between the inflexible and the permissive. Certain films would be "floored": the terms, once set, would not be lowered (although they could be adjusted during a run), regardless of the house nut, thus guaranteeing the distributor a minimum percentage of the gross and making it difficult for exhibitors to pad their operating expenses. Thus if a floor is set at, say, 70 percent, the distributor will not settle for less than 70 percent of the gross.[7]

Other films would be negotiable. The credits policy would be tightened: credits would be given only to paid-up exhibitors, and habitual delinquents would be sent films COD. Within nine months, Weltner had made enormous progress but not enough to satisfy Balaban. Weltner was exasperated: "You asked me 'Then, where's the money' and I can only answer 'So, where's the pictures?'"[8]

The pictures were the problem. No amount of marketing savvy could have turned *The Vagabond King* and *The Search for Bridey Murphy* (both 1956) into hits. Even making them a double bill failed to draw viewers. In fact, the combination resulted in the lowest volume of business in the history of the Loew's circuit. One could understand why Paramount made *Bridey Murphy:* the film was an adaptation of Morey Bernstein's controversial best-seller about reincarnation. But Paramount's decision to remake *The Vagabond King* is a mystery. *The Vagabond King* delighted audiences when Paramount made it in 1929; sound was a novelty, and the prospect of hearing Rudolph Friml's score sung by Dennis King and Jeanette MacDonald—in Technicolor, no less—enhanced its appeal. But in 1956, audiences expected musicals in color, and the team of Orest (a complete unknown) and Kathryn Grayson (a known quantity but never a box-office attraction) failed to dispel the memory of the original. In 1956 it was also impossible for any musical to compete with Fox's *The King and I,* which was released in July of that year and proved so popular with exhibitors that Weltner was forced to push the Paramount Weeks (the period during which the studio showcased its latest releases) back from September to midsummer, only to discover that the sales staff could not get play dates for Paramount product until late August because of the competition from *King,* United Artists' *Trapeze,* and Warner Bros.' *Moby Dick.*

What Paramount had going for it was primarily *The Ten Commandments* (1956), which grossed $43 million domestically and almost twice as much worldwide—not bad for a film that had cost $13 million, ran over three and one-half hours, and played at road show prices in major cities. Paramount's other 1956 epic, *War and Peace,* which cost only $6 million because it was filmed in Italy, had difficulty living up to the studio's expectations during its first run. Although floored at 60/40, *War and Peace,* which ran almost three and one-half hours, often failed to perform at that level, forcing Paramount to lower the floor and offer exhibitors credits from 5 to 10 percent. With high operating expenses, few films with broad appeal, and three-hour-plus epics restricted to a few screenings a day, exhibitors who insisted on remaining in the business began to rely more and more on the profits from the concession stand, which at least did not have to be shared with the distributor. Eventually, exhibition was dubbed the "popcorn trade" when it became evident that, after all the bills had been paid, theater owners were left with 10 percent of the gross.

As 1956 came to a close, Weltner realized that he would have to modify, perhaps drastically, the policy that he had wanted to implement. Hollywood's Golden Age had quickly turned to silver and was starting to rust. While he thought he had achieved a mean somewhere between the autocratic and the permissive, there was no way in the late 1950s that a studio could enforce a policy that could put exhibitors out of business. Thus first-runs would remain at 60/40 (with adjustments, when necessary), but sub-runs (post first-run bookings) would be subject to a sliding scale, with late sub-runs available at a flat rental of 35 percent of the gross.[9]

After the tepid response to the Bob Hope film *Beau James* (1957), Weltner began to wonder if Paramount should switch to straight percentage deals or raise the cost of flat rentals. *Beau James* proved that audiences who had once flocked to the Bob Hope–Bing Crosby–Dorothy Lamour "Road" movies would not accept Hope as New York's playboy mayor, "Gentleman Jim" Walker. Weltner had to abandon the floor that had been set for *Beau James* when exhibitors would not book it on those terms. *Beau James* might have fared better if Balaban had not rejected Weltner's proposal for a July 4 release in favor of a platform approach, which allowed for gradual audience buildup. Unfortunately, there was no audience to build. The truth was that Paramount had been offering the public a surfeit of Bob Hope: *Off Limits* (1954); *Seven Little Foys* (1955), which was moderately successful; and *That Certain Feeling* (1956), whose weak performance at the box office should have been a harbinger of things to come.

The following year saw no improvement. As 1957 began, the old problems of communication breakdowns and apathy returned with a vengeance. In May 1957, while Weltner was in Europe, Paul Raibourn, now a Paramount Pictures vice president as well as president of Paramount Television, convened a meeting with three of Weltner's executives to discuss—and supposedly implement—a consultant's report about Paramount's release patterns. When Weltner learned of the meeting on his return, his reaction was a mixture of anger, resentment, and a feeling of betrayal. He assumed, perhaps rightly, that Balaban had authorized the meeting and wondered why it could not have waited until he could be present. The logical explanation is that Balaban, who had grown aloof from the day-to-day activities at the studio, wanted an immediate solution to the lackluster performance of so many 1956 releases. As Weltner's memos imply, revenues were Balaban's chief concern. Weltner kept Balaban abreast of the grosses, even supplying him with comparative figures for similar films from other studios. Weltner was baffled by Balaban's decision to bring in an outside consultant, much less one who recommended an unworkable release pattern—or, rather, one that worked on paper but not in practice. An outsider might legitimately question a studio's releasing all of its major films during the summer, but Weltner knew from experience that those "golden months," as he called them, could fill a studio's coffers. The problem was that other studios had discovered the gold standard and found that midsummer, in particular, glittered.

Exhibitors had their standard, too. Knowing that gold varies in weight, they chose the most valuable, which, in 1956, did not include the Paramount product. Rather than experience disappointment again, Weltner recommended early summer and a broad release pattern that might mean a fallow July but would produce a fertile August, when a new batch of films would start arriving. Weltner's approach ran counter to the consultant's that favored September, which Weltner knew was not a golden month.

But as Weltner tried to point out, a release schedule, no matter how conscientiously prepared, requires the cooperation of personnel able to sell the films. Thus he begged Balaban to address the sales staff at a luncheon to be held in early September 1957 and commend them for a performance that, while not outstanding, was still better than it had been in 1956. Equally important were financial rewards for those generating the largest number of sales. It is one thing to push a new release; it is something else to move the backlog, especially if it includes pictures that few exhibitors want. In the past, Weltner argued, sales drives had always included monetary prizes, which had now been discontinued. Whether he convinced Balaban to reinstate the policy is unknown. But Weltner was right: in 1957, why would any salesman go out of his way to peddle the Paramount backlog unless there was the possibility of augmenting his paycheck?

Raibourn's calling a meeting of executives who did not even report to him was symptomatic of a studio in which lines of authority were being crossed and channels of communication ignored. The producing team of William Perlberg and George Seaton became part of Paramount in 1951 and provided the studio with films that ranged from the mediocre (*Somebody Loves Me* and *Aaron Slick from Punkin Crick*, both 1952) to the outstanding (*The Country Girl* and *The Bridges at Toko-Ri*, both 1954). Perlberg and Seaton were unhappy about the way their films were marketed and confided to Weltner that they had not been provided with information about new or established stars whom they might want to feature in their productions. Since others had ignored the chain of command, Weltner decided to "take this matter . . . into my own hands and supply Perlberg and Seaton with what they want at regular intervals [and] give them a greater feeling of confidence in the company."[10] The result was Clark Gable and Doris Day in *Teacher's Pet* (1958), Gable again in *But Not for Me* (1959), Fred Astaire and Debbie Reynolds in *The Pleasure of His Company* (1961), and *The Counterfeit Traitor* (1962) with William Holden and Lilli Palmer, who had appeared in *But Not for Me* and *Pleasure* and, no longer dwarfed by Gable and Astaire, gave an extraordinary peformance as Holden's ill-starred lover.

But Seaton and Perlberg were still unhappy about the way their films were marketed and their authority undercut. A case in point was the studio's scheduling a preview of *Teacher's Pet* before the one that Perlberg had arranged in Washington, D.C., thereby making the Washington screening anticlimactic. Nor were other producing teams (e.g., Norman Panama and Melvin Frank, Melville Shavelson and Jack Rose) bullish on Paramount. The producers had a common complaint: their frustration at being unable to ascertain the release dates for their films. One reason was the advertising department's tendency to change a release date because the ads that had been created for the film proved to be inappropriate for the original date. Another was Weltner's own schedule, which found him visiting exchanges in Bombay one week and Bangkok the next. When Weltner was out of the country, Raibourn made the decisions, which were often at odds with Weltner's; thus Raibourn changed the release date of *St. Louis Blues* (1958), thereby upsetting the ad campaign that had been planned for the film.

When Weltner was not pacifying disgruntled producers or having his authority usurped, he was placating self-absorbed stars. Once Jerry Lewis stepped out of Dean Martin's shadow and into his own spotlight, Lewis's self-importance grew, especially after the success of the first two films in which he appeared by himself, *The Sad Sack* and *The Delicate Delinquent* (both 1957). Like other studios, Paramount rereleased its films periodically. In April 1958 Paramount had found it profitable to reissue DeMille's *Reap the Wild Wind* (1942) and some Dean Martin and Jerry Lewis comedies, often as a double bill (e.g., *Scared Stiff* [1953] and *Jumping Jacks* [1952]). Lewis, however, had become a star in his own right and was loath to have the earlier movies, in which he shared billing with Martin, compete with his solo efforts. Paramount was less concerned about Lewis's ego than the box-office results, which justified rerelease.

As always, it was a question of the pictures, which, in turn, affected the balance sheet. While Paramount's 1957 domestic rentals averaged $49.9 million (up from $38.14 the previous year), neither 1957 nor 1956 was as profitable as 1955, which brought in $52.3 million. In fact, the 1956 revenues were almost identical with those of 1942 ($38.5 million). The box-office receipts were indicative of the films and the public's reaction to them. Clark Gable's name did not turn *Teacher's Pet* into a hit, and Doris Day was more successful in the 1960s with other costars such as Rock Hudson, Cary Grant, and David Niven. Shirley Booth and Anna Magnani both won Academy Awards for their first Paramount films—the Hal Wallis productions of *Come Back, Little Sheba* and *The Rose Tattoo*, respectively. But Wallis did the actresses an injustice by having them repeat their characterizations, as if audiences would flock to see Booth as another long-suffering wife (*Hot Spell* [1958]) and Magnani as an earth mother in search of sexual fulfillment (*Wild Is the Wind* [1959]). Audiences didn't; in fact, exhibitors were so put off by *Wind* that Weltner was forced again to lower the floor.

As the 1950s came to an end, it was becoming increasingly clear that Paramount's days as an autonomous studio were numbered. When the decade started, conditions had been different. Despite the consent decrees, Paramount's organizational structure had not been affected. The division-of-labor principle still prevailed: contracts with exhibitors were negotiated by the Contract Department; bookings, by the Playdate Department. By 1958, those departments no longer existed; sales managers handled such matters. Downsizing can be counterproductive, however, particularly in exchanges abroad where films were often reissued for immediate, rather than long-term, results. Since such a policy reduces a film's grossing potential, division managers—especially those in Asia—were expected to learn the difference between a reissue that is inconsequential enough for a spot booking and one that is too valuable to be treated like a piece of ephemera.

Again, the principle was commendable, but the implementation cost money. When an enterprising division manager in Asia was unable to carry out Weltner's reissue policy for lack of secretarial help, it was evident that Paramount was only interested in the short term. The future was up for grabs.

The bottom line was the competition. The summers had ceased to be golden; in July 1958, neither of Paramount's releases, *King Creole* with Elvis Presley and *Rock-A-Bye-Baby* with Jerry Lewis, could compete with MGM's *Gigi*. August was not much better: all Paramount had to offer was *The Matchmaker*, a far-too-literal adaptation of Thornton Wilder's play. The original included, among other suspensions of disbelief, periodic asides and monologues and a coda in which the cast summed up the moral. The film version was no different. But most moviegoers were not sophisticated enough to appreciate such comic conventions, time-honored as they were; and those seeking a light comedy that was urbane without being self-conscious gravitated to MGM's *The Reluctant Debutante*, also released that month. None of the studios, least of all Paramount, could compete with MGM's September release, *Cat on a Hot Tin Roof*, the highest-grossing film of 1958.

The rest of '58 was no better. All Paramount had to offer was *House-*

boat with Cary Grant and Sophia Loren, and the latest Jerry Lewis farce, *Geisha Boy*; by contrast, Fox had *Inn of the Sixth Happiness*, *The Sound and the Fury*, and *The Diary of Anne Frank*. The following year was more of the same. DeMille's last film, a mediocre remake of his 1938 swashbuckler, *The Buccaneer* (1958), paled alongside MGM's *Ben-Hur*, released the following year. As for musicals, *Li'l Abner*, with virtually no stars, lost out to Fox's *Can-Can* with Frank Sinatra and Shirley MacLaine, and Warner Bros.' *Damn Yankees*. Similarly, the popular films of 1959 were not Paramount releases but Warner Bros.' *The Nun's Story* with Audrey Hepburn; MGM's *Ben-Hur* with Charlton Heston; and United Artists' *Some Like It Hot* with Marilyn Monroe, Tony Curtis, and Jack Lemmon. Now the problem was not just the pictures but the stars: Paramount had no Monroe, Heston, or Hepburn, although, ironically, Heston and Hepburn had once been contract talent; no directors like Billy Wilder (*Some Like It Hot*), who had been the studio's premier director between 1942 and 1954, and William Wyler (*Ben-Hur*), who had given Paramount Oscar winners in the past (e.g, *The Heiress* and *Roman Holiday*).

As 1958 drew to a close, Weltner assessed the situation accurately: "The present level of our business in the U.S. is bordering on disaster."[11]

Weltner was the perfect example of a studio executive who knew exactly what he could and could not do, what lay within his purview and outside of it, and what he could control and what had to be left to others—or to chance—when a project got completely out of hand. His career was winding down when Paramount was most vulnerable; thus, if he had any grand vision, it was darkened by a Hollywood in which wily producers got their way because there was such a dearth of good scripts.

The Russian-born, Sorbonne-educated Samuel Bronston had a penchant for producing epics, not all of which were popular or critical successes. *King of Kings* (1961) was not; but *El Cid* (1961), which Bronston produced for Allied Artists, was. *El Cid* also won Bronston a Golden Globe and gave him celebrity status in Spain and Italy, mainly because the film was so overwhelmingly Christian in theme and imagery. Weltner was naturally pleased that Paramount had struck a deal with Bronston for two pictures. In fall 1962, Weltner visited Bronston in Madrid, where Samuel Bronston Studios was based. Like any independent producer in a Hollywood in flux, Bronston vacillated between playing host to Weltner and his group and playing hardball when the conversation turned to such matters as budgets, the studio's financial commitment to his proposed "Circus movie," and distribution rights.

Bronston was determined to produce a film with a circus setting starring John Wayne. The film eventually became *Circus World* (1964) and was only moderately successful. During their discussions, Weltner remained noncommittal, particularly about Paramount's sharing expenses should the film exceed the $6.5 million budget. Weltner held the line, though, on Paramount's commitment: $2.5 million, regardless of how high the budget went.

About Bronston's other epic, *The Fall of the Roman Empire* (1964), Weltner was quite vocal—not to Bronston, of course, but to Barney Balaban. Studio presidents have rarely felt comfortable discussing scripts—a matter generally left to production heads or executive producers. Weltner was no exception and admitted as much: "I fully realize that I am no authority on scripts." But he knew that if Paramount were to invest in "Roman papier-mache stuff," as he termed the revised screenplay (which he found no different from the first draft), the material would have to be considerably more substantial.[12]

Weltner realized that he had the final say, yet he was also aware that Paramount was at the mercy of independent producers like Bronston, who could fill the pipeline with films that Paramount could no longer produce in-house. Weltner joked that he could go down in history as the man who passed on *Roman Empire*, thereby inviting comparison with Jack Warner, who, after optioning *Gone with the Wind*, decided that nobody wanted to see a movie about the Civil War. There was hardly any comparison between the two films; despite the many revisions *Roman Empire* underwent, it was never a worthwhile project, much less one that had been budgeted at $13 million and ended up costing $20 million.

Weltner was, by nature, cautious and conservative, and he could sense a fiasco. His years in distribution had made him sensitive to films that had audience appeal and those that did not. When Weltner was in Paris in August 1962, he made it a point to check on the Audrey Hepburn–William Holden vehicle, *Paris When It Sizzles* (1964), which was just winding up production. The script bothered him, and the rushes convinced him that the material was far too sophisticated for a mass audience. He assumed there would be moments of zaniness, as there had been in *Breakfast at Tiffany's* (1961), and grew apprehensive when he found there were none. Then he realized that *Paris* would never be another another *Tiffany's*, despite the presence of Audrey Hepburn. But at this stage, there was nothing he could do except console himself with the fact that "everybody work-

ing on the picture seemed to be reasonably happy."[13] Their happiness was
not shared by the public.

Weltner's primary concern in 1962, however, was *Roman Empire*.
Except for writer Philip Yordan, who ended up with co-screenplay credit,
no one had any faith in the film—least of all, Weltner. It was only after
Yordan insisted that the script would reflect the results of exhaustive research that Weltner relented. After all, Will Durant had been hired as a
consultant. But when Weltner read the new script, he saw little, if any,
improvement. He tried desperately to make sense of the plot, which had
something to do with the breakup of the Roman Empire after the death
of Marcus Aurelius in A.D. 180. Roman imperial history is notoriously
convoluted, compared to the history of the Roman Republic. In terms of
plot, *Julius Caesar* (1952) and *Cleopatra* (1962) were more accessible films
because they dramatized events that fitted easily into a traditional narrative framework: Cassius conscripts Brutus into a conspiracy that results in
Caesar's death and later their own; Cleopatra forges an alliance with Caesar, whose assassination brings her into contact with Antony, with whom
she begins a celebrated affair that ends with their suicides. *Roman Empire*
cannot be summed up so succinctly. "There is none of the clarity that
surrounded the heroic character of El Cid," Weltner complained.[14] Weltner
was right; there was no central character, only a host of stereotypes enmeshed in a skein of relationships that might have been a suitable subject
for an operatic composer like Verdi, who knew how music could divert
an audience's attention away from a hopelessly confused libretto. Dimitri
Tiomkin, who composed many fine film scores, was not Verdi and could
do little to take the audience's mind off the hackneyed plot in which the
noble Livius yields the throne to the dissolute Commodus, who makes
Lucilla, Livius's true love, empress. Lucilla alternates between desire and
contempt for Commodus, but she is so preoccupied with her new position that she is incapable even of a love-hate relationship. The barbarians
attack, Livius and Commodus square off, Livius gets a chance to rule
what's left of the empire but walks away from the job like Gary Cooper at
the end of *High Noon* (1952), and the empire totters (the title is a misno-
mer) after three hours and twenty minutes (plus intermission) of turgid
writing occasionally relieved by epic combat.

Caesar, Brutus, Antony, and Cleopatra became so enmeshed in the
fabric of events that they ultimately selected the colors of the historical
tapestry they were weaving. Livius, Commodus, and Lucilla had their
colors selected for them by events in which they participated like som-

nambulists. When *Roman Empire* finally reached the screen, it elicited howls when Ballomar cried to his fellow barbarians, "Let us fall upon the Romans, killing them!" Even those who had never studied Latin and were unfamiliar with the hortatory subjunctive, sensed that this was pretty hoary dialogue. Although he found it difficult, Weltner tried to be upbeat: perhaps the battle scenes would camouflage the weakness of the script; perhaps the set that had been constructed outside of Madrid (and included a rather authentic Forum) could be reused for *Dear and Glorious Physician*, Taylor Caldwell's novel about St. Luke that Paramount had purchased (but failed to make). But no amount of rationalization could dispel the thought that a $5 million commitment on Paramount's part was a mistake. Bronston arrived at the $5 million figure because he had cut deals elsewhere, notably with Allied Artists, in order to raise enough money to make the movie. Weltner would have preferred an arrangement that gave Paramount international as well as domestic rights; the international rights were especially important in the case of marginal films that might perform poorly at home but do better abroad and might break even once the international revenues were tallied. But Weltner was afraid of committing more than $5 million, which gave Paramount only domestic rights to a film that cost $20 million.

There was no way Paramount could make a profit with *Roman Empire*, nor was it the first of Paramount's 1964–65 releases to disappoint the studio. Weltner was right about *Paris When It Sizzles*; it was a $3 million flop and should really have taught the studio a lesson: "If we ever need a 'horrible example' to epitomize all of the mistakes that could possibly be made in producing a picture, I think that PARIS WHEN IT SIZZLES would be the finest example."[15] But production had gotten so out of control that the example went unheeded. Desperate for product and willing to indulge those who could deliver it, Paramount went ahead with *Judith* (1966), a vehicle for Sophia Loren, improbably cast as a Holocaust survivor. Weltner felt uneasy about the film, which underwent a series of delays because Loren was unhappy with every version of the script she was shown. And when she was unhappy, her husband, Carlo Ponti, was doubly so. *Judith* was a nightmare for Paramount and a box-office failure.

To understand how out of control the quest for product had become, one has only to read Weltner's 29 April 1964 memo to Balaban, which Ed Weisl, chairman of the board's executive committee, received (although he was never copied on it). In it, Weltner inveighed against the making of the "ill-fated" *Paris When It Sizzles* and the writeoff it would cause. Scrawled at the bottom is Weisl's response: "I hope the studio is not making the same mistake with that picture in Israel." The reference, of course, is to *Judith*, which was being filmed there. Who greenlighted *Judith*? On paper, the project looked promising. But when Weltner had grown tired of Loren's and Ponti's pettiness, something apparently happened—there are no further memos—to convince Weltner to go along with the filming rather than become embroiled in litigation.

The *Judith* imbroglio was symptomatic of how a handful of people, possessed with the volatile combination of power and ego, can hold a studio hostage. When producer Ray Stark proposed that Tennessee Williams's one-act play, *This Property Is Condemned*, be converted into a film for Elizabeth Taylor, Weltner was interested, hoping to capitalize on the public's identification of Taylor with Williams on the basis of her Oscar-nominated performance in *Cat on a Hot Tin Roof* (1958). There was no way Taylor could play the role as written, since the character was a teenager. Weltner realized that the script would have to be tailored to an increasingly mature-looking Taylor. If Taylor was part of the package, so was her husband, Richard Burton—not as costar but as director. The fact that Burton had never directed before did not faze Weltner, who believed Burton's name would add spice to the project, especially after the head-lines-making affair the couple had had during the filming of *Cleopatra* (1963). The $3.5 million budget that Weltner had drawn up suggests how eager Paramount was to sign the couple, regardless of how inappropriate the role would be for Taylor even if it were revised and how foolhardy it was to entrust the direction of a $3.5 million movie to a neophyte. Neither was worth the proposed salary: Burton, one hundred thousand dollars; Taylor, $1 million. The rights and screenplay would cost four hundred thousand dollars, with Williams getting 20 percent of the net. As producer, Stark would receive one hundred thousand dollars. Eventually, Paramount made *This Property Is Condemned* (1966); the title was unchanged, but the stars, director, and producer were substantially different. Natalie Wood played the lead, and quite effectively, opposite Robert Redford; making his directorial debut was the young Sydney Pollack; John Houseman was the producer.

As more independent producers began supplying the studios with product, fewer studio employees were needed. The figures told the story: Paramount's branch offices numbered 957 in 1954 and 523 in 1959. Nationally, the figures were equally revealing: in 1959, there were 11,000 movie theaters, compared to the 14,760 in 1954; during that same five-

year period, film rentals in general decreased by 22.63 percent—from
$350 million in 1954 to $277 million in 1959. Hollywood had become a
seller's market, and Weltner knew it. Weltner also knew that Balaban was
saddling him with increasingly greater responsibilities, as if he were being
groomed for something higher.

In 1964, Weltner had already been given more authority than most
distribution heads. If Balaban was concerned about anything, it was the
balance sheet. He relied so heavily on Weltner's judgment that Weltner
found himself dealing with independent producers, not just catering to
their preferences for release dates but also handling more mundane matters like office space. But Balaban had parceled out Weltner's authority,
making it applicable to one sphere but not to another: "I do not have any
actual control over our Studio," he wrote, urging Balaban to see that
Joseph E. Levine, who had produced the class-trash hits *The Carpetbaggers*
(1964) and *Where Love Has Gone* (1964), be better treated.[16] Apparently,
no one had found a permanent office for Levine, who was being given
whatever space was available when he came to the studio.

Weltner's concern was that Levine be accorded preferential treatment, despite the fact that he could offer Paramount only glossy sleaze,
which was not always that profitable, as *Harlow* and *Sylvia* (both 1965)
proved. Levine was, as Weltner reminded Balaban, "as important a producer as [Hal Wallis and Otto Preminger] . . . and has brought to us . . .
very important properties."

Paramount was at the mercy of producers "important" enough to
merit a production deal—importance being measured in terms of track
record (mostly hits, few misses), reputation (hits in the past, future less
certain), promising projects, access to bankable stars, and favorable distribution deals. That most of these producers ended up as footnotes in the
history of American cinema was irrelevant; short-run success was what
mattered. There were, of course, exceptions like Hal Wallis; but even a
director-producer like Otto Preminger was indulged purely because his
record was mostly hits—*The Moon Is Blue* (1953), *The Man with the Golden
Arm* (1955), *Bonjour, Tristesse* (1959), *Anatomy of a Murder* (1959), *Exodus*
(1960), and one blatant miss (*Saint Joan*, [1959], best remembered for Jean
Seberg's screen debut). Weltner had carefully researched the grosses for
Preminger's films. Since *Saint Joan* was commonly acknowledged as an
aberration, Weltner was not about to hold its failure against Preminger;
he was, however, bothered by *Anatomy of a Murder*'s lukewarm response
abroad. But since the film was still a commercial success, he welcomed

Preminger on board. The problem was the property: *In Harm's Way* (1964), an overlong World War II melodrama with a cast of luminaries in various stages of eclipse (John Wayne, Henry Fonda, Patricia Neal) saddled with a script that dimmed what wattage they could still generate. The public was indifferent, as it was to Preminger's other Paramount films: the notorious *Skidoo* (1968), *Tell Me That You Love Me, Junie Moon* (1970), and *Such Good Friends* (1971). Except for *Hurry Sundown* (1966), in which Jane Fonda performed fellatio on a saxophone for Michael Caine's erotic gratification, Hollywood found Preminger retrograde. Apparently no one remembered *Laura* (1944) or *The Man with the Golden Arm* (1955).

Weltner could not afford to think future, only present. When Eddie Lewis brought him a script called *Seconds,* an absorbing variation on the Faust theme in which the dissatisfied can purchase youth and a new identity, Weltner was interested. If Eddie Lewis's name is familiar at all, it is in conjunction with Dalton Trumbo, the best known of the Hollywood Ten. As executive vice president of Kirk Douglas's production company, Bryna, Lewis managed to get work for the blacklisted Trumbo on Bryna's *Last Train from Gun Hill* (1959), a Paramount release. But in 1964 the blacklist was no longer enforceable, and Lewis was trying to emerge as a bona fide producer, not a traveler in the nether world of pseudonyms and fronts. Weltner was wise in green-lighting *Seconds,* which gave Rock Hudson his best role in addition to attesting to his undervalued acting ability.

In his own way, Weltner was a visionary and, like most visionaries, was unheeded. In a "Personal and Confidential" memo to Balaban and Y. Frank Freeman, he strongly questioned the inordinate amount of money spent on advertising films in the New York area at a time when so much of the moviegoing population had moved to the suburbs.[17] Weltner advocated spending more on regional advertising, arguing that the success of a film in New York, unless perhaps it played at Radio City Music Hall (and that was no guarantee of a hit, either), would have no effect on suburban audiences. Interestingly, as new venues opened in malls, shopping centers, and on highways—and as America discovered the multiplex—advertising in local newspapers, once limited to the basics, began to emulate the major dailies. Equally prophetic was Weltner's views on trailers. He rightly believed that the trailers told more of the plot than was necessary, in some cases even giving it away. Whether he would have approved of trailers made up of flash cuts of scenes, often out of sequence, tailored to an audience weaned on MTV and expecting a shot a second, is doubtful. But he probably would have felt that the trailers of the 1990s were trying to do their job: lure audiences into the theater by offering them a taste—and nothing more—of what awaits them.

But it was difficult to convince Balaban, who was already past the usual retirement age, to bury the past. In 1959, a revolutionary approach to advertising and trailers would never have restored Paramount or any studio to its glory days. If Paramount had attempted either, historians would have lauded it for its vision, adding regretfully that nothing could have stemmed the corporate tide that was rolling in. All Weltner knew at the end of 1958 was that neither the system nor the films were working. Paramount was riding on the crest of *The Ten Commandments*, which had now reached $24 million in domestic revenues; but the other films were asleep in the deep. Paramount released 20 films in 1957, grossing approximately $27.060 million, or $1.353 million per film; in 1958, 24 releases brought in $23.360 million, or $974,000 per film. Included in both years' output were films that Paramount would never even have considered a decade earlier: *Hear Me Good, Devil's Hairpin*, and *Zero Hour* (all 1957); *Space Children, Party Crashers, Hot Angel*, and *Hell Broke Loose* (all 1958).

Given both the paucity and quality of product, Weltner was forced to eliminate five branch offices. Other changes were in the offing. The gerontocracy that Paramount had become started crumbling in 1959 when Freeman's health reached such a stage that he had to resign. However, the old guard, unlike old soldiers, rarely fades away. Freeman, then nearing seventy, stayed on with the title of consultant, which guaranteed him a place at the studio as well as on the payroll.

Paramount no more needed another consultant than it did another Bob Hope vehicle or a "Road" movie. Crisis time had arrived, and in March 1960 Balaban announced that all nonessential positions would be eliminated, employees leaving the company would not be replaced, travel funds would be allocated only to the sales staff and senior executives, and the "miscellaneous" category would be deleted from the budget.

Balaban's edict went into effect immediately. The sales staff was expected to limit road travel to three days a week, with trips scheduled so as to avoid duplication. Those who would be on the road for more than three weeks were to spend one week in the branch office, getting show dates for unplayed (and unplayable) films. Overtime would be allowed only in extreme cases (e.g., handling shipments arriving on a weekend) and for no more than four hours. Phone calls would be scrutinized and callers identified. Air mail would be the exception, not the rule—and never on weekends.

These measures may have sounded Draconian, but companies have traditionally resorted to them when the times called for belt-tightening. In Paramount's case, the belt had run out of notches. Except for Weltner, Paramount lacked a voice with a vision. Weltner's voice—unfortunately, known only through his memos—had a clarity that did not resonate through the hollows of the studio. Weltner knew the direction in which Paramount had to proceed; he simply could not map it out. But in the early 1960s, who could? Even in the early 1940s, Hal Wallis could not get his way at Warner Bros. Now Wallis was an independent producer at Paramount, cast in the role of adversary—courtesy of a changing Hollywood. And so, instead of being an irritant to the brothers Warner, Wallis had become one to Weltner. But just as Weltner had to indulge his producers, Wallis had to indulge Jerry Lewis.

By 1960, Lewis was no longer the box-office draw he had been; to Paramount he was a "standard," a known quantity whose name was familiar enough to allow for less expensive advertising. Wallis knew that Paramount allocated less advertising money for a Lewis movie (about 10 percent of the budget) than for, say, *Conspiracy of Hearts* (1960), which needed more publicity because of its lack of big names and Holocaust theme (Catholic nuns helping Jewish children reach Palestine during World War II). The 1960 Jerry Lewis movie was *A Visit to a Small Planet*, which even Lewis afficionados find difficult to defend.

Conspiracy was clearly the better film, although neither found favor with the public. Still, Wallis kept pressuring the advertising department to spend more on *Visit*, probably because he knew that only hype could save it. Nothing could.

Lewis had become as much of a problem as Wallis. By 1960, Lewis's ego had increased in inverse proportion to his box-office appeal. He was now at a stage in his career where the right combination of script, marketing, and timing might—and only might—guarantee a hit. Lewis may have thought of himself as the heir of Chaplin, and French critics may have agreed; but the American public thought differently. Lewis still mattered to his fans, but even they were reaching a state of surfeit. Since 1949, Lewis had been averaging a movie a year; in some years, more. In 1953, there were three Martin and Lewis films in release; after his breakup with Martin in 1956, Lewis made two films in 1957, two in 1958, and three in 1960.

The 1960 releases were a problem. *The Bellboy*'s appeal was primarily to those who enjoyed watching Lewis in a series of comic routines unencumbered by a plot. Although one could sympathize with Lewis's attempt to update silent comedy by using routines that would have made Mack Sennett smile, the truth was that Lewis was not Sennett. Although Lewis had now become a producer, he was also an actor-director-star-coscreenwriter. Sennett never aimed so high.

Lewis could chalk up *The Bellboy* as an artistic failure, but neither he nor Wallis could have made a case for *A Visit to a Small Planet*, which was simply a Jerry Lewis vehicle based on Gore Vidal's Broadway success without the wit of Vidal and the genius of the original visitor, Cyril Ritchard. The most problematic of the 1960 films was *Cinderfella*, which, as the title implies, was a variation on the Cinderella story—with Lewis as a mistreated stepson turned into Prince Charming.

Cinderfella was another of Lewis's attempts to augment his repertoire, which, by 1960, included the stooge, the sidekick, the bumbler, the transformed waif, and the alien. By 1960, Lewis had become an auteur. After he and Martin stopped working together, Lewis not only went solo but also turned to producing, and often directing, his own pictures. Correspondingly, Wallis produced fewer Jerry Lewis vehicles—three between 1957 and 1960; and of the 1960 releases, only *Visit* was a Hal Wallis production. *Cinderfella* was a Jerry Lewis production.

It was also a movie that had a special significance for him: Lewis as Hollywood waif turned into leading man, able to play both clown and impresario. As clown, he "made 'em laugh"; as impressario, he attempted to revitalize the careers of two sopranos, Anna Maria Alberghetti and Gloria Jean. Alberghetti's talents had been wasted in Hollywood; the same year that *Cinderfella* opened to mediocre reviews, Alberghetti triumphed on Broadway in *Carnival*, the stage version of *Lili* (1953), with a score by Bob Merrill. Alberghetti at least found work in theater and television, doing an occasional stint as Maria in *West Side Story* and appearing in commercials. But Lewis could do no more for her than he could for child star Gloria Jean, whom he idolized and hired for *The Ladies' Man* (1961), which also gave former opera star Helen Traubel a larger role than she had had in the Sigmund Romberg biopic, *Deep in My Heart* (1954). Traubel's part, a nonsinging one, at least remained intact, but Gloria Jean's was so severely cut that her brief appearance was a waste of both talent and time.

Weltner was ambivalent about Lewis. He realized that, while Lewis's track record was spotty, the actor still had a following—but one that was growing younger as the slapstick quotient increased. However, now that

Lewis had turned producer-director (and, in some cases, coscreenplay author), Lewis, who had once appeared *in* Paramount films, now was providing Paramount *with* films. Thus, Weltner continued to keep a promise that he had made to Lewis when Lewis and Martin were still working together: never to arrange a multiple opening for one of his movies. Instead, a Jerry Lewis film would premiere in one city at one theater.

Weltner knew that if anything could save *Cinderfella*, it would be a multiple opening during Christmas week. But he would not renege on his promise, perhaps sensing the film had special meaning for Lewis, who functioned as both star and producer. Obviously, Lewis identified with the subject matter (transformation of clown into prince). Besides, Lewis had developed a formula that could make his films appealing to audiences who would ordinarily never attend a Jerry Lewis movie: he deliberately featured well-known actors of the past in the supporting cast not only to provide them with work but also to attract middle-aged moviegoers, eager to see how well or poorly the stars of their adolescence were aging. Thus Lewis cast Peter Lorre in *The Sad Sack* (1957) and *The Patsy* (1964), Marilyn Maxwell and Reginald Gardiner in *Rock-a-Bye Baby* (1958), Marie "The Body" McDonald in *Geisha Boy* (1958), Lee Patrick in *A Visit to a Small Planet* (1960), Judith Anderson and Ed Wynn in *Cinderfella*, Brian Donlevy in *The Errand Boy* (1962), Agnes Moorehead in *Who's Minding the Store?* (1963), and Thelma Ritter in *Boeing Boeing* (1965).

The formula was not an original one. Television had gone a similar route in the 1950s, giving stars like Loretta Young, Barbara Stanwyck, and Jane Wyman roles they could never have had on the big screen. Even at Paramount, producer A.C. Lyles embarked upon a series of low-budget westerns between 1965 and 1970 with such B movie stalwarts as Rory Calhoun, Corinne Calvet, Scott Brady, Jean Parker, Jane Russell, Dana Andrews, and Terry Moore.

Unlike A.C. Lyles, Lewis was not a low-budget producer. Initially, *Cinderfella* was budgeted at $400,000, then $434,800. It ended up costing over $2 million.[18] Worse were the *Cinderfella* previews. Producer Lewis informed Paramount that he had a final cut ready for a Nyack, New York, preview in August 1960. The truth was that it was probably more of a rough cut, although Lewis insisted "'this was it'—and there would be no changes."[19]

To make matters worse, *Cinderfella* was previewed after the main attraction, Billy Wilder's *The Apartment*, now an acknowledged classic. But because Lewis was unhappy about everything connected with the preview (the town, the theater, the manager who leaked the news to the press that Lewis would be in attendance), he vilified the audience, claiming it had come to see a "dirty" picture. *The Apartment* is now included in the Library of Congress's National Film Registry, created in 1989 to single out films of historical and cultural significance. The subject matter—an accountant who lends his apartment to an executive for dalliances, unaware that the executive's current mistress is the woman with whom he (the accountant) is in love—might have sounded "dirty." In Wilder's hands, *The Apartment* became a special kind of comedy—and one that Lewis would have found alien: a comedy that never loses its sense of humor even when exploring the vagaries of the human heart.

Lewis thought otherwise; he did not just call the film "dirty" but used the same epithet for the audience, which had actually come to the screening on the strength of Lewis's name, even overlooking the fact that the preview started twenty minutes late. At the end, the audience, knowing Lewis was sitting in the back, rose, turned around, and applauded. Lewis made a quick departure, alienating a group consisting largely of parents and children.

Lewis behaved similarly at the New York preview at the Capitol Theatre on Broadway and Fiftieth Street. Again, he arrived late—this time, shortly before 9:00 P.M., although the preview had been scheduled for 8:30 P.M. Lewis also wanted the Capitol for the premiere, but the theater had already been booked. The best Paramount could do was the Victoria, five blocks north—a smaller theater but better than *Cinderfella* deserved. Disgruntled, Lewis showed up but, sensing a disaster, made a hasty exit before the movie ended.

Weltner had sized up the situation: "[Lewis] seemed to be angry or annoyed or displeased or perhaps drowned in a sense of his own importance."[20] It was all of the above. Weltner could do nothing; Lewis's contract had five more years to go, and even if Balaban had agreed to buy him out, Weltner probably would have hesitated. Somehow, Weltner thought Lewis capable of delivering a breakthrough movie that would redeem him.

That was not the case. *The Ladies' Man* cost $3.32 million; even so, Weltner argued—in vain—for its being the studio's Christmas release instead of the Shirley MacLaine vehicle, *My Geisha* (1961). "Jerry is a staple," Weltner insisted; yet in the same breath, Weltner admitted that there was "reason to be scared about...a LADIES' MAN at $3,325,000."[21] Gone were the days when a Jerry Lewis film like *The Delicate Delinquent*

(1957), the comic's first movie after splitting with Martin, could come in at $486,000. Actually, *Delinquent* was vastly superior to the more expensive films that followed.

Weltner must have sensed he was witnessing the transformation of a studio. Always the company person, he made the cuts that were required. Yet, as he wrote, "We chip away but this is not the full answer. . . . These things are all good but they do not reach very far when I look at the astronomical costs of our pictures. To my non-production mentality, the attack must be made on the below-the-line-costs . . . so that we can afford to pay the talent the enormous sums of money that they are getting today."[22]

One of those "below-the-line-costs" was advertising. If Paramount was having trouble paying for the so-called talent (of which there was little in 1960), part of the problem lay in the disparity between the quality of the films and the amount spent on advertising them. What is truly frightening is that Weltner, despite his position, had no control over the advertising budget: "Our Advertising Department spends more money in a year than many sizable businesses gross."[23]

Studios have traditionally engaged in "creative accounting," thereby making it impossible to determine exactly what a film's net profits actually were; they have also been reluctant to share budgetary information with film scholars. Yet Paramount's advertising budgets, which Weltner considered inordinately high, only reflected what is now known to be a fact: "The strong relationship between attendance and advertising . . . shows filmgoers' reliance on outside sources."[24]

In the 1980s, a studio might have spent $10 million to advertise a movie; by the 1990s, the figure was $20 million—at least. Yet, if Balaban gave advertising free rein, it was understandable. How else could some of Paramount's movies of the early 1960s have ever attracted an audience?

Weltner understood how radically the industry had changed since he had entered it; what he found hard to fathom was the preeminence given to advertising, which had once fallen under the purview of distribution. Weltner firmly believed that the advertising budget should be 10 percent of a film's estimated gross unless the film warranted more. He was therefore shocked to receive the advertising budget for Lewis's *The Nutty Professor* (1963): $504,000, over and above the $150,000 that had been approved for Lewis to promote the film. Weltner recalled a time when a Jerry Lewis movie would get two hundred thousand dollars for advertising, on the assumption that it would net around $2 million.[25] Since Lewis was both directing and producing *The Nutty Professor*, he was apparently able to call the shots, despite the fact that the "Jerry Lewis audience" was much smaller than it had been a decade earlier. Still, Lewis got his way; he also received the $150,000. At Paramount, Jerry Lewis was still a name that mattered. Thus Weltner was forced to approve a budget he would have once rejected. Although he realized that "the profit factor is practically nil," he was still forced to admit: "I have no other recourse but to approve this particular budget."[26]

Weltner probably never imagined the day, which was not that far off, when "advertising" would not be limited to print (newspapers and magazines, lobby cards, one-sheets, etc.) but would also include such tie-ins as novelizations, T-shirts, sweatshirts, caps, magnets, comic books, mugs, and all the other paraphernalia for sale at studio shops and theme parks. If, at the end of the century, marketing a movie could cost almost as much as making it, the reason is that every movie, mainstream or independent, needs as much hype as it can get, regardless of its quality. For example, in 1995, a movie that cost $35 million to produce could cost $30 million to advertise.[27] The moviegoers, who remember Hollywood's palmy days, now turn out for *a* movie; they do not go to *the movies,* as they once did. And no one, not even the most astute marketers, can predict the movie of the month.

Thus, Weltner's 1961 recommendation that a comptroller be assigned to the treasurer's office to monitor advertising, overseeing its procedures and practices, might have made sense in 1941—except that then it would not have been necessary.

In 1961 Weltner had become an anomaly: he had a clear enough title (distribution chief) but not the job description to go with it. Weltner was expected to read scripts, which he did conscientiously when he was given them. In some cases, particularly when the script had not yet been written, he was only told the plot, as happened with the film that became *Hatari!* Although he was intrigued by the African setting, what really convinced him of the movie's potential was that Howard Hawks would direct it. Weltner respected Hawks's films. While Hawks had worked at Fox, Warner Bros., RKO, Columbia, and United Artists, he had never made a film for Paramount.

Throughout the 1950s, Hawks had directed a number of highly successful films that may have lacked the art of his earlier work (e.g., *His Girl Friday* [1940], *The Big Sleep* [1946], *Red River* [1948]) but were at least moneymakers: (e.g., *Gentlemen Prefer Blondes* [1953], which gave Marilyn

Monroe her first important role; *Land of the Pharoahs* [1955], which, although Hawks detested it, made a profit for Warner Bros.; and *Rio Bravo* [1959], which reunited Hawks with John Wayne). The Wayne-Hawks combination is apparently what sold Jack Karp, Freeman's assistant who became studio head when Don Hartman left, on the as-yet-untitled *Hatari!* (1962), known in 1960 as "The African Story" and dealing with the big-game hunters who supply zoos with wild animals. Wayne was on the verge of cutting a deal with Paramount, where he had not worked since DeMille's *Reap the Wild Wind* (1942), in which he battled a giant squid and lost. Wayne's career was coming full circle; it was at Paramount where Wayne would make his last two films for John Ford: *The Man Who Shot Liberty Valance* (1962) and *Donovan's Reef* (1963); it was also at Paramount where Wayne made his very last film, *The Shootist* (1976), before he died in 1979.

Karp, a Columbia law school graduate who, like Freeman, had no production experience, reacted like the neophyte he was. Karp was so eager for the Wayne-Hawks film to materialize that, without seeing a script (for none had yet been written), he made commitments to both Wayne and Hawks that would have proved difficult to rescind. Weltner, who had not been privy to the negotiations, realized that Paramount had passed the point of no return: "Walking away from this picture . . . would be a very expensive procedure, more than I care to estimate at this time."[28] However, Weltner suspected that the combination of Hawks, Wayne, and Africa might work. *Hatari!* was neither vintage Hawks nor memorable Wayne, nor was it worth the $150,000 (plus 50 percent of the profits) that Hawks received for producing and directing and the $750,000 plus the unspecified share of the net that went to Wayne. Yet Weltner was right: *Hatari!*, which cost around $4 million, grossed $7 million domestically and about the same internationally.

Weltner hoped that Paramount could make at least six hundred thousand dollars in overhead since *Hatari!* was a Hawks production, with the negative owned jointly by Hawks and Paramount but with Paramount's having perpetual distribution rights. Weltner's concern about overhead echoed the studio's, the difference being Weltner's conviction that a studio remains in business by making movies to satisfy audiences, not to absorb the overhead.

Paramount thought otherwise. Although Weltner had always been candid with Balaban, he was never more so than in his eight-page letter of 5 November 1962 in which he expressed his disillusionment with the conservatism of Karp and Freeman and his own frustration at being unable to bring about the changes that were needed. Although Freeman had more or less retired and Karp had replaced him as vice president of production, nothing had changed. "Whether our Studio people will admit it or not, they compulsively produce pictures because of the need of absorbing our Studio overhead."[29] This philosophy explains the mediocre-to-worthless releases of the 1959–62 period, during which Paramount could lay claim to only three films of any significance: *Psycho* (1960), which was filmed at Universal; *Breakfast at Tiffany's* (1961); and John Ford's *The Man Who Shot Liberty Valance* (1962).

Although Academy Awards are not the sole index of a studio's worth, they still reflect its standing in the industry. After the mid-1950s, Paramount's films were rarely nominated. When they were, the nominations were pro forma (as in Hitchcock's case) or in minor categories. Given the public's perception of *Psycho* as slasher schlock (rather than the masterpiece of gothic horror it is), Hitchcock's Best Director nomination was the Academy's way of acknowledging his existence (which it had been doing periodically since 1940) rather than his artistry, which at the time was considered nonexistent. *The Five Pennies*, based on the life of cornetist Red Nichols, deserved the 1959 nomination for Best Scoring of a Musical; yet even if the film had won, that kind of award carries no weight so far as the public is concerned. There were two reasons to see *The Five Pennies*: Danny Kaye's performance as Nichols and the great Louis Armstrong as himself. *Breakfast at Tiffany's* deserved the Oscar for Best Song, Mancini and Mercer's "Moon River," although Audrey Hepburn, nominated for Best Actress, lost out to Sophia Loren for *Two Women*, the first time any actor (or actress) won for a foreign film.

What Paramount was doing wrong, United Artists (UA) was doing right, as Weltner emphasized. During the same period (1959–62), UA released a spate of outstanding films: *Some Like It Hot* (1959); *On the Beach* (1959); *The Magnificent Seven* (1960); *Elmer Gantry* (1960); *Exodus* (1960); *Judgment at Nuremberg* (1961), for which Maximillian Schell and Abby Mann won Oscars for Best Actor and Screenplay (Based on Material from Another Medium), respectively; *Bird Man of Alcatraz* (1962); and *The Miracle Worker* (1962), for which Anne Bancroft was voted Best Actress and Patty Duke, Supporting Actress. Even more impressive was the fact that UA's films received Best Picture awards two years in a row: *The Apartment* (1960), which also won for Best Director (Billy Wilder), Original Screenplay, Art Direction, and Editing; and *West Side Story* (1961), which picked up Oscars in eight other categories, including Supporting Actress (Rita Moreno) and Director (Robert Wise and Jerome Robbins).

The UA comparison was not entirely apt. Although UA was often referred to as a studio (one of the "Little Three," along with Universal and Columbia), it was actually a distribution—not a production—company formed in 1919 by Mary Pickford, Douglas Fairbanks, D.W. Griffith, and Charlie Chaplin, and intended for independent producers who did not want to release their films through the major studios. Samuel Goldwyn, for example, frequently distributed his films through UA, as did David Selznick, Alexander Korda, and Walter Wanger, along with such lesser-known producers as Edward Small and Hunt Stromberg.

There were even two occasions when Paramount distributed UA features. In 1924, D.W. Griffith's finances were at their lowest ebb because of a series of flops: *One Exciting Night* (1922), *The White Rose* (1923), and particularly *America* (1924). Zukor came to his aid, enabling Griffith to secure a bank loan to make *Isn't Life Wonderful* (1924), which fared no better than his last three. But Griffith was now indebted to Zukor for four films, all of which, with the exception of *Sally of the Sawdust* (1925)—produced by Paramount but released by UA—were failures.[30]

Then, in 1942, UA, with only about twenty films scheduled for release (and four of them British), prevailed upon Paramount to provide it with others in order to supplement its meager slate. Since Paramount was planning to release around thirty-five films that year, the studio supplied UA with twenty-one features between 1942 and 1944, including some Hopalong Cassidy westerns. Except for René Clair's *I Married a Witch* (1942), none of the castoffs were outstanding. But the days of lend-lease were over. Although UA went through a dry period in the 1940s, it reaped a harvest of awards two decades later. Certainly five Best Picture Oscars in one decade—*The Apartment, West Side Story, Tom Jones* (1963), *In the Heat of the Night* (1967), and *Midnight Cowboy* (1969)—proved Weltner was right about one point: UA could attract talent that Paramount could not. The last time Paramount had won a Best Picture Oscar was in 1952 (*The Greatest Show on Earth*); there would not be another until 1972 (*The Godfather*).

There was no way a studio like Paramount could emulate a company like UA, where profits came from distribution. At UA, profits were not immediate, nor could they be. They came in steadily over a period of time. In 1962, Paramount's best-known producer was Hal Wallis, whose production company, much to Weltner's distress, had made $11 million on its films between 1954 and 1962; on the other hand, Paramount's take was only $792,000.[31] UA was formed to serve independent producers, who would be responsible for the advertising expenses.

At Paramount, it was different: the studio had its own advertising department, whose extravagance drove up the final cost. An even more serious problem was the overhead, which hovered around 25 percent, although sometimes, as in the case of *Hatari!* it was a flat fee. *Hatari!*'s overhead was six hundred thousand dollars, based on a projected $4 million budget, which, in view of the location shooting (entailing, at the very least, unit managers and their staffs, as well as extras from the native population) must have been higher.

Weltner wanted to reduce the amount of overhead as a film approached break-even, but, with so few films turning a profit, his plan was impossible to realize. Perhaps Paramount was right: the studio should keep making movies to pay for the overhead. Weltner began to wonder if a move to other quarters could reduce the overhead and make working at Paramount more attractive to producers.

In 1962, such a move was a distinct possibility. That year, the entertainment industry's premier talent agency, MCA (Music Corporation of America), also known as the octopus because of its tendency to throw out its tentacles and envelop whatever talent was worth representing, decided to accomplish a goal toward which it had been heading since 1958: ownership of a studio—specifically, Universal-International, still thought of as Universal despite its merger with International in 1946.

In 1946, Lew Wasserman, once just an agent and in 1952 Hollywood's most powerful one, became head of MCA and started laying the foundation for his empire: a mega-conglomerate that would not only represent talent but also showcase it—first on television, then in movies. In 1952 MCA formed a subsidiary, Revue, which produced such television shows as *Wagon Train*, *Ozzie and Harriet*, and *Alfred Hitchcock Presents*. Wasserman wanted more: a movie library, a movie lot, and a movie studio. In February 1958, MCA paid Paramount $50 million to distribute most of the studio's pre-1948 films to television.[32] In December of the same year, MCA paid Universal $11.25 million for its back lot.

MCA's next conquest was Universal itself; however, the Justice Department intervened, forcing MCA to give up its talent division if it wished to remain in film and television production, as MCA clearly did. And so, as 1962 came to an end, MCA became Universal's parent; no longer was it representing talent but rather featuring it on both the small and the big screen. And to bury the past, in 1963 MCA restored the name of Universal to its original unhyphenated state.

In many ways, Wasserman resembled Zukor, who was always working deals and augmenting his studio-empire through annexation and talent raids—buying up first-run theaters, including the Balaban-Katz circuit, thereby depriving his rival, First National, of one of its most profitable outlets and wooing D.W. Griffith away from UA even though it was for just a few pictures, none of them outstanding. Within a month of MCA's acquisition of Universal, Wasserman set his sights on Paramount.

In February 1962, Hitchcock, who had been one of Wasserman's most famous MCA clients, left Paramount for Universal. The timing was not accidental.

In November 1961, Weltner was traveling in Italy, where he learned that Hitchcock was dissatisfied with his treatment at Paramount.[33] Hitchcock had come to the studio in 1953; by 1960, he had given Paramount six films—*Rear Window* (1954), *To Catch a Thief* (1955), *The Trouble with Harry* (1955), *The Man Who Knew Too Much* (1956), *Vertigo* (1958), and *Psycho* (1960).[34] However, until *Psycho,* Hitchcock felt he was "nothing but a salaried employee [who] never had the opportunity to make the real money his talents deserved."[35] Hitchcock insisted he never received his share of the gross from *Window* and *Thief.* Even Weltner had no idea what it should have been, except that in the case of *Window* the percentage deal netted Hitchcock only $37,798; the director did somewhat better with *Thief:* $86,240.[36]

Hitchcock presented Paramount with what Weltner described as a "pretty tough" deal. The director knew exactly what his next two films would be: *The Birds* and *Marnie,* in that order. And he intended to make them, either at Paramount or elsewhere. If at Paramount, *Window* and *Thief* would have to be reissued with a better percentage arrangement. Otherwise, Hitchcock would jump studio. Paramount refused, and Hitchcock moved over to Universal.

It was the right choice. *Psycho* was not even filmed on the Paramount lot. Paramount threw up so many obstacles that Hitchcock had no other choice but to shoot the film at Universal, where his television show was filmed. In fact, he used the crew from *Alfred Hitchcock Presents* to shoot *Psycho.*[37]

While it seemed that Paramount had made a fortune with *Psycho,* it only distributed the film. Paramount was not the sole owner of the negative; Hitchcock owned 60 percent of it. In view of Paramount's original disdain for *Psycho*, Hitchcock was happy to leave for Universal, where he was given his own attractively furnished bungalow. Whether MCA decided to remain a talent agency or move into film production, the Hitchcock-Wasserman association would continue, with Wasserman either as Hitchcock's agent or the owner of the studio where Hitchcock worked. It turned out to be the latter.

Wasserman's overtures to Paramount in fall 1962 were probably linked with Hitchcock's joining Universal earlier that year. Having lured Hitchcock away from the Paramount lot, Wasserman may well have thought of luring the lot away from Paramount. Weltner's 5 November 1962 memo alluded to the "Wasserman Plan," which would make Revue Paramount's production center—in effect, transferring operations to Universal City. Such a move would free the Paramount soundstages for television production and attract independent filmmakers other than the ones currently distributing through Paramount. The move would also make Paramount ripe for a takeover, a merger, or a stock swap; and if MCA and Paramount should merge, MCA, which already owned the pre-1948 Paramount library, would get the rest; and that, along with Universal's own library, would keep television stations supplied with product indefinitely.

Karp and Freeman were opposed to the move even though serious discussions were never held with Wasserman, who appears only to have proposed the idea. Yet this was Wasserman's way: bait the hook and wait for a bite. Although Paramount was ailing, Karp and Freeman objected to the plan for reasons having nothing to do with its viability but rather the length of time needed to relocate (twelve to eighteen months, which was an exaggeration), crowded production facilities, inadequate parking, and second-class citizenship. Weltner, however, was willing to consider the plan. More logical than his colleagues, Weltner knew that, since overhead had become the bane of Paramount, it would be lower at Revue because the rent would be less; furthermore, Paramount would no longer be forced to make movies to absorb the overhead and could then become more selective. Nothing came of the "Wasserman Plan," but Weltner's reasons for considering it were far more compelling than parking spaces and face-saving.

A few weeks after Karp and Freeman turned down the Plan, Karp wrote a "strictly confidential" memo to Balaban with a copy to Weltner, who was then in London.[38] Karp reiterated what, for the most part, was already being implemented: eliminating in-house pictures and turning the lot over to independent producers whose films would be financed and distributed by Paramount or through coproduction deals; encouraging relationships with producer-directors, actor-producers, and actor-directors who can offer some assurance that their projects will reach the screen; retaining only such stars and producers whose presence might not guarantee a top-grossing film but one that at least would not be an abysmal failure like DeMille's final production, his $5 million remake of *The Buccaneer* (1958), or Marlon Brando's $6 million *One-Eyed Jacks* (1961), now a cult film but at the time a disaster. Karp's final recommendation—reducing the overhead—must have amused Weltner, who had made Paramount's high overhead into a personal crusade. Karp reasoned that the greater the number of independent productions, the lower the overhead: $3.92 million for 1963 as opposed to $4.6 million the previous year. However, the overhead was still high in comparison with the profits for those years: $3.4 million and $5.9 million, respectively. Keeping the soundstages busy with independent productions was not the answer. Quality product was.

The most frustrating part of Weltner's job was its lack of real power. That was still held by Balaban, whom Weltner served faithfully, always apologizing for an overlong memo or phrasing his suggestions so carefully that they could never be misinterpreted as advice (e.g., requesting that he and a few others be exempt from the ban on flying first-class when traveling abroad, not for their comfort but for Paramount's image). However, in 1961 Weltner became excited about Al Dewlen's courtroom novel, *Twilight of Honor*. Although Balaban had literally gone fishing, Weltner, apologizing for writing to Balaban on vacation, urged him to buy the rights, adding that it would be a good vehicle for Paul Newman. The letter was never sent, not because Weltner was reluctant to disturb Balaban, but because Balaban could not be located. MGM eventually made *Twilight of Honor* (1963) with Richard Chamberlain, hoping to capitalize on the actor's fame as television's Dr. Kildare. That *Twilight of Honor* did nothing for Chamberlain's film career is not the point. The letter is revealing for what it implies about Balaban and, indirectly, Paramount itself. Weltner even went so far as to have a synopsis of the novel written for Balaban: "I know that you are loath to reading scripts or even synopses . . . and you may wish to leave story appraisals to the Studio."[39] If Balaban was loath to read scripts or even synopses, who made the decisions? It could have been Jack Karp, who made his determination on the basis of plot, familiarity with the writer's and director's work, and the producer's arrangement with Paramount; or Weltner, who was guided by similar criteria.

Balaban apparently signed off on whatever was recommended by someone he respected.

There is no doubt that Balaban respected Weltner; but he also took advantage of Weltner's loyalty to Paramount and his willingness to shoulder greater responsibilities, which, by 1960, went far beyond those of the vice president of distribution. Accordingly, Weltner was promoted to executive vice president in 1962. Although production was an area in which he always felt uncomfortable, Weltner was not shy about expressing an opinion on a project or a proposal that he knew was not right for the studio. He encouraged Balaban to pass on releasing *Requiem for a Heavyweight* (1962). *Requiem* had been produced for Columbia, which was now trying to unload it, perhaps because Columbia anticipated poor box office. When Balaban decided to take Weltner's advice, Columbia ended up releasing the film. Weltner advised against optioning King Vidor's proposal for a movie about a famous director (modeled perhaps on himself) who, unable to cope with a changing Hollywood, returned to his small-town roots, where he found true happiness.

Hollywood had changed, and Weltner did not need King Vidor to tell him. Weltner understood the problem, articulating it with frightening clarity: "The heart of this entire problem is the tremendous scarcity of big box office names, either of actors, producers or directors, which scarcity is being magnified all the time."[40]

Frank Sinatra was a case in point. While Weltner had no objection to Paramount's making *Come Blow Your Horn* (1963) with Sinatra as a 1960s swinger, he warned Balaban about details in the proposed contract that he found unacceptable: the producers' (Norman Lear and Bud Yorkin) complete control of the production even though Paramount would be putting up the money; reduced overhead; and ownership of the film by the producers, who would also receive a "service fee" of $300,000 as well as 50 percent of the net profits, with a guarantee that the amount would not be less than $250,000 (or less than 27 percent of the gross profits). What really bothered Weltner were Sinatra's terms: a salary of $250,000 for ten weeks' work and prorated thereafter. Weltner knew there would be prorating, probably a good deal of it: "I have heard that [Sinatra's] track record of finishing a picture on time is not of the best and that he has been known to take time away from the shooting schedule to engage in other activities."[41]

No studio, even in its darkest hour, could accede to such terms. It was now "give a little, take a little" time. Because *Come Blow Your Horn* was not only the movie version of Neil Simon's hit comedy but also a Sinatra vehicle, the producers came off better than Paramount, which at least succeeded in having the service fee waived and the advertising budget limited to $350,000. There were undoubtedly other concessions—enough to convince Weltner that a $2.8 million budget would allow Paramount to break even at around $6 million. The studio did, and five other Neil Simon plays became Paramount films: *Barefoot in the Park* (1967), *The Odd Couple* (1968), *Star-Spangled Girl* (1971), *Plaza Suite,* (1971), and *Last of the Red Hot Lovers* (1972), along with Simon's first original screenplay, *The Out of Towners* (1970), based on discarded material from *Plaza Suite.*

The *Come Blow Your Horn* trade-offs made it clear that all deals are negotiable. The terms could be as simple as a fifty-fifty arrangement with the producers; as complex as a two-picture commitment, with a designated percentage of the profits from the first going toward financing the second; or as demarcated as a director-producer-star-script-distribution-overhead package.

There was no way that *All the Way Home* (1963)—the film version of the play based on James Agee's Pulitzer Prize–winning novel, *A Death in the Family*—would make a profit for either the producers, David Susskind and Ronald Kahn, or Paramount. Weltner had no love for Susskind, whom he found cantankerous (as did many in the industry); he was further incensed at the antipathy Susskind displayed toward commercial moviemaking on his syndicated television program, *Open End.* However, Weltner would not let his feelings prejudice him against a film that could bring Paramount prestige, if not profits. Besides, Weltner reasoned, the terms were fair: *All the Way Home* would be budgeted at five hundred thousand dollars, with each putting up half; Paramount would distribute the film in the Western hemisphere, the producers in the Eastern, with each party retaining the profits from its respective hemisphere. The profits, however, were negligible, although *All the Way Home* was worth making, if, for no other reason, to bring James Agee's poignant novel to the screen.

When Joseph E. Levine arrived at Paramount in the early 1960s, Weltner thought Levine could provide the studio with films that were both commercially and artistically successful. Levine was an eclectic producer—respected, on the one hand, for distributing the early films of Fellini, DeSica, and Rossellini; mocked (but secretly envied), on the other, for the Japanese-made *Godzilla* (1954), which he acquired for a mere twelve thousand dollars and which brought in $1 million; and for *Hercules* (1959), which he distributed to critical ridicule but great box office.

Levine's childhood reads like copy for a movie mogul's biography.[42] Born in a Boston slum in 1905, he left school at fourteen, having done everything from shining shoes to selling pretzels and safety pins, to delivering papers and driving an ambulance. Nightclubs were his introduction to the world of entertainment as well as the dark side of the business. Marriage to Rosalie Harrison put an end to that phase of his career when Rosalie decided her husband should be engaged in a more reputable line of work. But Levine was too entrenched in show business to return to sales, which was Rosalie's idea of respectability.

Levine's next venture met with Rosalie's approval: film exhibition. Like Louis Mayer, whose purchase of a New England theater introduced him to a world he never knew existed when he was scavenging for scrap iron, Levine experienced a similar awakening when he bought his first theater in New Haven. He favored rereleases such as old Ken Maynard westerns because they were cheap and exploitation films about venereal disease and World War II atrocities because they attracted the curious.

In 1942, Levine formed his own distribution company, Embassy, with himself as president and Rosalie as vice president. Levine's taste ran the gamut from dreck to art: dreck for cash, art for accolades. With the end of the war, European cinema experienced a rebirth. Levine was particularly impressed by a new kind of Italian film that was later dubbed "Italian neorealism." Few Italian filmmakers would have appreciated the label; the realism—neo- or otherwise—of such films as *Paisan* (1946), *Open City* (1945), *Shoeshine* (1946), and *The Bicycle Thief* (1947) was the result of expediency. The lack of soundstages required location shooting in trattorias, apartments, and particularly streets.

These films introduced American audiences to the other Rome, a city of squalor and poverty that differed radically from the one in the travel brochures. They were also known as art films, which were shown in art houses—small, independently owned theaters that catered to a discerning public, not a mass audience. But there was another kind of Italian film, Levine discovered, that was not all that different from the lower-grade American product: the pseudo spectacle that substitutes tacky grandeur for imperial splendor. Although *Attila* was made in 1954, it did not find an American distributor until 1958 when Levine took a chance on the film, which grossed $2 million. *Hercules* (1959) did considerably better: $20 million. Levine did not receive "Showman of the Year" awards in the 1960s for nothing.

Levine decided to bypass the press and promote his latest Italian import, *Hercules*, on television, targeting drive-in audiences, mostly the young, whose idea of the ancient world consisted of superhuman heroes with bronzed torsos and diaphanously clad heroines with heaving bosoms. Levine also hoped his audience might recognize the Hercules—the muscle-bound, Montana-born, former Mr. Pacific, Mr. America, Mr. World, and Mr. Universe: Steve Reeves. Levine convinced Warner Bros. to distribute *Hercules*, which was both typical and atypical of the kind of film Levine eventually distributed. As someone who started out at a time when Hollywood was grinding out flag-wavers and anti-Axis propaganda, Levine knew that exploitation films and faux epics were not ends in themselves and the only way to bring quality films to the public is by distributing films of little or no quality like *Hercules* to become financially able to do so. Like Hal Wallis, who produced blatantly commercial movies to finance pictures of substance, Levine realized that cheap imports would not give him the kind of stature he craved. His motives were not entirely artistic: the market for the Italian pseudo-spectacle was drying up. Still, Levine believed that the kinds of films Vittorio DeSica and Federico Fellini were making, especially with stars like Sophia Loren and Marcello Mastroianni, had the right ingredients to attract wide audiences, despite the language barrier.

Levine returned to the art film, starting with DeSica's *Two Women* (1960). He did not, however, use art film advertising. *Two Women* was publicized as a film with one of the most graphic rapes ever seen on the screen: a mother (Sophia Loren) and daughter (Eleanora Brown) are viciously attacked in a church by Moroccan soldiers. The publicity paid off with impressive box-office receipts and an Oscar for Loren, the first performer to win an Academy Award for a foreign language film. But Levine would not be bringing films of such caliber to Paramount—or, for that matter, to any studio. In the 1960s, no studio would even think of releasing art house products like *Two Women* and Fellini's *8 1/2* (1963).

In 1963, Levine entered into a multipicture, $30 million arrangement with Paramount in which the studio would put up the money (including a producer's fee) and he would provide the package, the contents of which would consist of "sex, violence, and action—just the things that sell."[43] Predictably, Levine gave Paramount high-gloss trash (e.g., *The Carpetbaggers* [1964], *Harlow* [1965], *Sylvia* [1965], *Where Love Has Gone* [1964], *Nevada Smith* [1966])—sex lacquered to a glossy finish, whose shiny veneer concealed a complete lack of substance. Yet it was trash that was, for the most part, commercially successful.

Levine negotiated a cross-collateralization deal with Paramount consisting of *The Carpetbaggers* and *Nevada Smith*. The source of each was Harold Robbins's potboiler novel, *The Carpetbaggers*, the kind of Hollywood exposé that the 1960s embraced on the assumption that there was dirt beneath the tinsel. The decade delighted in *Valley of the Dolls* (1967), wondering if Neely was really Judy Garland and Helen Lawson was Ethel Merman and if everyone in show business popped as many "dolls" as Sharon Tate. There were also Levine's own skeleton-rattlers, *The Oscar* (1966), *Harlow*, and *Where Love Has Gone*—the last derived from another Harold Robbins best-seller loosely based on the murder of Lana Turner's lover, mobster Johnny Stomponato, supposedly by Turner's own daughter.

Weltner found the cross-collateralization proposal "as complicated a business as I have read for a long time."[44] Within eighteen months of the release of *The Carpetbaggers*, Paramount would get two-thirds of the net, which then would be applied to *Nevada Smith*—with the remaining one-third divided between Paramount and Embassy. Within the second eighteen months, Paramount would apply one-third of *The Carpetbaggers* profits ("whatever they may be") to *Nevada Smith*—the remaining two-thirds divided between Paramount and Embassy. The *Nevada Smith* arrangement was similar: within the first and second eighteen–month periods, the same percentages of the profits (first, two-thirds, then one-third) would be applied to any outstanding production or distribution costs incurred by *The Carpetbaggers*.

In 1966, Levine, disturbed by Paramount's instability, which also made it a takeover target, decided to sell his stock in the studio. Ironically, his integrity as a producer returned when he left Paramount. Within the next two years, he produced three widely admired films, all Embassy releases, that were neither violent nor particularly sexy: *The Graduate* (1967), which made a star of Dustin Hoffman; *The Producers* (1968), which won Mel Brooks an Oscar for Best Original Story and Screenplay; and *The Lion in Winter* (1968), for which Katharine Hepburn received an Oscar, sharing the honor with Barbra Streisand for *Funny Girl* when voters could not decide whether Hepburn's Eleanor of Aquitaine or Streisand's Fanny Brice was the better performance.

In 1968, Levine sold Embassy to Avco, a diversified company specializing in aerospace equipment but with real estate and broadcasting interests as well, hence Embassy's appeal to Avco. But except for *Carnal Knowledge* (1971), Avco Embassy's releases were poorly received. Although Levine continued to produce until shortly before his death in 1987, he was dismissed as a flamboyant hustler who relied on the profits from his class trash to produce art. The record shows that he succeeded on both counts.

The Levine experience showed that Paramount was running on empty. That Levine could produce three masterpieces for Embassy after leaving a trail of trash at Paramount was indicative of the depths to which the studio had sunk. Weltner knew the times were bad; he also knew that if there would always be an England, there would always be a Paramount—of some sort.

Paramount, on the other hand, knew there would not always be a Weltner. Yet Weltner was the youngest of Paramount's senior executives. In 1963, he had been with the company for forty years; he was now sixty-two. Naturally, Paramount was "desirous of insuring the retention of Weltner's services until such time as he retires," as was stated in the five-year contract that he was offered, giving the studio "an exclusive call on Weltner's services on a full-time basis for the period commencing [14 August 1963] . . . and ending January 1, 1967." Furthermore, Weltner was guaranteed $93,000 a year during that 5–year period; he could also stay on as a consultant for 8 more years at an annual salary of $23,500.

When Weltner retired in 1967, it was not as executive vice president but as president of Paramount Pictures Corporation. Weltner must have known his tenure as president would be brief when, less than a year after he was made executive vice president, he was approached to succeed Balaban. The board was desperate. Balaban had turned seventy-six, and, at sixty, Jack Karp was just two years younger than Weltner. Yet no one at Paramount could equal Weltner in experience. George Weltner was the only game in town.

When Weltner agreed to be Paramount's president in late spring 1964, it could not have been for the money: $115,000 was not that much more than what he was making. Besides, his contract made it clear that he could receive "additional amounts during . . . his active employment." More likely, Weltner viewed the presidency as the natural culmination of a career spent in one company where he literally started at the bottom and ascended through the ranks to the top.

At the 2 June 1964 stockholders meeting, Balaban announced that he was yielding the presidency to a "younger man" so that the company "might be better served" and that he would become board chairman, with Zukor as chairman emeritus. What Weltner did not know in the summer of 1964, as congratulations poured in from exchanges throughout the world, was that within a year his job and the studio's future would be imperiled.

What Weltner did know, however, was that Paramount needed a production head. Karp, sensing his days were over, resigned the same day as Weltner's appointment. His successor was Martin Lee Rackin, a former journalist-turned-screenwriter who became a producer in the mid-1950s (e.g., *The Helen Morgan Story* [1957], *Fort Dobbs* [1958]). Since Rackin had more screenwriting than producing credits, he was only an interim appointee.

In June 1964, shortly after Weltner became president, Howard W. Koch received a phone call asking him to go to the Beverly Hills Hotel to meet with some Paramount executives.[45] Koch was then working for Frank Sinatra as vice president of production at Sinatra Enterprises, where he had already produced *Sergeants Three* (1962) and the film that once baffled audiences and now is regarded as a Cold War masterpiece as well as one of Sinatra's best pictures, *The Manchurian Candidate* (1962). Although Koch was scheduled to fly to Rome later that day to complete work on Sinatra's latest film, *Von Ryan's Express* (1965), he agreed, provided the meeting be brief. It was. Weltner was there to make him a job offer: vice president, worldwide production, at Paramount.

Koch did not commit himself. He knew he needed Sinatra's blessing, which, to his surprise, came without the confrontation scene that Koch envisioned en route to Rome. Sinatra, in fact, was delighted that "his man" would be production chief at a major studio.

Koch's credentials were ideal; so was his age—forty-eight. Koch had entered the business at eighteen when he joined Universal's contract and play date department at the studio's New York office. Within a year, Koch was in Hollywood; his stint as assistant cutter at Fox led to his being hired as second assistant director of *The Keys of the Kingdom* (1944). He graduated to first assistant director of such films as MGM's *Million Dollar Mermaid* (1952) and *Julius Caesar* (1953), and Universal-International's *The Naked Spur* (1954).

Once he and producer Aubrey Schenck formed their own company, Bel-Air, releasing through United Artist, Koch had even more opportunities to work behind the camera—first, as codirector of *Shield for Murder* (1954), then as director of *Big House, U.S.A.* (1955) and *Fort Bowie* (1958).

Although Koch would continue to direct throughout his career (mostly in television for such series as *Cheyenne*, *Maverick*, and *The Un-*

touchables), he was primarily a producer. Understandably, Sinatra hired him in 1961 to be his new company's production head.

If anyone should have been asked to head production at Paramount, it was Koch. The *Hollywood Reporter* (16 September 1964) spoke for the entire film community: "It's about time someone who knows how to make motion pictures is finally named the head of a Hollywood studio."

Koch was never meant to be production chief at a time when the studio system was crumbling. Although he could claim to have been a producer for thirty years, his tenure as Paramount's production chief lasted for all of two.

Within less than a year after Koch became production chief, two men whose names meant little or nothing to him, Herbert G. Siegel and Ernest H. Martin, had decided Paramount needed a change of leadership: themselves.

3

Barbarians at the Spanish Gate

Of the eight studios that dominated the movie business during Hollywood's Golden Age, Universal was the first to lose its independence and acquire a succession of parents, corporate and otherwise.[1] First, it was Decca Records in 1952. This was not as incongruous as it might seem; Decca, which had pioneered the original cast albums of Broadway musicals, could at least claim an affinity with Hollywood, given the number of Decca recording artists who had appeared in Universal releases during the 1940s (e.g., the Andrews Sisters, Ella Fitzgerald, Martha Tilton, Deanna Durbin, Dick Haymes). Universal's next parent was no outsider, either, compared to Coca-Cola, which took over Columbia in 1985; or Sony, which did the same four years later.

In 1952, MCA (Music Corporation of America) was the talent agency of choice, whose clients were represented in every branch of entertainment (radio, television, theater, music, and movies). It was MCA's privileged status that emboldened it to enter a realm usually closed to talent agencies (less euphemistically known as "flesh peddlers"): televison production. Lew Wasserman, at the time MCA president and a confirmed Democrat, prevailed upon Ronald Reagan, then a Democrat, to aid MCA in circumventing the Screen Actors Guild's (SAG) policy that prohibited talent agents from engaging in production without a waiver.[2] SAG's reasoning was simple: the artist employs the agent, not vice versa. If MCA were involved in both production and representation, the agency would be employing the artist.

In 1952, Ronald Reagan was in his last year as SAG president—a position he had held since 1947. (He would be reelected again in 1959, having served an unprecedented six terms.) Reagan was also an MCA client; most important, Wasserman was his agent.

Reagan, who projected an ingenuousness that only a cynic would question, used his influence to secure a blanket waiver for MCA to enter TV production, arguing that the advent of television and the corresponding cutbacks in film production made it difficult, if not impossible, for most actors to work exclusively in movies and that such a waiver could only benefit the SAG membership, since it would provide work on both the big and small screens.

MCA then created its own television production company, Revue, which produced such shows as *Stars over Hollywood, Alfred Hitchcock Presents,* and *General Electric Theatre,* which was hosted by Reagan. But MCA was not satisfied with producing just for the small screen any more than it had been with booking dance bands and soloists in the 1920s. MCA clearly had designs on a studio, especially one with a sizable backlot that would provide a home for Revue Productions, which was then renting space. So, in 1958, MCA bought Universal's back lot; in 1962, MCA bought the studio.

Between 1958 and 1962, the political climate had changed. Reagan's film career was coming to a close, ending officially with *The Killers* (1964). He had also changed parties and had become a Republican. Reagan continued to perform but in a different capacity: first as governor of California, then as United States president. However, in 1962, John F. Kennedy was president, and Lew Wasserman might have thought that, in view of his reputation as a Democratic fundraiser and Kennedy supporter, the Justice Department would have blinked while a talent agency defied the Sherman Antitrust Act by taking over a studio. Given MCA's roster of stars (Marlon Brando, Warren Beatty, Doris Day, Dean Martin, Ingrid Bergman, Gregory Peck, Sophia Loren, and Paul Newman, to cite a few of the fourteen hundred performers MCA represented), it would have been more than a conflict of interest; it would have been a travesty of the labor-management distinction: the employee would pay the employer to work for the employer. Thus Attorney General Robert Kennedy gave MCA two choices: the talent business or film production, but not both. MCA chose the latter. On 16 September 1962, MCA Artists ceased to exist; MCA was officially out of flesh-peddling and into moviemaking.

In 1965, it seemed as if history was repeating itself when Herbert J.

Siegel, president of the talent agency General Artists Corporation (GAC) and board chairman of the Baldwin-Montrose Chemical Company, and Ernest H. Martin, the other half of Feuer & Martin (the Broadway producing team responsible for such hits as *Where's Charley?*, *Guys and Dolls*, *Can-Can*, and *How to Succeed in Business without Reallly Trying*), staged a battle for control of Paramount.

Since the insurgents did not have the same aura as Wasserman, Reagan, and Robert Kennedy, their bid for the crown was not fraught with the Machiavellian melodrama of Reagan's blanket waiver for MCA and MCA's attempt to absorb Universal. Actually, Siegel and Martin were more concerned about legality than the earlier cast of characters. But since neither Siegel nor Martin was exactly a media icon, the story of their attempt to wrest control of Paramount from a lethargic management has never been fully told.

As Willy Loman might have said, Siegel and Martin were known but not well known. The Philadelphia-born Siegel graduated from Lehigh University in 1950 with a B.A. in Journalism. A few weeks after graduation, he married Ann Levy; through her, he became part of a family that made broadcasting history: Ann's father, Isaac "Ike" Levy, and his brother Leon were instrumental in the formation of CBS.[3] Siegel's marriage opened doors that would otherwise have been closed or extremely difficult for the son of a coat manufacturer to enter.

Ike Levy was a lawyer whose poker companions included Irving Berlin and Harpo Marx. Ike was more interested in being an entrepreneur than in practicing law, but whatever business he entered would have some connection with popular entertainment. In 1922, it was impossible to remain indifferent to the spell of radio, which seemed to have done the impossible by bringing entertainment into the home. Thus, when Philadelphia's WCAU became available in 1922, Ike bought it. The next question was what to do with it. More oriented toward the art of the deal than its consequences, Ike prevailed upon his dentist brother, Leon, to manage the station. Like Ike, Leon dreamed of something more satisfying than extracting teeth and filling cavities. Leon agreed to manage WCAU, since it would not interfere with his practice: the station broadcasted at night, so he could play dentist by day.

But once a lawyer and a dentist enter the world of entertainment, there is no turning back except for failure. And the Levy brothers would not fail.

There was another Philadelphian, soon to eclipse the Levys, who had graduated from the Wharton School of Finance the same year Ike Levy bought WCAU: William S. Paley, the son of Sam Paley, co-owner of Philadelphia's Congress Cigar Company, whose most popular brand was La Palina—a name designed for no other reason than to evoke "Paley." Always on the lookout for sponsors, Leon persuaded Sam Paley to advertise La Palina on WCAU, which was not difficult since the popularity of cigarettes had affected cigar sales.

Meanwhile, William Paley, who, like the Levys, enjoyed the good life, had to justify his Wharton degree—which he did by joining the family business; within three years of graduation, he had become vice president and secretary of Congress Cigar.

Leon Levy became part of the Paley family in 1927 when he married William's sister, Blanche. That same year, a series of events occurred that eventually led to the formation of CBS and the first chapter of the William S. Paley legend. In 1926, Arthur Judson, business manager of the Philadelphia Orchestra and New York Philharmonic (and representative of such artists as Vladimir Horowitz, Bruno Walter, and Ezio Pinza), approached NBC about the possibility of featuring his artists on the air. When NBC showed no interest, Judson spearheaded a group that called itself the United Independent Broadcasters (UIB). Once WCAU guaranteed UIB ten hours of air time, WCAU became a UIB affiliate.

That same year, the prospect of a merger between two recording companies, RCA and Victor, drew Victor's rival, the Columbia Phonograph Company, into UIB's orbit. The result was the Columbia Phonograph Broadcasting System, which premiered on 25 September 1927 with a live performance of Deems Taylor's opera, *The King's Henchman*. Although the transmission was affected by a thunderstorm that reduced the number of listeners, the performance was a significant event in the history of broadcasting. Two months after the *King's Henchman* broadcast, CPBS became CBS. William Paley, vice president of Congress Cigar, was so impressed by La Palina's sales (which were largely attributed to the commercials on the Congress Cigar–sponsored programs) that he obtained a controlling interest in CBS; by September he was president. The Levy brothers also became part of CBS: both went on the board of directors. Ike resigned in 1951 when CBS was reorganized into separate divisions (CBS Radio, CBS Television, Columbia Records, etc.) but still remained a major stockholder; Leon stayed on, and by 1965 owned almost 367,000 CBS shares.

When Herbert Siegel married Ann Levy, William S. Paley was already a legend; the legend would grow. For anyone bent on a career in some form of popular entertainment, Siegel had married into the right family.

The world of media appealed to Siegel, although he was as yet uncertain of his own place in it. At least he knew that if he had to be bicoastal, his base of operations would be the East. In a way, Siegel was a throwback to the days when distribution was centered in New York and production in Los Angeles. Certain East Coast types—Zukor, Harry Warner, and Columbia's Jack Cohn, Harry Cohn's brother—preferred to stay in close proximity to the banks and the stock exchange; they relished the business—not the creative—end of moviemaking.

So it was with Siegel. With the Paley connection, he could easily have wangled a job at CBS, but the prospect of being a squire in Paley's kingdom did not sit well with a twenty-two-year-old who wanted to succeed on his own. And yet CBS indirectly played a role in his failed attempt to take over Paramount.

In 1950, the same year that he graduated from Lehigh, Siegel became secretary and director of Official Films, a New York outfit that produced and distributed educational films—a position he held until 1955. The next significant entry on Siegel's resumé gives one pause: in 1960, Herbert Siegel became chairman of the Baldwin-Montrose Chemical Company—the result of a merger betwen Baldwin Rubber, which manufactured automotive and industrial rubber products, and the Montrose Chemical Company. The switch from movies to tires might have seemed a comedown except for one crucial fact: Baldwin-Montrose had a 70 percent interest in the talent agency General Artists Corporation (GAC), whose president Siegel became in 1963. Thus, when Siegel and Martin made their move to free Paramount from what they considered ossification, neither was a show biz novice.

In 1950, the year that marked Siegel's less-than-spectacular entry into film, Broadway witnessed the opening of one of the most beloved musicals in American theater: *Guys and Dolls*, which ran for twelve hundred performances, spawned a movie version in 1955, and continues to enjoy frequent revivals. *Guys and Dolls* was a Cy Feuer and Ernest Martin production. It was not, however, their first. In 1948, Feuer and Martin confounded the skeptics with a musical version of *Charley's Aunt. Where's Charley?* not only enjoyed a healthy run (792 performances) but also provided the star, Ray Bolger, with his signature song, "Once in Love with Amy." In 1962, the Feuer and Martin production of *How to Succeed in Business without Really Trying* received, among other honors, the Pulitzer Prize for drama (a rarity for a musical), the Critics Circle Award as best musical, and Tony Awards for Feuer and Martin. As successful Broadway producers, the team appreciated Paramount's longstanding relationship with the theater, which harked back to the time of Zukor, who had respected stage talent, and Jesse Lasky, who had always looked to the New York stage for potential film properties before proceeding elsewhere. While the movie musical's golden age was coming to a close in the mid-1950s, Paramount was still releasing movie versions of Broadway shows, both musicals and nonmusicals as well as films interlaced with musical numbers (e.g., the Elvis Presley films *Loving You* [1957], *King Creole* [1958], *G.I. Blues* [1960], *Blue Hawaii* [1961], and *Roustabout* [1964]). The bona fide musicals included *Anything Goes* (1956), which at least preserved most of the Cole Porter score; Rudolph Friml's *The Vagabond King* (1956), which failed to equal the success of MGM's ventures into operetta (*The Student Prince* and *Rose Marie*, [both 1954]; *Funny Face* [1957], a glorious resetting of George Gershwin's music to a fashion world script; and *Li'l Abner* [1959], which seemed more cartoon-like on film than it did on the stage).

Paramount was fortunate in having producers like Hal Wallis and William Perlberg, and producer-directors like William Wyler and Billy Wilder who understood how stage drama could work on the screen without losing the immediacy that can easily happen in a medium where the action is fragmented into shots of various size and duration. Significantly, Paramount's most successful stage adaptations came from Wilder (*Sabrina* [1954]); Wyler (*The Heiress* [1949], and *Detective Story* [1952]); Perlberg (*The Country Girl* [1954] and *The Pleasure of His Company* [1961], both directed by George Seaton); and Wallis (*The Rose Tattoo* [1955]; *The Rainmaker* [1956], in which a (perhaps) too old Katharine Hepburn played the unfulfilled Lizzie, a role created by Geraldine Page; *Summer and Smoke* (1961), which allowed moviegoers to see Geraldine Page in the role that had made her a star; and *Becket* [1964], which confirmed Richard Burton's status as a classically trained actor, in case anyone had forgotten).

Perlberg and Wallis were not always successful in their choice of vehicle or star. Why Perlberg thought *The Rat Race* (1960) would succeed on the screen when it had lasted a mere eighty-four performances on Broadway a decade earlier is puzzling. Since Wallis does not even mention *A Visit to a Small Planet* (1960) in his autobiography, it is impossible to know if he envisioned Gore Vidal's 1956 comedy as a romp for Jerry

Lewis or if Lewis envisioned it as a romp for himself. Lewis could not erase memories of the patrician Cyril Ritchard, who had originated the role of the extraterrestrial visitor. Consequently, Vidal's sophisticated satire degenerated into buffoonery.

Still, between 1949 and 1964, Paramount vied with Warner Bros. in the number of stage adaptations it released. There were miscalculations, of course, such as *My Three Angels* (1955); *Desire under the Elms* (1958), which proved that, without the right director, Eugene O' Neill is better read than seen; and *The Matchmaker* (1958), in which Shirley Booth had the unenviable task of performing the role that Ruth Gordon had created on Broadway. There were a few plays that were never distinguished theater to begin with and remained such on the screen (e.g., *The World of Suzie Wong* [1960] and *Come Blow Your Horn* [1963]). But the best were worthy replicas of the originals. To producers like Feuer and Martin, who appreciated Paramount's predilection for the theater, the studio served a dual purpose: it could invest in Feuer and Martin productions and later release the movie versions.

Paramount, however, was not the force that brought Martin, Feuer, and Siegel together. CBS was.

After graduating from Juilliard, where he was a scholarship student with a concentration in trumpet, Seymour "Cy" Feuer moved to Los Angeles where he became musical director of CBS-owned Columbia Records in 1933.[4] Around the same time, Feuer joined the CBS orchestra, whose chief function was to provide musical interludes in the absence of any scheduled programs. In 1938 Republic Pictures hired him to compose and conduct background music for its films; by 1942, Feuer had scored some three hundred Republic films, mostly B westerns. Even when Feuer was toiling at Republic, he was musical director of such CBS radio shows as *Escape* and *Studio One*—the latter devoted to literary adaptations and soon destined to make the transition to television under the same name, becoming one of most celebrated live drama series of the 1950s. Finding neither Republic Pictures nor CBS radio particularly challenging, Feuer joined the army in 1942.

Because of a respiratory ailment, Ernest Martin (born Ernest Markowitz) did not serve in the armed forces during World War II. Almost nine years older than Feuer, Martin also had a CBS connection that had begun when he was a UCLA political science major working part-time as a CBS tour guide at the Sunset Boulevard studios.[5] After graduating in 1942, Martin returned to CBS in a variety of full-time jobs, eventually becoming program director, producing or supervising such shows as *My Friend Irma, Suspense,* and *Life with Luigi.*

Once World War II ended, Martin suspected radio was nearing the end of its heyday. To Feuer, the end of the war had more to do with returning to civilian life than it did with the future of radio. Neither Martin nor Feuer had formally met until Martin was invited to a welcome-home party for Feuer, after which they not only became best friends but also producing partners.

In 1965, Feuer and Martin were contemplating something far grander than a Broadway musical. So was Herbert Siegel, who had cast his net even earlier. While all three came from diverse backgrounds, they were united by a common bond: CBS, which proved invaluable at the time they decided to take over Paramount.

In 1963 Siegel had higher aspirations than running GAC, now located on Santa Monica Boulevard not far from the former home of MCA Artists. With MCA's departure from the talent business, Siegel hoped that, by affecting the MCA look (agents in dark suits to suggest uniformity and team spirit), GAC could become what MCA had been. Siegel even hired MCA alumni including MCA's former president, Lawrence Barnett, whom he made GAC board chairman. After just a year as GAC president, Siegel managed to acquire four other talent agencies: IMA Talent Ltd., UTM Artists Ltd., the Harold D. Cohen Agency, and International Talent Associates.

In 1965, Siegel believed he had the professional standing and credibility to move into the big time. Of all the studios, Paramount seemed the most susceptible to takeover, if only because the average board member's age was seventy! Paramount needed new blood, and the thirty-seven-year-old Siegel and the forty-six-year-old Martin intended to supply it.

On 20 May 1965, Siegel informed the Securities and Exchange Commission (SEC) that he would solicit proxies to obtain control of Paramount because, as *Newsweek* (31 May 1965) reported, the company "has not been managed to realize its full potential." Siegel's goal was to buy 125,000 shares (approximately $8 million worth) at $64 a share, thereby securing a position on the board. As the press intimated, Siegel would have no difficulty raising the $8 million because his father-in-law, Ike Levy, was a major CBS stockholder; and his brother-in-law, Dr. Leon Levy, owned CBS shares valued at $14.6 million.

Siegel also did not think it would be difficult; although he himself owned only one hundred shares of Paramount stock, Baldwin–Montrose owned ten thousand. The arrangement seemed foolproof: Baldwin-Montrose would buy sixty-five thousand shares; Feuer & Martin Productions, fifteen thousand; and FMI, Ltd. (a holding company the team set up for the Paramount shares), forty-five thousand. Well aware of the Justice Department's decision that forced MCA to choose between flesh-peddling and production, Siegel—on the same day that he filed notice with the SEC—resigned from GAC, in which he had very little stock. He was determined to play by the rules.

That Paramount's gerontocracy was being challenged augured well for stockholders. Paramount stock rose from 56 1/2 on 17 May to 67 3/4 on 21 May. Once Martin and Siegel went on the board, however, the stock dropped 5 5/8 on 25 May, suggesting that the takeover was a fait accompli. Still, it was an improvement over Paramount's past performance. To the stockholders it seemed that the din of battle had subsided; actually, it was intensifying.

In the coming months, a great many facts about Paramount emerged that explain why Siegel and Martin thought it was easy prey. Although the studio reported a profit of $6.559 million for 1964 (a bit better than 1963's $5.908 million), the revenues came largely from leasing films to television. In fact, by 1965, television leasing had made Paramount $23.3 million richer.

Siegel believed Paramount was becoming more of a television conduit than a studio. Certainly the hits of the early 1960s were few. There was *Psycho,* of course, but what was not known at the time was that *Psycho* was more profitable to Hitchcock than to Paramount—and, finally, more profitable to Universal, when Hitchcock exchanged his rights to the film for MCA stock after moving to Universal.[6] *Breakfast at Tiffany's* (1961) and *Hud* (1963) were deservedly popular but not as profitable as the two big moneymakers, both of which were models of mediocrity: *Hatari!* (1961) and *The Carpetbaggers* (1964), the latter costing $3.3 million and grossing $8 million. Two anticipated blockbusters, *Circus World* and *The Fall of the Roman Empire* (both 1964), fell considerably short of expectations.

Weltner could not have been surprised when Siegel's name was mentioned so often as his replacement. Weltner had known of Siegel's intentions for at least a month before they were disclosed; he was also aware that Siegel and Martin were not the only ones who were critical of his performance as president. In fact, Weltner had not been president a year before being openly criticized at a board meeting. In a "personal and confidential" memo, Weltner identified the critic as Stanton Griffis, an investment banker, Cornell graduate, and longtime board member who used the 7 April meeting to launch a double attack—on Paramount for its increasingly "salacious" films and on Weltner for his poor judgement and ineffectual leadership.[7]

Weltner's memo went through several drafts, each carefully purged of emotive language until the tone was as dispassionate as possible for one who had been deeply hurt but was unwilling to show it. Weltner had to defend himself against charges that were patently unfair. Although Weltner did not directly attribute Griffis's prudery to his age (mid-seventies), he could not resist noting that "if we are to listen to the pleas of an older generation, we must walk on eggs, ever mindful of the birds and the bees and similar fare." At sixty-three, Weltner did not think of himself as belonging to Griffis's generation. He also understood that youth must be served, staunchly defending the "younger" generation, which every studio was courting: "Let us not sit back in criticism of our young people ... and feed them Alice in Wonderland, Little Red Riding Hood pablum, pap and balderdash. If we want to stay in business, we must move with the times. . . ."

What truly bothered Weltner was Griffis's behavior. Griffis had become the board member every company fears. So overextended that he frequently missed meetings and so self-absorbed that he ignored the agenda of the ones he chose to attend, Griffis had outlived his usefulness. He was prone to reliving the past, particularly the mid-1930s, when he was a Paramount stockholder and helped Balaban put the studio on a firm financial footing after it had emerged from bankruptcy in 1935. Then, Griffis's Wall Street connections were invaluable, enabling him to wipe out Paramount's $98 million debt through a series of short-term loans and stock purchases.[8]

But that rescue mission had occurred thirty years earlier. In the interim, Griffis went on the Paramount board, eventually becoming chair of the executive committee. However, he was the kind of financier who is never satisfied being associated with just one company. For a time he was even treasurer of Cornell-McClintic Productions, which Guthrie McClintic and Katherine Cornell had formed to produce Cornell's stage vehicles. Nor was politics alien to Griffis; he served as United States ambassador to Poland in 1947, Egypt in 1948, Argentina in 1949, and Spain in 1950.

Exactly what Griffis wanted from Paramount in 1964, except dividends and a soapbox, is uncertain. Like many an elder statesman, he had assumed the right to hold forth on whatever he considered pertinent, regardless of the occasion. Yet anyone who found Paramount's films of the early 1960s salacious (presumably, Griffis meant *The Carpetbaggers, Harlow,* and *Nevada Smith*) was simply out of touch with the times. Griffis also chose to grandstand at the April meeting, contrasting his efforts that were "spent . . . getting [Paramount] out of the banks" with Weltner's that succeeded in "putting Paramount back into the banks."

The reason, Griffis insisted, was the production deals with Levine and Preminger. Weltner admitted that Preminger went way over budget with *In Harm's Way,* yet that was not unusual. Besides, it was Preminger's first Paramount film. Weltner also bristled at being called "the father of the Joe Levine deal"; that distinction belonged to Jack Karp. But instead of laying the blame on Karp, which many CEOs would have done, Weltner exonerated him. Karp, Weltner argued, was in a bind: Paramount was reaching the stage of having no films in the pipeline. At least Levine could keep the product flowing.

As gently as he could, Weltner recommended that Griffis be replaced by someone younger—someone more attuned to the moviegoing public and less cavalier about attending board meetings.

Neither Balaban nor Ed Weisl, chairman of the board's executive committee, saw the earlier drafts of the memo in which Weltner described Paramount as "raider bait to a whole myriad of vultures," two of whom had already descended, causing the takeover rumors that started in spring 1965. Weisl must have been aware of these rumors; according to Weltner's memo, one scenario had Weisl "ready to push Weltner out." Understandably, the final draft made no mention of a possible ouster. Even if there had been some truth to it (and there probably was), Weltner would have accomplished nothing by confronting Weisl; he was also too much of a professional to accept rumor as fact. Weltner, however, was not loath to name a few of the vultures in the memo: in addition to CBS president James Aubrey, there were "Norton Simon, Siegel and others." "Siegel" could only have been Herbert J. Siegel, then a substantial Paramount stockholder and board member. Weltner, therefore, was unusually gracious when he introduced Siegel and Martin at the 1 June 1965 stockholders' meeting in the Versailles Room of the Hotel Astor. First, he made it quite clear that they were replacing Duncan Harris and the seventy-five-year-old Y. Frank Freeman, both of whom had been board members since the mid-1930s. Weltner also emphasized the newcomers' "fine background of experience"—Siegel's in representing talent and Martin's in producing shows. Interestingly, Weltner also alluded to Martin's pre-Broadway days at CBS. After Weltner saw the two of them in action, he could no longer be gracious. It was now evident that neither Siegel nor Martin had any respect for seniority. Balaban recalled that at one board meeting they behaved "like bulls in a china shop." Siegel called one board member an "idiot" and demanded that others be "thrown out"; Martin pounded the table so fiercely that Zukor was heard to remark, "If this keeps up we'll have to get a new table."[9]

A few weeks after joining the board, Siegel and Martin met with Weisl to inform him that they intended to take control of Paramount, with Siegel replacing Weltner as president and Martin replacing Howard W. Koch as production head. It was odd that they sought out the sixty-eight-year-old Weisl, whose age made him one of the old guard. Evidently, Siegel and Martin sensed that Weisl would be sympathetic to their cause, perhaps because he gave some indication that he, too, believed Weltner and Koch should go; hence, the rumor—or fact—that Weisl wanted Weltner out.

Ed Weisl was atypical of Paramount's board: a lawyer with degrees from the University of Chicago who had been director of the University of Chicago Alumni Foundation, special assistant to the United States attorney general, and a member of various committees of the United States Senate. Once Siegel and Martin were convinced that Weisl believed Paramount was out of joint and needed straightening, as he later implied, they felt justified about their own realignment campaign. However, they failed to recall that Weisl was a lawyer who weighed his words so carefully that neither side would benefit from his testimony and, more important, that Weisl's reputation made it impossible for him to support a team that had become so outspoken about a studio in which he had a vested interest.

By August, the we/they stage had been reached. The "we" were Siegel and Martin; the "they," the Paramount board.[10] Paramount enlisted the aid of attorney Louis Nizer, who in 1956 had been instrumental in preventing Louis Mayer from staging a comeback and gaining control of Loew's Inc., the parent company of MGM—the studio that Mayer had run from 1924 to 1951, when he was forced to resign. Paramount hoped Nizer could do the same with an unwanted presence on its own board. The difference, however, was not only that Mayer had been terminally ill with leukemia in 1956 (and died the following year at the age of seventy-two); he was also not a threat to Loew's Inc. Siegel and Martin, on the other hand, constituted a menace; and, unlike Mayer, they were in their prime.

Paramount cried conflict of interest, charging that, even though Siegel had stepped down as GAC president, he could still be privy to negotiations between GAC's clients (e.g., Jackie Gleason, Robert Cummings, Martha Hyer, Michael Caine) and Paramount because he was still chairman of Baldwin-Montrose, which had a 70 percent interest in GAC. Furthermore, few talent agencies would be willing to do business with a studio on whose board sat the ex-president of a rival agency, particularly one that was part of a company in which the board member owned 22.8 percent of the stock and controlled 21.7 percent of the voting power. According to the SEC, Siegel was the "parent" of Baldwin-Montrose, which, in turn, was the parent of GAC.

On 25 August, Paramount filed suit in federal district court, accusing Siegel and Martin of antitrust violations and harassment. The suit barred Siegel and Martin from the board and prohibited them from voting their shares (now 135,000) until Baldwin-Montrose divested itself of GAC, as it had to in order to comply with the SAG regulation restricting talent agencies to 5 percent of a studio's stock.

Naturally, Baldwin-Montrose had to relinquish its share in GAC. But Paramount went further, alleging that Martin's five-hundred-thousand-dollar arrangement with Capitol Records for the financing of three Feuer and Martin productions represented a conflict of interest with Paramount's subsidiary, Dot Records. Paramount was grasping at straws. Dot specialized in country and western; unlike Capitol, Dot neither backed Broadway musicals nor produced original cast albums.

The suit had evolved into a free-for-all. Producer Albert Zugsmith claimed he was asked to head a stockholders' protective committee, purely in a fact-finding capacity. Zugsmith really wanted his voice to be heard, but what he had to say was self-serving. He complained that Paramount had disregarded his real estate suggestions, which included selling the back lot to Desilu, the Lucille Ball–Desi Arnaz television production company that had formerly been the home of RKO and was adjacent to the studio. (Ironically, Paramount *bought* Desilu the following year.) What really irked Zugsmith was that his rival, Joseph Levine, was making—so he thought—the same kinds of films as he was and releasing them through Paramount, which Zugsmith was not. Zugsmith could not appreciate the distinction between pulp cinema like Levine's *The Carpetbaggers* and *Harlow* and exploitation pictures like Zugsmith's *Teacher Was a Sexpot* (1960), *The Private Life of Adam and Eve* (1961), and *Fanny Hill* (1964), all of which Paramount refused to distribute.

Then two dissident stockholders got into the act. Burton Goldberger, a New York dentist, filed suit against Baldwin-Montrose, accusing the company of acting in its own interest, not the stockholders.' The company should, he charged, relinquish its Paramount stock and retain GAC. Next, Harry Lewis, a Brooklyn attorney, lodged a similar stockholders' suit, arguing, like Goldberger, that Siegel cared more about Paramount than he did about the stockholders. It was one thing for a plastics and chemicals company like Baldwin-Montrose to have a controlling interest in a talent agency; it was another to have a controlling interest in a movie studio.

The cast of characters began to swell. In September, Sumner Redstone, then president of the Theatre Owners of America (and twenty-five years later owner of Paramount), organized the Paramount Stockholders and Customers Protective Agency, which represented fourteen theater circuits. The group had a legitimate complaint: a Paramount embroiled in suits and countersuits would be an economic disaster for exhibitors, particularly in 1965 when the film industry was relying more and more on independent producers, the best of whom would be loath to work at a beleaguered studio.

By November, Baldwin-Montrose finally arranged to divest itself of GAC and arranged to sell its 70 percent stake for $2 million to a four-person management group consisting of GAC's vice president and treasurer, the senior vice president, the president of the personal appearance division, and the president of the television division.

Even so, Paramount would not give up. Nizer insisted there was still conflict of interest, which could only be resolved if Siegel resigned from Baldwin-Montrose or Paramount; and Martin, from Paramount or Feuer & Martin Productions.

In December Paramount's antitrust case against Siegel and Martin reached the New York federal court in Foley Square. On Friday, 10 December, Martin's lawyer, Paul Connolly, questioned Weisl about the meeting that had been held the previous June at the home of New York publicist Benjamin Sonnenberg at which he, Siegel, and Martin were present—the meeting at which the insurgents described their takeover scenario. While Weisl admitted that such a meeting took place, he denied that Weltner's job was ever offered to Siegel. Being a lawyer himself, Weisl took issue with the statement that he had been "critical" of Paramount's leadership; Weisl insisted he had merely said, "There is always room for improvement," which, to him, did not imply criticism. When asked his opinion of some of the arrangements that had been made with independent producers, Weisl hedged again; after admitting that he was not exactly pleased with all of them, he then added, "All major companies are compelled to make them."[11] Weisl's testimony was so ambivalent that it was worthless—which is probably what he intended.

The decision that Judge Edmund L. Palmieri handed down on 24 January 1966 favored the insurgents: Paramount and GAC were never in competition, nor were Paramount and Feuer & Martin Productions; Baldwin-Montrose acted in good faith when it gave up its stake in GAC; there was no evidence that Paramount lost any projects or sustained any financial losses during the battle; and, as the ultimate blow to Paramount, Siegel and Martin were to return to the board.

On 23 March 1966, without any fanfare, a newcomer joined the Paramount board: Charles G. Bluhdorn, the thirty-nine-year-old chairman of Gulf + Western.

It is hard to imagine Siegel's being unaware of Bluhdorn, styled "the mad Austrian" and, according to one insider, "the most ruthless conglomerateur of them all."[12] Although Bluhdorn cultivated a persona that was intentionally enigmatic, it is at least possible to reconstruct a skeletal biography, if not a fleshed-out one. He was born in Vienna on 20 September 1926 to Czech parents who left Austria for England ten years later. If the family was Jewish, as many believed (although Bluhdorn had a habit of both downplaying and emphasizing his origins, depending on the occasion), it was the right year to leave Vienna. After Austrian chancellor Engelbert Dollfuss was assassinated in 1934 by Nazis disguised as Austrian soldiers, only a naif would have thought that Hitler would give up his dream of annexing Austria, particularly after Dollfuss's successor, Kurt von Schuschnigg, signed a treaty with Germany that virtually made Austria a German satellite in matters of foreign policy.

In 1942, the Blitz and repeated rumors of a Nazi invasion made England less of a refuge. That year, the Bluhdorns emigrated to America. When the war ended, Charles, who spent 1945 in the Army Air Force, was nineteen. But he had already learned that the American dream could become a reality if one were willing to take calculated risks. Whether or not he knew what an entrepreneur was, at nineteen he had become one. Commodities became an obsession with him. Once he discovered America's passion for coffee, he began importing it, mainly from South America. Soon he learned that coffee prices fluctuated because they depended on such factors as the quality of the crop, the current import tax, and the public's taste. While Americans appeared to be diehard coffee drinkers during World War II, they consumed less of it after the war was over, partly because of cost and partly because of the popularity of caffeine-free brands like Nescafé and Sanka.

The year that the Bluhdorns arrived in the United States was especially hard on car owners. In 1942, automobile production was drastically curtailed; the cars that remained were only available to civilians in vital occupations. And drivers, except those working in defense plants, were limited to three gallons of gas a week.

World War II forced Americans to take better care of their cars by replacing defective parts, since in most cases a trade-in would have been impossible. In 1947, $2.52 billion worth of replacement parts were produced, 34 percent more than the previous year. Although there was a 23 percent decline in 1949 ($1.96 billion), Bluhdorn realized there was more money to be made selling and distributing replacement parts than in importing coffee from Brazil.

By 1949 Bluhdorn was a millionaire, thanks to fan belts, hub caps, and oil filters. In 1956, he purchased a controlling interest in the Michigan Plating and Stamping Company, which manufactured rear bumpers for Studebakers; the following year, he merged it with his next acquisition, the Beard and Stone Electric Company of Houston, an auto replacement parts distributor. In 1958, he combined the two to form the Gulf & Western Corporation, whose name was suggested by the locations of the two companies: Houston evoked the Gulf of Mexico; Michigan, the Midwest. Two years later Gulf & Western became Gulf + Western Industries, madly diversifying until it became a conglomerate with divisions in everything from agricultural products to metals.

In 1965, the year of the Siegel-Martin push for Paramount, Bluhdorn was sporting Gulf + Western's newest acquisition: New Jersey Zinc, the biggest zinc producer in the United States. But metals and their alloys would not satisfy Charles Bluhdorn.

When Bluhdorn came on the Paramount board in March 1966, he must have known who Siegel was—and vice versa. Among Gulf + Western's many subsidiaries was Consolidated Cigar (formerly Congress Cigar), which included name brands such as La Palina, which the Levy brothers used to tout on WCAU.

Siegel and Bluhdorn represented the new movie mogul—someone interested not so much in making movies, as the previous generation had been, as in making money *through* movies. To both of them, filmed entertainment, movies and television, was just the name of a division on a little rectangle within a company's organizational chart—a box linked to other boxes that, in turn, are connected to a central one.

While Baldwin-Montrose was nowhere near the behemoth that Gulf + Western was rapidly becoming, it was guided by the same principle: diversification. In some ways, it was Gulf + Western in miniature—the result of a merger between Baldwin Rubber (automotive and industrial rubber products) and Montrose (chemicals and plastics). Bluhdorn might even have thought that Baldwin-Montrose was something he could eventually absorb; whether, at the time, Bluhdorn thought he could absorb Paramount is doubtful. But there was someone at Paramount who thought he could: Martin S. Davis, who, curiously, in early April—a few weeks after Bluhdorn went on the Paramount board—was made vice president of Paramount Pictures and Weltner's executive assistant.

A native New Yorker, Davis was a mere twenty when he was discharged from the army in 1946, having lied about his age to enlist; that same year found him working in public relations at the Samuel Goldwyn Company's New York office on Sixth Avenue. Within two years, Davis had become assistant national director of advertising and publicity at Goldwyn. For the next ten years, he remained in the same general area: midtown Manhattan.

Fascinated by the movie business but determined to stay in New York, Davis left Goldwyn in 1955 to become eastern publicity head at Allied Artists, located a short distance away at 1560 Broadway. In 1958 he moved to 1501 Broadway as Paramount's director of sales and marketing. By 1960, he was head of publicity at Paramount, and in 1965, executive vice president and COO, reporting to George Weltner.

Weltner knew Paramount was vulnerable and that it was only a matter of time before it would become a subsidiary of some conglomerate, but not Siegel's, if he could help it. A studio under siege needs a deliverer, and Weltner wanted to be selective. He resented Siegel's linking him with the gerontocracy that had made Paramount a senior citizens' center; he had also not forgotten Siegel's uncivilized behavior at board meetings. Perhaps it was Weltner who charged Davis with the task of rescuing Paramount from Siegel's clutches, even if it meant falling into someone else's. However, one doubts that Davis needed much encouragement, especially if he sensed there was a potential buyer who could find a place for him in the new regime.

At any rate, Davis did not have to conduct a nationwide search. The deliverer was already on the board.

Paramount appealed to Bluhdorn for the same reason that Columbia appealed to Coca-Cola twenty years later: profits, of course. However, if a company has interests in electric wire and cable, beef, sugar, marine hardware, car batteries, and zinc alloys, like Gulf + Western, the prospect of consorting with Hollywood's elite and having access to a society synonymous with glamour makes a studio an even more desirable commodity. Coca-Cola executives in Atlanta felt similarly about Columbia in 1985; there was just so much one could say to beverage distributors and managers of bottling plants. And while there would be less to say to movie stars, attending a premiere, followed by a private reception, compensated for the speechlessness that comes from awe. Besides, a premiere is more exciting than a sales convention.

Here is where Siegel and Bluhdorn differed. Siegel was indifferent to the glamour part; he was essentially a New Yorker whose marriage had introduced him to the world of media. Siegel never aspired to the creative end of the business. Bluhdorn did—vicariously. He delighted in visiting a set and posing with a star. Then there was the special kind of power that comes from owning a studio: the power over those who create mass entertainment but lack the autonomy that all filmmakers crave yet rarely achieve. Thus, Bluhdorn could run Paramount on the creative energy of others.

It took little effort on Davis's part to persuade Bluhdorn to bring Paramount under the Gulf + Western aegis. Even had the glamour angle not worked (which it did), Davis had only to remind Bluhdorn that Paramount could fall prey to a company like Baldwin-Montrose, which was Gulf + Western in embryo.

It should have been clear to Siegel that Bluhdorn's presence on the board augured ill, as did another event that occurred that March. At a special meeting of the board, a proposal was made to eliminate cumulative voting in favor of straight voting; in the latter, voting is determined by shares, with each share counted once. Thus, in order to elect anyone to an eleven-member board like Gulf + Western's, the rule would be one vote per share. Under cumulative voting, however, shareholders could allocate their votes among as many, or as few, candidates as they wished. This method was ideal for directors wishing to remain on the board. The vote to eliminate cumulative voting passed 8–2, with one member absent. Naturally, the two nays were Siegel's and Martin's; since straight voting enabled a simple majority to elect the entire board, Siegel and Martin, who then controlled only 9 percent of the outstanding shares, could easily be outvoted. It was obvious that the proposal to eliminate cumulative voting also eliminated the threat the men posed.

During the court battle, Paramount's stock rose. Siegel and Martin needed more than the 143,000 shares (or 9 percent) they managed to acquire. Of that 143,000, Baldwin-Montrose owned 80,000; Feuer & Martin Productions and FMI Ltd., the rest. In mid-April, when Bluhdorn offered to buy their stock at $83 a share ($9.50 higher than what it was selling for and considerably higher than the $64 a share they had originally paid), Siegel and Martin had no other choice but to sell, once they realized that Paramount could count on proxies constituting 27 percent of the outstanding stock (about 438,000 shares) from loyal shareholders who were savvy enough to know that Gulf + Western, whose gross sales had gone from $8.4 million at the end of fiscal 1958 to $271.3 million seven years later, was Paramount's *deus ex machina*—and theirs as well.

Siegel tried to save face, claiming that Baldwin-Montrose at least made a profit (about $1.6 million) from the sale of the stock. He also prided himself on making the industry aware of Paramount's geriatric board, which was rendered less senescent by the departures of Y. Frank Freeman and Duncan Harris. Siegel, however, discreetly avoided any reference to the ninety-three–year-old Adolph Zukor, who got the hint and was rewarded with the title of chairman emeritus for life.

Six months after Bluhdorn bought out Siegel and Martin, he bought Paramount. On 19 October 1966, Paramount Pictures Corporation went out of existence as an autonomous studio and became a Gulf + Western subsidiary. The last stockholders' meeting at the Americana Hotel was anything but nostalgic, except for Zukor's standing ovation; cigar in hand, he said nothing but merely smiled.

As if any further proof were needed that Gulf + Western was in control of Paramount, G+W's president, John H. Duncan, and executive vice president, David N. Judelson, joined the board following the resignations of Siegel and Martin.

Organizationally, Gulf + Western resembled a quilt, partitioned into seven sections of various widths, with each section representing a group: *Manufacturing* (die castings, auto bumpers and bumper parts, precision parts for jets and missiles, life-support systems, electric wires and cables, and, interestingly, government-classified ordnance items provided for military use in Vietnam); *Distribution* (auto parts warehouses and outlets, a supply source for dealers, repair shops, and service stations); *Metals and Chemicals* (New Jersey Zinc, mining operations, zinc oxide and titanium pigments); *Agricultural* (sugar manufacturing and beef, vegetable and citrus fruit processing); *Consumer Products* (notably Consolidated Cigar, including such brands as Dutch Masters, Muriel, and La Palina); *Forest and Paper Products* (towels, tissues, paper cups and plates, egg cartons, and matches); and *Insurance, Financing Services, and Banking* (various kinds of financing and loans through Gulf + Western's 92–percent-owned Associates Investment Company; fire, theft, and collision coverage through Emmco Insurance; and life and accident insurance through Capital Life).[13]

With the acquisition of Paramount, the Gulf + Western quilt received another patch: *Leisure Time.* "Paramount" was not a group designation like "Manufacturing" or "Consumer Products"; it was part of Leisure Time, which, like the other panels on the quilt, was multipartite. Paramount Pictures alone would not have been worth $144 million. Bluhdorn bought Paramount Pictures Corporation, which was more than just a movie studio; in 1966, it consisted of a 31.8–acre backlot with 19 sound stages (which became 52.4 acres and 31 sound stages after Paramount bought Desilu; the 10.2–acre Sunset Studio, once owned by Warner Bros., which Bluhdorn would shortly sell to Gene Autry's Golden West Broadcasters; Paramount TV Enterprises, responsible for such popular series as *Star Trek, Mannix,* and *Mission: Impossible;* 51 percent of the Canadian theater chain, Famous Players; music publishing (Famous Music and Paramount Music); and Dot Records. Bluhdorn had not bought a house; he had purchased an estate.

Even though it was part of a division, Paramount's performance as a studio was measured not only against other units within its group but other groups as well. For fiscal 1967, Manufacturing brought in the most money ($224.58 million). Leisure Time, however, did not do badly; it provided G+W with 33.5 percent of its gross income (of which 19.9 percent came from film). Thus, of the $215.69 million that Leisure Time generated, $127.88 million was derived from film—but not from 1966 releases. Paramount had only one hit that year, *Alfie;* the revenues came largely from film library rentals and licensing agreements with television stations.

While it is unfair to compare a division with a group, it was evident that without Manufacturing (and such basic items as air conditioners, timers, cables, plastics, automotive parts, and aluminum) Paramount would have been a liability to Gulf + Western; it was also evident it could never have survived as an autonomous studio if its 1966 releases were any harbinger of the future. *Is Paris Burning?* was not only a critical and commercial failure; it also went $1 million over budget, eventually costing $7 million. *This Property Is Condemned,* which featured a sensitive performance by Natalie Wood, also exceeded its budget by almost $1 million, coming in at $4.62 million rather than the anticipated $3.65 million. *Oh Dad, Poor Dad, Mamma's Hung You in the Closet and I'm Feeling So Sad* should have been released in 1966 but was held up a year because Paramount did not know what to do with this piece of oedipal absurdism that worked on the stage with Jo Van Fleet but not on the screen with Rosalind Russell; with Russell as the mother from hell (and giving a performance that left a bitter aftertaste), the absurd became the grotesque. *Oh Dad* also went over budget—$2.175 million as opposed to $1.65 million.

Alfie, the best of the lot, came in on budget: a mere $638,000 for a career-making performance by Michael Caine. Another inexpensive but impressive release that year was Cornel Wilde's *The Naked Prey,* in which Wilde doubled as star and director; given the African setting, the film cost $647,649—only $20,000 over budget. Until *Prey* Wilde was remembered, if at all, for his portrayal of Frédéric Chopin in *A Song to Remember* (1945). Twenty years later, Wilde was no longer seated at the piano; instead, he was racing through the jungle in a loincloth, pursued by natives who saw him as no different from the animals they hunted.

Howard Hawks's *Eldorado* should have been released in 1965, but it was not in the theaters until 1967. *Eldorado,* too, exceeded its budget by almost $1 million ($4.653 versus $3.846 million)—far too much for a recycled and spiritless *Rio Bravo* (1959) and unworthy of the director of *His Girl Friday* (1940), *Sergeant York* (1941), and *Red River* (1948).

A studio survives in corporate Hollywood by cutting deals with canny producers, powerful agents, and bankable stars so that it can intersperse its yearly releases, most of which will be unmemorable, with a couple that will make up for the mediocrity of the rest. In Paramount's case, it was not even a couple of films a year. Until the turnaround in 1970, Paramount released only a handful of films of any significance during the 1960s: *Breakfast at Tiffany's* (1961), *The Man Who Shot Liberty Valance* (1962), *Hud* (1963), *Seconds* (1966), *Rosemary's Baby* (1968), *Medium Cool* (1969), and *True Grit* (1969). But at least the studio lasted.

And it would have lasted whether Bluhdorn or Siegel took it over; Paramount would have been a cog in someone's industrial wheel—Bluhdorn's Gulf + Western's or Siegel's latest trophy, Chris-Craft's. In 1968, Siegel, determined to score at least one conquest, staged a takeover of Chris-Craft. That Chris-Craft has been synonymous with the name of

Herbert J. Siegel since 1968 was the result of a series of transactions and transformations—some engineered by Siegel, others by his predecessors. Siegel's becoming chairman of Chris-Craft in 1968 came as no surprise to readers of the *Wall Street Journal* or the financial pages of any major newspaper. Baldwin-Montrose was Chris-Craft's biggest stockholder, and while Siegel had resigned as head of GAC, he never resigned from Baldwin-Montrose. Strangely, the conglomerate that Siegel constructed out of old ruins and new foundations was not that dissimilar to Bluhdorn's; it was merely less imposing. But it was built from the same materials: auto accessories and rubber.

Chris-Craft originated in Detroit in 1926 as National Automotive Fibers (NAF), which produced upholstery and foam rubber for auto manufacturers. In the 1940s, NAF acquired the Montrose Chemical Company and, in 1960, Chris-Craft. Chris-Craft had been known for generations as a world-class boat manufacturer, so much so that people used the company name in speaking of the boats. "I own a Chris-Craft" or "I sailed on a Chris-Craft" were common boasts in the 1930s and 1940s.[14]

By 1962, the corporate name was Chris-Craft Industries, which proved so profitable that, when Siegel assumed control of it six years later, he began to emulate Bluhdorn—first by diversifying, then by restructuring. Siegel reorganized Chris-Craft into three divisions: boats, television broadcasting, and industrial (e.g., rubber and latex products, foam rubber for upholstery and shoes). Unable to acquire a studio but determined to be an investor, if not a player, Siegel went into a frenzy of buying and selling—but always selling at a profit. There was no difference between Siegel's ethics and his approach to business: "A guy once said, 'You lie on the banks like an alligator and wait to snap up the right deal.'"[15] Siegel knew the right bank on which to lie.

After obtaining a controlling interest in Piper Aircraft, Siegel sold it in 1975 and invested in Fox, Warner Bros., and Paramount. With the creation of Time-Warner in 1990, Chris-Craft reaped a profit of $2.3 billion.

Although Fox seemed ripe for takeover in 1981, Siegel, who controlled 20 percent of the stock through Chris-Craft, decided to remain on the bank once he realized that, if he acquired Fox, Chris-Craft could fall prey to a corporate raider (as if Siegel were not one himself). Thus Siegel sold his shares to oil tycoon Marvin Davis, Fox's next owner, in exchange for a couple of Fox's television stations.

Television brought Siegel's career full circle, placing it concentrically within the much bigger circle started by the Levy brothers and completed by William Paley with the formation of CBS. Siegel's investment in Warner made it possible for him to establish a television subsidiary, BHC Communications, through which Chris-Craft owns and operates eight television stations, the best known being WWOR-TV. Chris-Craft's investment in Paramount led to its becoming a joint owner of the United Paramount Network (UPN).[16]

Siegel's empire may not have extended as far as Bluhdorn's, but it was large enough for Chris-Craft to qualify as a mini-conglomerate. One could easily see Paramount becoming part of Chris-Craft: Siegel would simply have added a fourth division to include it. And like Bluhdorn, he would have found a place for his children. Siegel's sons, William and John, became senior vice presidents of Chris-Craft and would probably have ended up on Paramount's organizational chart like Bluhdorn's son, Paul, who went as far as vice president of acquisitions until he withdrew from the Hollywood scene.

How long Paramount would have lasted under Siegel is problematic, especially with so many bigger companies studio-shopping in the 1980s (e.g., Coca-Cola, Sony, Matsushita, Time Inc.). What was Paramount anyway but real estate, rentals, and a film library, most of whose greatest movies (pre-1948) were owned by MCA and, when telecast, are introduced by the Universal globe, followed by the Paramount mountain?

At least Bluhdorn had a vision—nebulous, perhaps—of a studio that, with the right people making the right deals, might produce the right films. If Chris-Craft is any indication of the way Siegel would have run Paramount, the studio would merely have been one more curve in an ever-expanding spiral, to be spun off for something better or sold when something sexier landed on the alligator's bank. Siegel lacked both vision and, equally important, persuasive charm. If Paramount was to be sold, Bluhdorn was the buyer of the moment.

Contrary to F. Scott Fitzgerald's belief, some American lives do have a second act; Siegel's and Bluhdorn's lives did. However, George Weltner's was what Fitzgerald had in mind: a one-acter with a single set. In July 1967, when Weltner left his office high above Broadway with its grand view of Times Square, he would not be returning. Weltner had officially retired, and when the announcement was made the letters Weltner received from branch managers throughout the world revealed the affection they had for him.

Weltner had a few good years left but not many. He and Bertha retired to a West Palm Beach condominium, where he looked forward to fishing, boating, and traveling. But in the early 1970s, he began to suffer from memory loss. In 1973, upon arriving in Switzerland, he became disoriented, unable to claim his baggage. Diagnosed with Alzheimer's disease, he deteriorated slowly, lingering for twelve more years before dying on 15 November 1985. By then, even Gulf + Western was about to fade into oblivion. Had he had been alive, Weltner would probably have greeted the news with a shrug and then gone fishing.

4

Charlie's Boys

The Paramount purchase only fed Bluhdorn's megalomania. Not content with just being Gulf + Western board chairman, Bluhdorn also decided to assume the title of president of Paramount Pictures after George Weltner's retirement in July 1967. For Bluhdorn, "president" was merely an honorific; the actual moviemaking process meant little to him. He may not even have known what films Paramount had in the pipeline except the ones he had personally approved; his favorites were those with European settings (e.g., the 1970 releases *The Adventurers* and *Darling Lili*) or "American dream" plots (the 1969 *Paint Your Wagon*). Bluhdorn was poor at picking winners, but he understood authority; one way he had of wielding it was by dropping in on location shoots. Only an industry newcomer would find location filming exotic; when a helicopter deposited Bluhdorn on the Oregon set of *Paint Your Wagon*, he could scarcely conceal his delight at witnessing a film in the making—particularly one about the California Gold Rush, with whose "get rich quick" philosophy he could identify. He was less ebullient when the film, based on the Alan Jay Lerner–Frederick Loewe Broadway musical with only a fraction of Loewe's glorious score intact, turned out to be a critical and financial failure.

Bluhdorn was gradually wising up to Hollywood, at least to the extent of realizing that his taste in film was unreliable. *Darling Lili* featured two box-office favorites, Julie Andrews and Rock Hudson, each of whom had costarred in successful movies with other actors (Andrews with Dick Van Dyke in *Mary Poppins* [1964], and Hudson with Jane Wyman in *Magnificent Obsession* [1954] and Doris Day in *Pillow Talk* [1969]). Unfortunately, the lack of chemistry between Andrews and Hudson produced awkwardness instead of passion, resulting in love scenes that must have been as frustrating to perform as to watch. Worse, *Darling Lili* cost $20 million, the same as *Paint Your Wagon*.

Although *The Adventurers*, based on Harold Robbins's novel, came in for less ($13 million), audiences were alienated by the three-hour length, and critics by the Eurotrash plot. Bluhdorn had finally learned the difference between running a studio and running a company. Gulf + Western may have needed Bluhdorn, but Paramount needed a production head and, eventually, a president. And Bludhorn was savvy enough to know that, if Paramount should sink into the red, the production chief and the president would take the heat. Paramount was merely a band within the Gulf + Western spectrum; should it fail to generate enough energy, it could be replaced or discarded without disturbing the system. By functioning only as Gulf + Western chairman, Bluhdorn could spin off Paramount, if necessary. But until then, he first had to find a production head; and then someone to whom he could relinquish the presidency.

Peter Bart and Robert Evans seemed an unlikely combination. Bart, who held degrees from Swarthmore and the London School of Economics, began his career as a staff reporter for the *Wall Street Journal* and *New York Times*, where he was assigned to write a daily column covering trends in the media. The column led to a stint as the *Times* Los Angeles correspondent and greater latitude in subject matter, although the movie industry—generally, from a business perspective—was a frequent topic. His approach to Hollywood—namely, that of an economist—was unusual in the early 1960s, when journalists covering the movie scene focused on celebrities and scandals. Bart prepared the way for later *New York Times* writers such as Geraldine Fabrikant and Bernard Weinraub, who succeeded in making corporate Hollywood's mergers and spinoffs readable.

It was in Los Angeles that Bart became aware of Robert Evans, whose resumé reads like a rung-to-rung guide up the Hollywood ladder: teenage radio actor, disk jockey, model, television performer, boutique clothier, and (almost) movie star, best remembered as Irving Thalberg in the Lon Chaney biopic, *The Man of a Thousand Faces* (1957), Ava Gardner's matador lover in *The Sun Also Rises* (1957), and the title character in *The Fiend Who Walked the West* (1958).[1] One could easily see Evans working for Bluhdorn; Bart, less so.

Bart seemed to belong behind an editor's desk. Eventually, that was where he ended up but not until 1989, almost a quarter of a century after joining Paramount. Bart's twenty years as a film producer at Paramount and elsewhere led to his being named editor of *Daily Variety* in 1989 and, soon thereafter, editor-in-chief.

By the time Bart became aware of Evans in the mid-1960s, Evans had reached the producer's rung, where he remained throughout his career. Bart was especially intrigued by the way Evans found his material. Evans relied on trackers, whom he paid to scout around for books, either nearing completion or already in galleys, that could be made into successful films. Evans would then fly to New York, read the manuscript or the galleys, and option whatever had potential. When he read the manuscript of Roderick Thorp's *The Detective*, he was so convinced it would be a best-seller that he offered Thorp a thousand dollars for each week the book remained on the best-seller list, plus an additional fifty cents per copy after the first fifty thousand copies were sold.[2] *The Detective* became a best-seller with its publication in 1966, and a hit film with Frank Sinatra two years later.

It was at the time Evans was pitching *The Detective* to Twentieth Century–Fox that he made Bart's acquaintance. Bart was a friend of Abby Mann, whom Evans had hired to write *The Detective* screenplay. Evans was already aware of Bart's *Times* pieces and was genuinely flattered when Bart expressed an interest in making him the subject of one of them. Either Evans failed to appreciate the humor of what Bart wrote or was so awestruck at having made the *New York Times* that he claimed Bart referred to him as "the next Thalberg."[3] On the contrary, Bart made no reference to Evans's most famous movie role; rather, he described Evans as so obsessed with finding film material that he once booked a midnight flight to Cleveland to hear tapes that supposedly revealed the innocence of Dr. Sam Sheppard, who had been convicted of killing his wife in 1954.

Bart's piece was mildly satirical, as even the title indicated: "I Like It. I Want It. Let's Sew It Up." Evans had not only mastered the art of the deal but the vernacular as well. Yet Bart was obviously fascinated by this newcomer who, in turn, was taken with Bart's intelligence. Such complementarity could translate into a successful partnership if the two had the chance to work together—which happened in 1966, the same year in which Bart's piece appeared.

There was someone else besides Bart who had become interested in Evans. Whether Charles Bluhdorn learned about Evans from the *Times* piece or from his scouting system (which, in Hollywood, was the equivalent of networking without affirmative action and equal opportunity) is unimportant. Evans was the kind of hustler that Bluhdorn admired. When Bluhdorn offered to make him head of European production, based in London, Evans accepted immediately, believing he had the qualifications for the job; the press, however, thought differently. Evans then knew he had to prove himself—and did. Whether Evans succeeded or failed mattered little to Bluhdorn. If Evans failed and foreign grosses plummeted, Bluhdorn had a fall guy.

When Evans arrived in London in autumn 1966, he discovered the same kind of gerontocracy there that Herbert Siegel had found in the States. Evans dealt with the problem as Siegel might have: he fired the loyalists who insisted that, if Tommy Steele could charm audiences in *Half a Sixpence* on the stage, he could do the same on the screen. When the musical premiered in London in 1963, Vietnam meant little to British theatergoers. Perhaps some knew that it had once been part of French Indo-China and was now partitioned into the Communist North and the anti-Communist South. Even those who did would never have let Cold War politics interfere with their enjoyment of a show with one of Britain's best-loved musical comedy performers.

In America, the situation was different. By the mid-sixties, the threat embodied in the Communist North under Ho Chi Minh grew into an undeclared war polarizing not only America but the world at large. Evans knew that musical whimsey, British style, was not what moviegoers wanted. Since the film version of *Half a Sixpence* (1968) had been scheduled for production before Evans came on board, he viewed it as a barometer of his staff's expertise. When the mercury sank along with the picture, Evans's suspicions were confirmed.

The mid-sixties were far from Paramount's best years, and Evans thought he knew why. As Vietnam cast a pall over American life, terms like "the war" (World War II) and "postwar" (post World War II) had become passé, at least to the baby boomers. "The war" was the one being fought in southeast Asia, and "postwar" lay in the future. The last commercially successful World War II film was *The Longest Day* (1962), whose audience-friendly recreation of the Normandy invasion was in keeping with the age of Camelot. By the mid-sixties, "the war" was acceptable only in escape films like *Von Ryan's Express* (1967) that were really prison movies in a different guise. However, a World War II movie set in Hawaii on the eve of Pearl Harbor, or in Paris during the liberation, would have had little appeal except to an older generation. Realizing Paramount was making films for middle-aged audiences that had stopped being regular moviegoers, Evans confronted Bluhdorn with the evidence that World War II had become a hard sell.

Since that was Bluhdorn's war, he had assumed audiences would feel the same and turn out en masse for *Is Paris Burning?* which, he hoped, would do for World War II what *The Birth of a Nation* (1915) and *Gone with the Wind* (1939) had done for the Civil War. *Is Paris Burning?* was nothing more than a star-studded semi-documentary that ran nearly three hours and featured a French and American cast including Kirk Douglas, Anthony Perkins, Yves Montand, and Simone Signoret. Bluhdorn had such high expectations for *Is Paris Burning?* that he insisted on a Paris premiere. Unfortunately, the evening was marred by torrential rain, as if the elements were presaging the critical and financial disaster the film turned out to be.

Evans had to explain to Bluhdorn that an America wracked by an unpopular war whose progress was charted on the late news had little interest in World War II, "good war" that it was. The proof existed earlier when another overlong Paramount release about World War II, *In Harm's Way* (1965), failed to interest audiences despite a similarly impressive cast that included John Wayne, Kirk Douglas, Patricia Neal, and Henry Fonda. If World War II was to have any meaning in the Age of Aquarius, it would be in a film like *Patton* (1970), which deflated the myth of heroism by portraying a military icon as a megalomaniac, alternately perverse and compassionate, wedded to a code of honor that young audiences could at least understand, if not respect. *Patton*, however, was a Twentieth Century–Fox release.

Evans's candor paid off. Once Bluhdorn realized that Evans understood movies to the extent of predicting what might fail and suggesting what could succeed, Evans was elevated to vice president of worldwide production; in short, production head.

Evans knew he could not do the job alone. Since he was no longer an independent producer, trackers were out of the question. But he needed someone who could perform the same function, someone who kept up with current fiction and could offer an informed opinion on what was filmable. For Evans, that meant only one person: Peter Bart. Bart's title varied over the seven years he spent at Paramount. For the first few years he was listed as either "production executive" or "executive assistant to Robert Evans." By 1972, he was "vice president, creative affairs." In an earlier time, he simply would have been a contract producer like Warner Bros.' Henry Blanke or MGM's Arthur Freed. In corporate Hollywood, titles that were once self-explanatory now require translation.

Bart and Evans had the synergy that Bluhdorn hoped would result in "pictures that people in Kansas City want to see."[4] To Bluhdorn, Kansas City audiences were, for some reason, representative of America's taste in film.

Bluhdorn had now gotten over his Eurocentric phase; instead of movies in which historical events or authentic settings overshadow the drama, he wanted ones with sympathetic characters caught up in situations that could even end tragically and still succeed at the box office. Bart and Evans failed neither Bluhdorn nor Kansas City.

Supposedly, it was Evans who urged Bluhdorn to hire Stanley R. Jaffe, although one doubts that Bluhdorn needed much persuasion. Bluhdorn was obviously aware of the Jaffe name. He also knew that a name by itself does not translate into a studio presidency. Although Bluhdorn was willing to bring Jaffe on board, he expected Jaffe to prove his worth before offering him the crown. Stanley R. Jaffe was part Young Turk, part old regime. He was twenty-nine when he arrived at Paramount in 1969. In an industry noted for children who follow in their parents' footsteps, Jaffe was no exception. While many things had changed in Hollywood between the time Leo Jaffe, Stanley's father, had graduated from New York University in 1930 and Stanley from the University of Pennsylvania's Wharton School of Finance in 1962, there was one that had not: connections.

Leo Jaffe came to Columbia in 1930 because he had a contact there: Abe Schneider, whom Leo had known at NYU where they were accounting majors, joined Columbia in 1922 and by 1930 had become assistant treasurer. Jaffe, in turn, became Schneider's assistant, then his brother-in-law, and eventually studio president.[5] By 1962, would-be film executives had more prestigious credentials, including M.B.A.s and J.D.s, as higher education grew less elitist and more accessible, and the degree became a union card. But even for college grads eager to break into the business, there was entry level, Hollywood style: sorting mail at a talent agency or playing gofer at a studio, despite a title like "administrative assistant" that would only fool outsiders.

Stanley Jaffe was able to bypass the mailroom; his was a name that inspired awe even among Hollywood's jaded. By the mid-sixties, his father had achieved elder statesman status; he spent his entire career (1930–81) at Columbia in a variety of positions (vice president and treasurer and finally president and board chairman) that, for the most part, required only financial and administrative decisions. The closest Leo Jaffe came to the creative side of the business was persuading Ray Stark, who was producing the movie version of *Funny Girl* (1969), to allow Barbra Streisand to repeat her Broadway triumph on the screen despite objections from marketing executives that she was an unknown quantity; and brokering deals with such producers and directors as Sam Spiegel, Preminger, Richard Brooks, and Stanley Kramer to provide Columbia with badly needed product. Yet Leo Jaffe would never have expected credit for *Lawrence of Arabia* (1962), a Spiegel production; Preminger's *Anatomy of a Murder* (1959); Richard Brooks's *In Cold Blood* (1962); and Kramer's *Guess Who's Coming to Dinner* (1968). Leo Jaffe only brought the players together; the players made the films.

Spiegel seems to have had as much, if not more, of an influence on Stanley Jaffe than his own father. It was at Columbia where Spiegel had enjoyed one of his greatest successes, *On the Waterfront* (1954). Stanley was fourteen when the film was released. While most teenagers were mesmerized by Marlon Brando's performance as well as the film's pulsating realism at a time when realism seemed to have retreated from the screen, Jaffe was taken with the Spiegel mystique, which was the stuff of Hollywood mythology—except that in Spiegel's case the myth had a kernel of truth.

It would have been impossible for a son of Leo Jaffe—even one who grew up away from the film epicenter in New Rochelle, New York—to be unaware of Sam Spiegel. True, Leo Jaffe was more interested in net profits than art and felt more comfortable talking to his brother-in-law about golf than studio politics. Yet even Leo could not help but be awed—and perhaps amused—by the Spiegel saga. For Spiegel's rise to prominence was in keeping with similar success stories of an earlier era.

Spiegel was a throwback to the time when Central and Eastern European Jewish immigrants created an empire of their own in Hollywood.[6] He was born in the Galician town of Jaroslaw in 1901 when Galicia, once ruled by Russia and Poland, was part of the Hapsburg Empire. That would change with the coming of World War I and the Russian Revolution. Jews, who had felt protected under Emperor Franz Josef, were no longer safe; with the emperor's death in 1916 and the end of World War I two years later, they were subjected to the most barbarous form of anti-Semitism: pogroms.

Since Galicia was teeming with refugees, Spiegel emigrated to Palestine, where he lived on a kibbutz. He gradually acquired a resumé that was considerably more diverse than any mogul's. Jack Warner and Harry

Cohn may have worked in vaudeville, Laemmle in a clothing store, and Zukor in the fur trade; but Spiegel had been—among other things—a ditch digger, cotton broker, talent scout, stock promoter, felon, and deportee. That much is true. Then there are the famous Spiegel fabrications: Spiegel the polymath, University of Vienna graduate, and lecturer on drama at the University of California at Berkeley.

Although Spiegel invented some details of his checkered past, he was truthful about his love of film, which went back to the time he saw his first movie at a Jaroslaw nickelodeon. Naturally, he was drawn to Hollywood, where he arrived in 1939, passing himself off as "S.P. Eagle" to avoid deportation because of his criminal record. But by 1945 Spiegel, with a combination of wily charm and brazen cunning, had acquired enough friends in high places to apply for American citizenship as a Polish immigrant. It was inspired timing. Galicia, which had been returned to Poland after World War I, was about to change hands again and become part of the former Soviet Union.

In 1948, Spiegel and director John Huston formed Horizon Pictures, whose first release was Columbia's *We Were Strangers* (1949), produced by "S.P. Eagle." The film was a failure; undaunted, Spiegel briefly renamed the company Horizon Enterprises and came up with a winner, *The African Queen* (1952), which won Humphrey Bogart his only Oscar. Two years later, "S.P. Eagle" felt sufficiently confident to drop his alias. When *On the Waterfront* opened in 1954, the credits read "Produced by Sam Spiegel." As the famous *Variety* headline put it, "The Eagle Folds Its Wings"; the best unkept secret in Hollywood had been divulged. Henceforth, the name was Sam Spiegel, who went on to produce two more classics, *The Bridge on the River Kwai* and *Lawrence of Arabia*, and others like *The Chase* (1966) and *The Happening* (1967), which did nothing to enhance his reputation.

Stanley Jaffe probably heard from his father how instrumental Spiegel had been in getting *On the Waterfront* made: how "the Eagle" persuaded Harry Cohn, Columbia's president and production head, who had vetoed the project in 1953, to release the film as a Horizon production once Marlon Brando agreed to play the leading role of Terry Malloy, and how he dissuaded director Elia Kazan from giving the part to Frank Sinatra even though Kazan had gone so far as to sound out Sinatra about shooting the film in Hoboken, New Jersey. As a Hoboken native, Sinatra was amenable: he understood the milieu (dockworkers) and the subject matter (waterfront crime).

Leo Jaffe was far from a bystander during these behind-the-scenes machinations.[7] While Kazan was negotiating with Sinatra, Spiegel and Jaffe were doing the same with Brando, who eventually agreed to play the part for a mere $125,000. But Spiegel did not do badly, either: 50 percent of the net. As Leo Jaffe told Spiegel's biographer, "He was an excellent negotiator."[8] Understandably, Spiegel was Stanley Jaffe's inspiration: "A long time ago I began to know that I wanted to be a producer in the sense that Sam Spiegel is a producer.... Five of his films were up for Best Picture Oscars and they were directed by four different men. So I grasped the importance of producing early on."[9]

Stanley Jaffe wasted no time in pursuing his dream. Two years after graduating from Wharton, Stanley was executive assistant to Eliot Hyman at Seven Arts, which Hyman and Ray Stark had formed in 1958, ostensibly for licensing films to television (but ultimately for making movies). Stanley's first job in the business was the result of chance. Leo Jaffe was well acquainted with Ray Stark, whose interests were not limited to movies. In 1962 Stark was eager to produce a stage musical based on the life of his mother-in-law, Fanny Brice. Two years later, *Funny Girl* opened on Broadway, "A Ray Stark Production in Conjunction with Seven Arts." The 1968 film version, a Rastar production, was a Columbia release—the result of a deal that Leo Jaffe had brokered.

In 1967 Seven Arts merged with Warner Bros. to become Warner Bros.–Seven Arts (a union that lasted for only four years, when Warner Bros. became part of Warner Communications). For someone as determined to enter production as Jaffe, a movie studio, however hyphenated, would have been the ideal berth. But Jaffe knew his chances were limited in a company where he had already been pegged as "television," specifically "television programming." In corporate Hollywood, typecasting is not limited to actors; job titles become adhesives that stick to careers until the wearers have the courage to peel them off, or fortune does it for them. If Jaffe were to be "television" for any length of time, it would be as a producer. Thus, when the opportunity arose to join CBS-TV in 1968, he accepted; although he never intended to make network television his career, he was at least able to create *The Professionals*, a half-hour show about sports figures that later went into syndication.

Jaffe's break came in October 1969 when Bluhdorn made the proverbial nonrefusable offer: the dual title of executive vice president and COO, positions that would test his production and management skills. As COO, he would be replacing Martin S. Davis, who was delighted to return to the parent company as senior vice president of Gulf + Western—a position, as well as a power base, more suited to his corporate style. Within three months, Jaffe acquired another title on the basis of his previous experience: president of Paramount Television.

Jaffe's rise, even in New Hollywood, was swift, especially for a twenty-nine-year-old. After producing his first film, *Goodbye, Columbus* (1969), which was a huge success in addition to introducing Ali McGraw to moviegoers, Jaffe was promoted to president of Paramount Pictures in July 1970. Bluhdorn was then able to divest himself of a title that, luckily for Paramount, was just that. Jaffe's appointment freed Bluhdorn to return to the one role at which he excelled: Gulf + Western chairman.

Like his father, Jaffe chose to remain in New Rochelle with his wife and two children and commute to Los Angeles. For Jaffe, an East Coast address made sense: while he occasionally gave interviews, he was ill at ease schmoozing or socializing, and thus did little of either. His impersonal manner, as well as his disdain for hustlers, was perfectly acceptable in New York; on the West Coast, where open-necked shirts, jeans, and even sneakers were considered proper attire, Jaffe's corporate look would have been out of place. But then, Jaffe was only president, not production head.

As president, Jaffe found himself in a situation where income from film rentals seemed to be increasing annually ($37.4 million in 1967; $40 million in 1968; $60 million in 1969) but not at the rate that Bluhdorn and Davis expected. It was *The Odd Couple* and *Rosemary's Baby* (both 1968) that brought Paramount out of the economic doldrums; in 1969 it was *Goodbye, Columbus* and *Romeo and Juliet*, which cost $1.8 million and grossed over $20 million. On the other hand, at the end of fiscal 1970, film rentals, although up 8 percent over 1969, accounted for only 5 percent of Gulf + Western's total income ($1.63 million).

Paramount's few hits of the late 1960s, especially the above-mentioned that continue to delight viewers, tell only part of the story. In 1967, eager to provide more space for independent filmmakers and television producers, Gulf + Western purchased Desilu Studios for $40 million. Before there was Desilu Studios, there was Desilu Productions, formed by Lucille Ball and Desi Arnaz to produce such television series as *I Love Lucy*, *December Bride*, and *Our Miss Brooks*. When RKO ceased production in 1957, Ball and Arnaz, both of whom had worked briefly at RKO before becoming television icons, seized the opportunity to provide Desilu with a permanent home. The couple purchased the RKO lot on Gower Street and its two Culver City facilities to create Desilu Studios. In paying

The Lasky barn (1913), Paramount's first "studio," now on exhibit at the Hollywood Heritage Museum. Museum of Modern Art/Film Stills Archive (hereafter MOMA/FSA)

The Squaw Man (1914) cast in front of the Lasky barn. MOMA/FSA

(Above) Paramount's founders: key figures in the 1916 Famous Players–Feature Play merger. Left to right, Jesse Lasky, Adolph Zukor, Samuel Goldfish (Goldwyn), Cecil B. DeMille, and Albert Kaufman (Zukor's brother-in-law and Famous Players's general manager). Academy of Motion Picture Arts and Sciences (hereafter AMPAS) *(Below)* The Paramount presence in Hong Kong (1926). AMPAS

A break during the filming of *She Done Him Wrong* (1933). Left to right, script girl, Cary Grant, Mae West, and producer William Le Baron. AMPAS

Did they or didn't they? Gary Cooper and Marlene Dietrich in the Lubitsch production *Desire* (1936). Paramount Pictures

The Paramount logo in a 1923 *Photoplay* magazine ad. AMPAS

Claudette Colbert, who made more than thirty films for Paramount between 1929 and 1944. Private collection

Mitchell Leisen at the piano with Paramount star Betty Hutton, whom he directed in *Dream Girl* (1948). MOMA/FSA

(Above) The Paramount "white look" replicated at Columbia in Leisen's *The Lady Is Willing* (1942), with Fred MacMurray and Marlene Dietrich. Columbia Pictures *(Below)* The adaptable "white look," including the telephone, in the thriller *Sorry, Wrong Number* (1948) with Barbara Stanwyck as a murder victim. Paramount Pictures

(Above) Gary Cooper
as a Mountie and
Paulette Goddard as
Louvette, a role
originally intended
for Marlene Dietrich,
in *Northwest Mounted
Police* (1940).
Paramount Pictures

(Left) Marlene
Dietrich as the gypsy
Lydia in Leisen's
Golden Earrings
(1947), looking much
as she might have if
she had appeared in
*Northwest Mounted
Police*. Paramount
Pictures

Billy Wilder and Marlene Dietrich, whom he directed in Paramount's *A Foreign Affair* (1948) and UA's *Witness for the Prosecution* (1958). MOMA/FSA

Paramount comedy teams: (above), Bing Crosby (left), Dorothy Lamour, and Bob Hope in *Road to Bali* (1952), the trio's sixth Road movie; (below), Dean Martin (left) and Jerry Lewis in their sixth film, *Jumping Jacks* (1952). AMPAS

Hal Wallis (center) relaxing with Robert Cummings and Lizabeth Scott on the set of his production, *You Came Along* (1945), Scott's film debut. AMPAS

The screenwriter (William Holden) and the silent screen diva (Gloria Swanson) dancing a tango in *Sunset Boulevard* (1950). Paramount Pictures

A global affair: Paramount president Barney Balaban (left) and George Weltner,
then Paramount's head of international distribution, in the early 1950s. AMPAS

(Above) The famous Paramount gate at night in the late 1940s. AMPAS
(Below) The gate used for the scene in *Sunset Boulevard* when Norma Desmond
arrives in her Isotta-Fraschini. AMPAS

The Paramount Building (1501 Broadway) by night in 1934. AMPAS

A quartet of Oscar winners (clockwise from above): Olivia de Havilland (Best Actress) and Montgomery Clift in *The Heiress* (1949); Ray Milland (Best Actor) in the year's Best Picture, *The Lost Weekend* (1945), for which Billy Wilder was named Best Director; Buddy Rogers and Clara Bow in *Wings* (1927), winner of the first Best Picture Oscar; and Robert Redford (Best Director) and Timothy Hutton (Best Supporting Actor) in *Ordinary People* (1980). AMPAS

Adolph Zukor's one-hundredth birthday celebration in 1973. Left to right, Frank Yablans, Charles Bluhdorn, and Robert Evans standing behind the seated centenarian. AMPAS

Like father, like son: Don Vito (Marlon Brando) in *The Godfather* (1972), standing over his son Michael (Al Pacino), the next Don. AMPAS

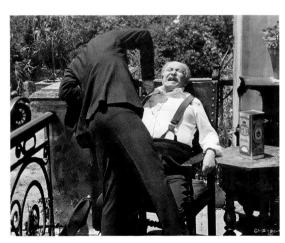

Vengeance is mine: the killing of Don Ciccio in *The Godfather Part II* (1974). Paramount Pictures

(Above) Paramount in the 1970s. Left to right: Robert Duvall (Tom Hagen), Diane Keaton (Kay), and Al Pacino (Michael) in *The Godfather Part II* (1974), winner of six Oscars. Paramount Pictures *(Below)* Robert Redford as Jay Gatsby and Mia Farrow as Daisy in *The Great Gatsby* (1974), whose authentic costumes and musical scoring were acknowledged at Oscar time. Paramount Pictures

(*Above*) Movie fans turned monsters as Homer Simpson (Donald Sutherland) becomes a sacrificial victim in *The Day of the Locust* (1975), a superb adaptation of Nathanael West's novel. MOMA/FSA (*Below*) Keith Carradine as a rock star in Robert Altman's *Nashville* (1975), which interweaves the lives of twenty-four people over a five-day period. MOMA/FSA

Barry Diller, Paramount chairman (1974–84), with his then companion and future wife, Diane von Furstenberg, at a 1993 reception. AP/Wide World Photos

(Opposite page) Michael Eisner, Paramount's COO under Diller,
who moved on to the Mouse House as Disney CEO. AP/Wide
World Photos

Dawn Steel, who started in merchandising at Paramount in 1978 and advanced to production head in 1985, only to encounter the lethal combination of sexism and cancer. AP/Wide World Photos

(Above) Brandon Tartikoff (left), seated next to Paramount Communications chairman and CEO Martin S. Davis, at a 1991 press conference announcing his short-lived appointment as Paramount Pictures chairman. AP/Wide World Photos *(Below)* Sherry Lansing, once president of Twentieth Century–Fox, who replaced Brandon Tartikoff in 1992 with the title of motion pictures group chairman. AP/Wide World Photos

(Above) Tom Hanks and Sally Field, as Forrest Gump and his mother, in *Forrest Gump* (1994), whose phenomenal success made Paramount the second-highest-grossing studio in 1994. Paramount Pictures *(Below)*Viacom chairman and CEO Sumner Redstone (left) and CBS Corp. chairman and CEO Mel Karmazin celebrating the $36.75 billion Viacom-CBS merger on 7 September 1999. AP/Wide World Photos

$40 million for Desilu, Bluhdorn planned to merge the Paramount and RKO lots, which were adjacent (and at one point separated only by a fence), and rent the property—Paramount/RKO and the Culver studios—to television and independent film producers.

Bluhdorn always tended to act before considering the legal ramifications of his actions. Gulf + Western would now be in possession of three studios besides Paramount. For almost fifty years RKO had been a functioning studio. Now the defunct RKO was merely real estate, as were the Culver studios—the fourteen–acre Culver Studio and the twenty-nine–acre Culver Backlot. But it was also real estate that had been used for film and television production; and if Bluhdorn had his way, it would be used for the same purposes.

The Justice Department thought differently. In 1967, the issue was not theater ownership, as it had been two decades earlier; it was control of a disproportionate amount of studio space at a time when the industry was in a state of retrenchment. It was one thing to annex the property of a former studio; it was another to acquire two additional properties that would enable Paramount to offer independent film and television producers a choice of four locations. The Justice Department decided that Paramount was returning to its monopolistic ways, and Gulf + Western was forced to sign a consent decree, requiring the Culver Studios to be sold within two years.[10]

The consent decree was a sobering experience for Bluhdorn. When the dream takes too long to become a reality, the dream must be deceptive: either abandon it or conjure up another. Rather than waiting to see if Paramount would awaken to a new dawn by the end of the decade, Bluhdorn started behaving as erratically as he did when *Is Paris Burning?* had failed to be the blockbuster he expected. It was time for the "Sell the studio" scenario or one of its variations: "Get out of the movie business" (which Bluhdorn and Davis had contemplated in 1967), "Sell the lot," or "Sell half of the lot and shack up with another studio." Stanley Jaffe arrived at Paramount for downsizing time. In fall 1969, Paramount dismissed close to 150 employees; branch offices in Seattle and New Haven were closed; film production was down; as for rentals, only *The Odd Couple* reached the $20 million mark; and the stages were being used primarily for television shows such as NBC's *Bonanza* and *High Chapparal* and ABC's *Mod Squad* and *Movie of the Week*. Furthermore, television producers only wanted studio space; they brought their own staff, including secretaries and set decorators, and had little, if any, need for Paramount personnel.

Because of his business background, Jaffe had no trouble espousing the party line, which, at the end of 1969, happened to be "Sell half of the lot." This time, the rationale was, in part, rational: Rent the stages to television producers and make movies in homes, apartments, restaurants, on the street, or on location. As Davis put it, sizing up the new generation of moviegoers the way a club bouncer might: "These kids aren't going to the movies to take home dreams."[11]

Davis's was a cynicism based partly on contempt for humankind but mostly on an obsession with the balance sheet that renders the obsessed indifferent to past and present. In the past, Hollywood had been known as "the dream factory" or, as critic Parker Tyler dubbed it, the purveyor of the "daylight dream." And dreams were precisely what the young needed in the late sixties. In 1968, the anti–Vietnam War movement had gained momentum, leading to campus riots, notably at Columbia University and the Sorbonne. That same year, another dream—the dream of racial harmony that Dr. Martin Luther King Jr. had envisioned five years earlier in his "I Have a Dream" speech at the Lincoln Memorial—became a dream deferred as an assassin's bullet ended his life and, shortly thereafter, the life of one of King's most ardent supporters, Robert Kennedy.

There were no dreams to take home because both Hollywood and the American government suspended dreaming for the duration. To the flower children, 1969 may have been the year of the Woodstock festival, but it was also the year that details of the My Lai massacre were revealed and the bombing of Cambodia began, setting off another round of protests that culminated in the tragedy at Kent State University in May 1970 when National Guardsmen opened fire on Kent State students, killing four of them.

While Davis was right in assuming that Paramount's 1969 favorite would be *True Grit*, which won John Wayne his only Oscar, *Medium Cool* (1969) was Paramount's only release that dared depict an America that had given up on its leaders and defected to the cool medium where bloodshed is recorded with dispassion. Set against the violence that erupted at the 1968 Chicago Democratic convention, *Medium Cool* dramatized Vietnam's tragic impact on two people, a television newsman and a woman he befriends, who under other circumstances might have had a life together. If, as T.S. Eliot wrote, "Human kind cannot bear very much reality," Hollywood assumed that Americans could get theirs on television; and with the end of the Production Code and the beginning of the ratings system in 1968, the industry offered an alternative reality, as if the real consisted only of bare bodies and obscenities. Naturally, *Medium Cool* reflected the times in the dialogue and discreetly photographed nudity (enough to earn it an "X" rating, which thirty years later would have merited a PG-13).

If Davis saw the film, his reaction would have been influenced by the gross, which was not impressive despite the superlative reviews. But Davis was no more a filmmaker than Bluhdorn, who was also eager to sell part of the lot because he thought more money could be made in home video and first-run movies via satellite. Each viewed Paramount as a cash cow to be milked to exhaustion, at which point it would be replaced by a fitter specimen.

Stanley Jaffe's business training made him sympathetic to Davis and Bluhdorn's thinking: "As for the studio, we're going to get rid of it and that delights me personally," Jaffe told *Life* magazine.[12] Jaffe was partially correct: only half of the lot was to be sold. Yet, in view of his promotion to president, Jaffe had no choice but to laud the deal (with which he probably concurred) and find a new location for the production staff.

Preparatory to the actual sale, Gulf + Western created a new subsidiary, Paramount Studio Properties Inc., to be administered by Executive Vice President Irving Horowitz. Separating film production from studio real estate also meant relocating it—freeing the stages for television and, in a sense, freeing moviemakers too by sending them into the "real" world to shoot their films. Thus a subtle distinction had been made between the studio lot and the movie studio. The movie studio was intact; the lot was negotiable.

Even selling half of the lot would not solve the problem. As a new decade was dawning, Paramount's real profits derived from a few successful 1969 movies, notably *True Grit* and *Goodbye, Columbus*. Perhaps Gulf + Western reasoned that, with a lucrative real estate deal, the future would be brighter. Actually, it was—but not because of the real estate deal, which only liberated production briefly from the corporate dungeon. Bluhdorn could never have known the lineup of great films that were on the horizon, thanks to the efforts of Evans and Bart. What Bluhdorn and Davis never realized—or if they did, never admitted—was that, in Bart and Evans, they had two of the most creative men in Hollywood, each of whom complemented the other: Bart, who could bring to completion a vision that was only partially his but needed his ego-free perspective to succeed, and the ego-driven Evans, who needed someone like Bart to provide that perspective. It was essentially the difference between being *of* and *in* the business: Bart was of it, but Evans was undeniably in it.

But neither Bluhdorn nor Davis was interested in prepositional distinctions; they did not have Lincoln's subtle sense of rhetoric with which he distinguished between "government of the people, by the people, and for the people" in the Gettysburg Address. Their solution for Paramount was simple: dump it, in whole or in part, and worry about the future when it comes. But to those who live in the now, there is no future—only an unending present that dissolves into the past as the future fades in to provide continuity.

In April 1970, Gulf + Western, which may have advocated long-range planning but never really planned ahead, was moving closer to a sale. The clue was the decision to transfer Paramount's production headquarters from Marathon Street in Hollywood to Beverly Hills; accordingly, the production staff, headed by Stanley Jaffe, Robert Evans, and Peter Bart, moved to a four-story building at 202 North Canon Drive, a few doors away from the industry's newest power restaurant, The Bistro. The move was a boon for Bart and Evans; less bureaucracy resulted in greater creativity, for it was during those five years on Canon Drive that some of the greatest films of the poststudio era were made—e.g., *The Godfather* (1972), *Paper Moon* (1973), *The Godfather Part II* (1974), *Serpico* (1974), *The Conversation* (1974), *Chinatown* (1974), *Murder on the Orient Express* (1974), and *Nashville* (1975), all of which were Paramount releases.

In 1975 Paramount received thirty-nine Oscar nominations. *The Godfather Part II* won for Best Picture, Supporting Actor (Robert De Niro), Director (Francis Ford Coppola), Screenplay Adapted from Other Material (Coppola and Mario Puzo), Art Direction, and Original Dramatic Score. Ingrid Bergman was voted Best Supporting Actress for *Murder on the Orient Express*; Robert Towne was rightly honored for *Chinatown*, the year's Best Original Screenplay. Although *The Great Gatsby* found little favor with reviewers, the film's recreation of the jazz age was acknowledged with awards for Nelson Riddle's orchestrations of vintage songs and Theoni V. Aldredge's authentic costumes.

Canon Drive would not be Paramount's permanent address, yet the brief period production was based there showed what could be achieved when creative people are left to themselves, with minimal interference from micromanagers and numbers crunchers. This did not mean that Bart and Evans were free to cut any deals they wished. Until he left Paramount in 1971, Stanley Jaffe, although living in New York, kept tabs on what was happening at Canon Drive. Bart and Evans ran everything by Jaffe and, according to Bart, won every argument.[13]

Within two years of his arrival at Paramount, Jaffe was ready to leave. It was not entirely a matter of choice, since he worked well with Evans and Bart. The problem was that Jaffe still considered himself East Coast, living with his wife and two children in the same town where he had grown up—New Rochelle. Although he commuted regularly to Los Angeles, he did not have a second home there; his home-away-from-home was the Beverly Hills Hotel. Like his father, Jaffe could never become an Angeleno, even later in his career when producing chores required his spending more time in Hollywood. But as president of Paramount Pictures, he had little choice but to reside within an easy commute to 1501 Broadway; and if he took the train from New Rochelle, he could walk to his office from Grand Central Station. However, working in New York caused him to see more of Bluhdorn and Davis than he would have if he were based in Los Angeles.

Jaffe rarely spoke of Davis; as for Bluhdorn, he was so effusive ("I love Charlie Bluhdorn") in an interview he gave five years after leaving Paramount that it seemed he was trying to rebuild a bridge that had been burned.[14] However, in an earlier interview, and one that may have piqued Bluhdorn, Jaffe implied that he, Bart, and Evans pretty much ran the studio:"Charlie is always kept apprised.... Otherwise he's quite uninvolved. I don't even think he knows most of the pictures we're doing."[15]

It must have been difficult for a would-be producer like Jaffe to realize he was expected to function as a hatchet man—streamlining budgets, reducing overhead, and, if neccessary, eliminating jobs. He also had to deal with Martin Davis, Bluhdorn's *capo*, as he was often called in Mafia parlance, whose reputation for incivility even surpassed his own. But more than anything, Jaffe was handicapped by his premature ascendancy in a business to which he was suited but in a role in which he was miscast. To achieve what he wanted, Jaffe would have had to break out of the East Coast mold, despite its attractions, and make his peace with Los Angeles.

Leo Jaffe played to his strengths, which did not include production; Leo was in the movie business but not in moviemaking. Theoretically, Stanley Jaffe was in both. Yet in 1971 he was neither running Paramount Pictures, in the sense of producing films, nor in conrol of Gulf + Western. He was in a situation where two uncommonly talented men were making Oscar-winning films for the studio over which he presided but whose direction he could not chart for a number of reasons, one of which being his lack of proximity to the creative center of moviemaking, and, more significantly, his lack of social grace, which made him a washout as a schmoozer and a dinner party deadbeat. If Jaffe was often more irritable than usual, it may have also been that his marriage was in jeopardy. The novelty of being the industry's youngest president had ended, and Jaffe had to face up to the nature of his job.

Although Gulf + Western never provided Jaffe with a job description, his successor, Frank Yablans, composed his own; and since Yablans was working with the same creative team of Evans and Bart, he was obviously speaking for Jaffe. A year after Jaffe left Paramount, Yablans had lunch with gossip columnist Earl Wilson at New York's "21." Wilson's syndicated column in the *Los Angeles Herald Examiner* (4 April 1972) quoted Yablans, who described his job with a conciseness of which most executives are incapable, because they are either inarticulate or, more likely, fearful of alienating higher-ups. Yablans was not the most sensitive of executives; hence his days were also numbered. However, rarely has anyone distinguished between the roles of studio president and production head so clearly: "Bobby [Evans] is without question head of production, but I am without question president of the company. . . . Any property Bobby wants to do must bear my stamp. I answer directly to Gulf & Western. At the beginning of the year I request certain funds. At the end of the year I answer for the funds. If they're not satisfactory, at the beginning of the next year I don't get the funds."

Jaffe's irritability was growing worse. When Bluhdorn wanted to star his latest discovery, Joanna Cameron, in the film version of Neil Simon's *Star-Spangled Girl* (1971), Jaffe told him in no uncertain terms to stay on his own turf and not trespass on unfamiliar terrain. According to Robert Evans, Jaffe was not only curt but abusive as well.[16] What Jaffe never understood about Bluhdorn was the latter's almost dynastic need for a surrogate son. Bluhdorn had little hope for his own son, Paul, as a future studio head, even though he found work for him at Paramount. Bluhdorn, unfortunately, was always underestimating his would-be protegés. Perhaps weaker men could be shaped along corporate lines, but not Jaffe, whose idea of a patriarch was his own father, not Charlie Bluhdorn. Jaffe's real problem was his inability to play the game, mainly because the game repelled him. As the late Samuel J. "Buddy" Silberman, former chairman of the board of Consolidated Cigar who joined the Gulf + Western board in 1968, put it: "Jaffe never got the true feel of the corporate style of management."[17]

By April 1971, Jaffe was no longer president, but Bluhdorn was loath to have him leave Paramount. Offered a production deal, Jaffe, always a sports enthusiast, produced *The Bad News Bears* (1976), which altered (for the moment, anyway) the prevailing belief that sports movies are bad box office. Although paying twelve-year-old Tatum O'Neal $350,000 raised some corporate eyebrows, the comedy about Little League baseball was enthusiastically received. At the time Jaffe did not know that he would be returning to Paramount. But that would be after Bluhdorn's death.

Less than a year before Jaffe left Paramount, an incident occurred that received little coverage in the press: Gulf + Western had found a buyer for half of the Paramount lot—a Rome-based outfit with a Vatican connection: Società Generale Immobiliare (SGI), Italy's largest real estate and construction company.[18] Since Bluhdorn was notorious for outlandish business schemes (including trying to interest Fidel Castro in a sugar cartel), the press may have dismissed the proposed sale as another of the mad Austrian's pipe dreams. Although several actors who had their own production companies were eager to buy, Bluhdorn preferred SGI. In June 1970, a stock swap was arranged: in exchange for 50 percent of Marathon Studio Facilities (the renamed Paramount Studio Facilities), Gulf + Western agreed to purchase 15 million shares (or 10.5 percent) of SGI common stock that may have been owned by the Vatican, a well-known SGI shareholder. In more practical terms, SGI was supposed to get half of the fifty-two–acre lot; and Bluhdorn, a seat on SGI's board.

The new half-owner would not be taking possession immediately. (As it happened, it would not be taking possession at all.) Gulf + Western announced a long-range study, causing various theories to circulate about the fate of the lot, the most common being its reconfiguration as a residential and commercial community with a streamlined studio somewhere in the vicinity.

But what exactly were SGI's plans? And why, if Bluhdorn could have sold to Danny Thomas or some other actor-producer, did he choose an Italian company that few in Hollywood had ever heard of?[19]

5

The Italian Connection

In 1970, any Hollywood insider asked to name the studio most likely to make the movie version of Mario Puzo's *The Godfather* (1969) would have said "Paramount." *The Godfather* was followed by the more impressive sequel, *The Godfather Part II* (1974). Then Paramount decided to make it a trilogy with *The Godfather Part III* (1990). Although Paramount was not known for crime movies, it seems to have developed a special interest in the genre in the late 1960s after *The Brotherhood* (1969), which, although unsuccessful, was at least well-timed. After 1963, it was impossible to deny the Mafia's existence; that fall, a low-ranking mob member, Joseph Valachi, then serving a life sentence, agreed to cooperate with Sen. John L. McClellan's subcommittee investigating organized crime in return for protection. Valachi had a good reason: Mafia kingpin and Valachi's former cellmate, Vito "Don Vito" Genovese, had taken out a contract on him, presumably for the same reason he was appearing before the McClellan Committee: informing.

Some of Valachi's revelations seemed too lurid to be true. *The Brotherhood*, on the other hand, provided a lexicon of Mafia conventions for the uninitiated: sons succeeding their fathers in the organization, the Sicilian law of silence (*omertà*), the Irish lawyer/advisor (*consigliere*), the dutiful wife who never inquires about her husband's activities, canaries stuffed in the mouths of slain informers, a code of honor that even requires kin to pay with their lives for violating it, a quick and easy guide to garroting violators, the ritual meal before the hit, and the kiss of death followed by a blast from the executioner's rifle (*lupara*).

Although *The Brotherhood* received some favorable reviews, it failed at the box office. Part of the reason lay in the casting. Except for the script, written by Lewis John Carlino, and a few character actors (e.g., Eduardo Ciannelli and Joe DeSantis) in minor roles, an Italian presence was largely absent. The closest any of the leads came to authenticity was the renowned Greek actress, Irene Papas, who looked Mediterranean enough to be married to a Sicilian, played by Kirk Douglas. As Frank, a Mafia kingpin, Douglas was Sicilian in makeup only, although he was genuinely moving in the final scene when, realizing his brother Vince has been sent to kill him for running afoul of the Cosa Nostra, he provides Vince with a *lupara*, the executioner's rifle, before they embrace for the last time.

Yet one has to suspend disbelief to accept the fair-complexioned Alex Cord as the avenging brother and Susan Strasberg as his wife. As directed by Martin Ritt, *The Brotherhood* seems like another crime film with a few Italian touches thrown in for good measure (a funeral with over-the-top wailing, a game of boccie, and a wedding with the older dons deliberately sitting apart from the younger). But the material proved too exotic for a director who understood mean streets, disaffected spies, and union organizers, but not "The Family."

Carlino's script, however, had potential. Carlino's Vince anticipates Puzo's Michael, the son who could have gone into a respectable profession but chose instead to remain in the Mafia. Both Vince (Alex Cord) in *The Brotherhood* and Michael (Al Pacino) in *The Godfather* are college-educated veterans who were not expected to continue in the family business. At the beginning of *The Brotherhood*, the Mafia father has already died, and Frank, the older son, has replaced him. Although Vince has a job lined up in Boston, he chooses to work for Frank, later breaking with his brother when Frank decides to remain in labor racketeering rather than branch out into other enterprises. In *The Godfather*, Michael's decision to enter the Mafia was not based on anything as frivolous as wanting to live in New York and have his hand kissed by underlings and petitioners. Michael turns mafioso after he sustains a broken jaw during a second assassination attempt on his father's life. Michael's Dartmouth degree did not prepare him for his new role of avenger, which he readily embraced, as if born for the part.

Here the similarities between *The Brotherhood* and *The Godfather* end. How *The Godfather* also came to be filmed at Paramount, where it originated as a story/outline that Puzo expanded into a novel, is a film historian's initiation into the Hollywood labyrinth, wherein dwell gossipmongers, talk-show hosts and their often uninformed but always voluble guests, spinmeisters, and press agents (both the pros who speak guardedly and the disaffected who care only about settling scores). How Paramount became home to *The Godfather* involves a trip through the studio's back roads, complete with detours, turn-offs, and an occasional dead end. Still, a detour generally brings the driver back to the main road, and, while taking the exit ramp into Paramount's Italy may not answer *The Godfather* question, it does explain how one of the world's most famous movie producers, the Neapolitan-born Dino De Laurentiis, became associated with the studio and made his own Mafia movie, *The Valachi Papers* (1972), which opened the same year as *The Godfather* (but was not a Paramount release), and also how, at the same time *The Godfather* was being planned, a real-life Mafia scenario was unfolding on the Paramount lot.

Of all the branch offices in Europe and Asia that George Weltner routinely visited, the one on Rome's Via Leonida Bissolati was special. The general manager of Paramount's Rome office was Pilade Levi, with whom Weltner enjoyed a relationship that was more than just cordial; theirs was a true friendship. In fact, Weltner's son, Jack, once stayed in Rome with the Levis for six months. There was nothing formal about the correspondence between Weltner and Levi, which always began with "Dear George" or "Dear Pilade." Levi kept Weltner informed about his wife and family, including his mother's health problems, and Weltner's replies showed genuine concern.

There was someone else at Paramount, four years younger than Weltner, who also knew Levi and proved to be an even more important Italian connection: Luigi G. Luraschi. London-born and Swiss-educated, Luraschi was destined for the international scene, moving quickly from the London Metal Exchange into the field of hotel management—the latter turning him into a seasoned traveler, like Weltner. Luraschi's linguistic skills and cosmopolitan background brought him to Paramount's Long Island facility in 1929. Luraschi, however, was not assigned to the processing lab, where Weltner was still working, but to foreign distribution, an area that had already captured Weltner's interest. Around the same time that Weltner was made president of Paramount International, Luraschi was transferred to the West Coast to head Paramount's foreign department. In 1953, during the height of the Cold War, Luraschi was put in charge of foreign and domestic censorship at the studio. A devout Catholic and militant anti-Communist, Luraschi used his position to furnish the CIA with information about forthcoming releases with racial or ethnic stereotypes that could discredit the United States in the eyes of the international community.[1] Although their paths crossed frequently, Weltner never knew Luraschi was a CIA informant (whose ability to influence film content turned out to be minimal). Weltner assumed their common interest was international distribution. In 1960, he discovered they also had Dino De Laurentiis in common.

Had De Laurentiis been born in the late 1800s like Sam Goldwyn and Adolph Zukor, instead of in 1919, and traveled to America in steerage instead of a jet, he would have become as legendary as they. Like the studio moguls, De Laurentiis wove myth and fact into a colorful bio that sounded more like a movie script than a life. He also had the right height: five feet-plus (depending on his shoes), which would have made the other moguls, all of whom were equally short, comfortable in his presence. De Laurentiis repeated the story of his entrance into the movies so often that it began to sound plausible, the way success stories often do, even though his rise from obscurity to fame probably never happened quite as he told it. When interviewed, De Laurentiis became a storyteller, collapsing time, coloring facts, and remaining silent about details that would have shed light on his access to big bucks, prompting many journalists to wonder if perhaps there was a Mafia connection (an allegation De Laurentiis has denied).

De Laurentiis always gave an impressionistic account of his childhood. He seems to have been a born maverick—running away from boarding schools, scoffing at the idea of working in his father's pasta factory in Torre Annunziata near Naples, and finally setting out for Rome, where he either studied film and/or worked as an extra. Drafted into the army shortly after Italy joined the Axis in 1939, De Laurentiis had to wait until the end of the second world war to realize his goal of becoming a film producer. His producing debut occurred in 1949 with *Bitter Rice* (*Riso Amaro*), a Lux Film release that arrived in the United States the following year.

Bitter Rice was an immediate hit, not so much because of its vestigial neorealism (the plight of female workers in the Po Valley rice fields) as for its sensationalism. The star, Silvana Mangano, was in the earth mother tradition of Anna Magnani and Sophia Loren. More voluptuous than Magnani and fleshier than Loren, Mangano may not have been as good an actress as either, but she epitomized what American audiences, just discovering the films of Fellini, DeSica, and Rossellini, perceived as the Italian version of the Hollywood love goddess: a force of nature with a face free of makeup and a body unfettered by foundation garments.

When *Bitter Rice* opened at New York's World Theater in 1950 (which two decades later played host to *Deep Throat*), one of the posters featured a recumbent Mangano with her dress hitched up well past her thigh, revealing the absence of panties. For once, the poster was accurate. Audiences accustomed to shaved armpits were also in for a surprise. The earth mother did not use a depilatory. The film's graphic (for 1950) depiction of sex, which included a rape in the rain, caused the Legion of Decency to issue a "C" (Condemned) rating, but that did not deter moviegoers. And, as often happens during a shoot, De Laurentiis and Mangano fell in love and were married in 1949, the year of the film's release.

Bitter Rice represented one side of De Laurentiis: the commercial. Although it had the authentic look of such neorealistic films as *Shoeshine* and *Paisan* (both 1946), the steamy sex made it evident that *Bitter Rice* was intended for a much wider audience than the art house crowd—which was indeed the case when it was released nationwide in a dubbed version in 1952. Although *Bitter Rice* made De Laurentiis a player, he was not satisfied. In a bid for respectability, De Laurentiis, like Joseph E. Levine, vigorously pursued properties that would give him the stature he craved, which would obviously not come from potboilers. His efforts were rewarded when two of his productions, Fellini's *La Strada* (1954), coproduced with Carlo Ponti, and *Nights of Cabiria* (1957) won Oscars for Best Foreign Language Films of 1956 and 1957. These were about the extent of De Laurentiis's prestige pictures. Once he went Hollywood, the gross took precedence over art.

At the time *La Strada* was playing in art houses, two other De Laurentiis films (also Ponti coproductions) were playing on the circuits. Only moviegoers who read credits carefully would have associated the producer of *La Strada* with *Ulysses* and *Mambo*, both 1955 releases. Eager to gain a foothold in Hollywood, which he eventually did, De Laurentiis was looking for affordable but recognizable stars like Anthony Quinn, who costarred in *La Strada*, to appear in his Italian-made films. In *Ulysses*, De Laurentiis succeeded in getting Kirk Douglas for the title role, with Quinn as Antinous, the chief suitor, and the ubiquitous Mangano in a dual role, presumably to showcase her versatility: the goddess Circe, who turns men into swine, and the faithful wife, Penelope, devising various stratagems to keep the suitors at bay until her husband returns. *Mambo*, which capitalized on the latest dance craze, also starred Mangano, reunited with her *Bitter Rice* costar, Vittorio Gassman.

Both films were as typical of De Laurentiis as the Fellini Oscar winners. Throughout his career, De Laurentiis vacillated between quality and pulp, realizing that the latter would never win him the approval of cineastes (who would never see the films, anyway) but would at least get wider distribution. Interestingly, *Ulysses* and *Mambo* had the same distributor: Paramount. De Laurentiis now had a major studio behind him, thanks chiefly to Luraschi, who not only knew him but also spoke his language. Within a few years, Luraschi would end his thirty-year career at Paramount and join De Laurentiis Productions in 1960 as the supervisor of the company's English-language films.

Feeling that he could now go solo, De Laurentiis severed his partnership with Ponti in 1957 after they coproduced *War and Peace* for Paramount. Neither seemed happy with the film. Budgeted at $4 million, *War and Peace* eventually cost $6 million and barely made a profit. *War and Peace* also occasioned a lawsuit, the reasons for which are somewhat murky, except that money was involved.[2] Paramount was supposed to pay 40 percent of the final cost as initial payment for the worldwide distribution rights. However, in a De Laurentiis production, only one thing is certain: Dino's cut is bigger than the studio's; if the studio wishes, it can recoup its investment quickly but without any guarantee of further earnings.

Paramount and De Laurentiis ended up suing each other over *War and Peace*: Paramount accused De Laurentiis of defaulting on a loan, and De Laurentiis countered by claiming Paramount owed him $127,000. By 1962, the suit was resolved—amicably, it seems, although the details are unknown. De Laurentiis would play a more prominent role in Bluhdorn's Paramount in the 1970s; in the meantime, between 1960 and 1968, he gave Paramount only three films: *Five Branded Women* (1960), *The Violent Four* (1968), and *Barbarella* (1968)—the last featuring Jane Fonda in the title role doing a strip over the opening credits.

In 1960, De Laurentiis began looking on Hollywood as a conduit through which he would release his own films. The distributor was unimportant; it could be Columbia, Fox, or Paramount—and was, at various times, all three. In 1960, De Laurentiis felt secure enough to start planning his own studio.

In January 1962, construction began on a 750–acre facility on the Via Pontina, some 13 miles south of Rome, that would be known as Dino De Laurentiis Cinematografica.[3] The facility cost $30 million, 60 percent of which was financed by the Italian government at 3 percent interest over a ten- to fifteen-year period. De Laurentiis christened it "Dinocittà," his answer to Rome's Cinecittà, one of the world's largest studios—and also one that he could never rival. That fall, while De Laurentiis' monument to himself was under construction, he and Luraschi flew to New York to set up offices for the Dino De Laurentiis Corporation of America. De Laurentiis' thinking had undergone a 180–degree reversal: no longer was he interested in distributing films with European actors for American audiences; henceforth, he would be producing films with American actors for the international market.

Believing that the industry needed another Cecil B. DeMille, De Laurentiis set out to make a biblical epic. Like DeMille, he did not favor the Hebrew Bible over the Greek New Testament; both had movie potential. Although he would have liked Paramount to distribute *The Bible* (1966), Weltner suspected the film would fail, as indeed it did, despite Luraschi's understandable enthusiasm for it. Fox released the $23 million flop, which is hardly the one for which director John Huston (who also played Noah) will be remembered. Columbia had had better luck a few years earlier with another De Laurentiis epic, *Barabbas* (1962), again with Anthony Quinn and Silvana Mangano. The film, which cost around $10 million, was vastly superior to *The Bible*. Fortunately, *Barabbas* was shot on a couple of standing sets on the site of Dinocittà before construction began. Otherwise, *Barabbas* might have cost as much as *The Bible*, which made full use of Dinocittà's four soundstages, three of which could be converted into one gigantic space.

During his 1962 trip, De Laurentiis also visited Los Angeles, where he deliberately avoided mentioning Paramount as a possible distributor. However, a new regime would change his mind.

It took a while before De Laurentiis became a sometime member of the Paramount family again. That only happened when Dinocittà went into receivership in the early 1970s after it became evident that epics like *The Bible* and *Waterloo* (1971), the latter released by Paramount, had nothing to offer but spectacle. And what was once a state-of-the-art movie studio outside of Rome became an industrial park.

By 1969, De Laurentiis had returned to the Paramount fold and was ready to provide the studio with more than castoffs. While De Laurentiis seemed to have been the logical producer of *The Godfather*, he appears to have made no effort to acquire the rights, possibly because he knew Paramount had already done so. In a typical De Laurentiis deal, "Dino puts up the initial money—to buy the book, commission a screenplay, and hire a director—*before* he approaches a studio."[4] Once he discovered that *The Godfather* was always intended as an in-house production that would not require his byzantine method of financing, he showed no interest in it. What Paramount did not know in 1969 is that De Laurentiis had lined up a Mafia property of his own, which he would later call the companion piece to *The Godfather*.

The Godfather is one of those films around which so much credit-claiming has accumulated that one can only cut a swath through the overgrowth and open up a path, realizing that the path was once part of a much longer paper trail that has since been covered over. In the absence of memos and transcripts of conversations and meetings, one has to depend upon the most reliable of Hollywood sources, even though skeptics would call "reliable Hollywood source" an oxymoron. Still, such sources occasionally emerge, and not always "on condition of anonymity."

Of those associated with *The Godfather*, Peter Bart, at the time Paramount's vice president of creative affairs, is the most credible. Unfortunately, Bart no longer has his notes, which he decided to burn when lawyer-to-the-mob Sidney Korshak reminded him that "the best insurance policy in the world that absolutely guarantees continued breathing . . . [is] silence."[5]

Even without his notes, Bart is quite adamant about several points: it was he who optioned the novel in 1969 before it was published and championed Francis Ford Coppola as director and co-screenwriter, not so much because Coppola was Italian as because he knew that Coppola, better than anyone else, could subordinate the novel's many subplots to the overriding theme of a family bound, for good or ill, to rituals and laws that might seem primitive to outsiders but not to its members. Coppola struck Bart as the kind of director who could make such archaic codes understandable, without necessarily sanctifying them. Bart was also influenced by Coppola's Oscar-winning script for *Patton* (1970), which managed to balance the general's bouts of megalomania and irrationality with moments of compassion and lucidity. However, *Patton* portrays the general's extremes of behavior as only one aspect of his character; what truly defines George S. Patton is his unswerving allegiance to a military code that demands unquestioning obedience of all who embrace it—not all that different from *omertà*, which makes similar demands on those bound to uphold it.

Coppola was, however, not production chief Robert Evans's first choice. According to Evans, Coppola was hired only after other directors (e.g., Arthur Penn, Elia Kazan, and Richard Brooks) turned *The Godfather* down, either because they felt the novel glamorized the Mafia or doubted that pulp fiction could metamorphose into art.[6] Still, it is strange to think that Penn, whose *Bonnie and Clyde* (1967) transformed a pair of bank robbers into tragic figures, victims of the Great Depression, would bypass another opportunity to engage in hagiography. As for Brooks and Kazan, *The Godfather* no more turned the Corleones into the Holy Family than Brooks's *In Cold Blood* (1964) turned Perry Smith and Dick Hickock into misunderstood youths; or Kazan's *A Streetcar Named Desire* (1951), rape into retaliation for putting on airs. More likely, none of the directors found the project worthwhile, since *The Godfather* was originally intended as a ninety–minute crime movie budgeted at $1 million.[7]

Kazan apparently never lost interest in *The Godfather*, particularly after the novel became a best-seller, the budget increased, and the concept changed from gangster flick to family saga. When the project seemed beyond Coppola's abilities, Evans seriously thought of replacing him with Kazan, who may have decided that, if he could wring lilies out of acorns in *Baby Doll* (1956) and *A Face in the Crowd* (1957), he could do the same with *The Godfather*. Bart admits that Coppola was on the verge of being fired (and, in fact, may have been on more than one occasion and then rehired). Fortunately, Bart and Evans realized that Coppola could control the narrative, never allowing *The Godfather* to veer off into sensationalism for its own sake and throw the film off kilter. For all its scenes of violence, *The Godfather* is essentially about familial relationships, which, in the case of the Corleones, extended well beyond blood relatives.

As for Kazan, the possibility of directing *The Godfather* proved to be a blip on the screen of his career; he does not even mention it in his autobiography, *A Life*.

From the beginning, there was no doubt that Puzo would be involved in the screenplay. The project originated as an outline, a hundred–page story, or a combination story-outline (accounts vary) entitled "Mafia," which both Bart and Evans read in 1968. Evans claims to have optioned the story for $12,500; what he optioned was just that—a rough draft, not even a treatment. That may have been acceptable at the beginning, but Bart insisted that the novel had to be written before the rights could be purchased, and Puzo involved in the adaptation.

In addition to being a novelist, Puzo was also a compulsive gambler who could support his habit more easily by writing screenplays than novels. Yet he knew Paramount needed the novel before the screenplay could even be discussed. Puzo first sought out Atheneum, the publisher of his earlier novel, *The Fortunate Pilgrim* (1965). When Atheneum showed no interest in "Mafia," Puzo tried Putnam's, which offered him an advance. And before *The Godfather*, as "Mafia" was finally titled, was published in April 1969, Bart bought the movie rights for Paramount; he claims to have provided Puzo with office space on the Paramount lot to complete the book, although Puzo has denied such largesse.[8] Regardless, Bart as vice president of creative affairs was the one who handled the negotiations.

Bart always intended that Puzo and Coppola coauthor the screenplay, not because they were both conversant with the subject matter but the opposite. Strange as it may seem, Puzo's knowledge of the Mafia was derived from secondary sources, as was Coppola's. And so, a high stakes gambler (Puzo) linked up with a writer-director (Coppola, M.F.A., UCLA), who had received a Best Screenplay Oscar for *Patton* (which he shared with Edward North), had an erratic record as director, a disdain for mainstream Hollywood, and an ignorance of the Mafia as profound as Puzo's, yet could bring in a musical like *Finian's Rainbow* (1968) at $3 million.

Still, Coppola managed to make one of the most honored films in the history of American cinema, as well as one of the finest crime movies ever produced. There were several reasons for the film's immediate popularity: the novel, which remained on the best-seller list for over a year; a public primed for violence after a decade of death that saw the assassinations of John Kennedy, Medgar Evers, Martin Luther King, Jr., and Robert Kennedy; race riots in Los Angeles and Newark, campus demonstrations, and the killing of four unarmed Kent State University students by National Guardsmen; and an awareness of organized crime that had been building up for two decades since Sen. Estes Kefauver's televised hearings in 1951 had enabled viewers to see how a real mobster like Frank Costello spoke and behaved.

That awareness became a fascination in the early 1960s when Joseph Valachi testified before Senator McClellan's subcommittee about the organization that he called "*cosa nostra*" (literally, "our thing"), thus flagrantly violating *omertà* by familiarizing the public with a phrase that Mafia members used among themselves. Valachi spoke exactly like the low-level hoods in low-budget crime movies, right down to pronouncing "th" as "t" so that "breath" and "death" became "bret" and "det." In 1971, the year before *The Godfather* opened, Joe Colombo, head of one of New York's leading crime families, was the victim of an assassination attempt at New York's Columbus Circle, which left him paralyzed for the rest of his life. The hit had been authorized by Mafia boss Carlo Gambino, who believed Colombo had called too much attention to the Cosa Nostra through the Italian-American Civil Rights League. The organization, more mythic than real, was allegedly Colombo's attempt to refurbish the image of Italian-Americans and shore up ethnic pride by downplaying the role of the Mafia to the point of denying its very existence. Since no one believed Colombo, it was not only a futile gesture; it also robbed him of his mobility.

To say that *The Godfather* appeared at the right time is to offer only one explanation for its popularity. Other films were similarly well-timed yet shunned by the public. One would have thought that *My Son John* (1952), a rabidly anti-Communist tract in which a Catholic mother (Helen Hayes) discovers that her intellectual son (Robert Walker) has become a Communist, would have attracted a wider audience; it appeared at a time when Senator McCarthy was insisting that subversives had infiltrated even the State Department and the military. While there are many reasons for *The Godfather*'s success (exclusive of its art), humankind's perennial fascination with the dark side of family dynasties (as distinct from criminal organizations) cannot be ruled out. It was the same fascination that inspired Aeschylus, Sophocles, and Euripides to take on the House of Atreus with its manifold crimes (infanticide, homicide, human sacrifice, and matricide) and make them, however reprehensible, consistent with the nature of the perpetrators.[9] But since the dramatic versions of the House of Atreus were all mythic, theatergoers could console themselves with the knowledge that Agamemnon's family was not like their own. Unlike life, myth is secure because it provides a buffer between the familiar and the fantastic.

The Godfather tapped into something deeper than an audience's historical awareness; it appealed to its sense of myth, recalling themes, characters, and situations that, depending on one's view of Carl Jung, derive either from the collective unconscious or, more simply, from an immediate identification with the archetypes we have all encountered earlier in fairy tales, folklore, children's stories (which are often allegorical, like "The Tale of the Runaway Bunny"), and even dreams. One does not have to be versed in classical mythology to understand the nature of vengeance, even when exacted by family members against their own. When Carlo Rizzi marries Don Corleone's daughter, Connie, he does not merely become a member of a family, acquiring Michael and Sonny Corleone as brothers-in-law, but of a family that observes *omertà*. When Carlo betrays Sonny, causing his death, he must die—kin or not. In one of the most brilliant examples of crosscutting in film, Michael, now a literal godfather as well as a symbolic one, is at the baptism of Connie's child, who will also be called Michael. While Michael is renouncing Satan, the assassination he has ordered is taking place, resulting in the deaths of various enemies, including the stigmatized Rizzi.

Such interfamilial killing is natural in the primordial world of myth. After Agamemnon sacrifices his daughter Iphigenia to get a fair wind to continue on to Troy, he is hacked to death on his return by his wife Clytemnestra; she, in turn, is killed by her son Orestes, who has no other choice but to avenge his father's murder. Clytemnestra's motives (Iphigenia's ritual slaughter; Clytemnestra's preference for her new lover, Aegisthus; Agamemnon's return from the war with a mistress, Cassandra) in a more civilized setting might have been considered circumstances placing Agamemnon's murder in a human context without condoning it. But there is no humanity in a universe that allows nothing to go unavenged and grants the avenger considerable latitude in both the nature and extent of his revenge.

The Corleones inhabit a universe where a request is a mandate, which, if ignored, results in a punishment far in excess of the action. When a Hollywood producer refuses to grant the don's request that his godson, Johnny Fontane, be cast in his next film, the producer awakens to find the head of his favorite horse in bed with him. Similarly, when Minos decided to keep the prize bull that Poseidon had sent him from the sea and sacrifice another instead, Poseidon caused Minos's wife, Pasiphae, to lust after the bull and conceive an offspring, the Minotaur. Retribution in myth is never a case of like for like; because such retribution even transcends conventional morality, it has no place in a society where justice is tempered by mercy. However, to the Corleones, neither society nor justice has evolved to such a degree. Theirs is a world the Greeks would have understood, one in which even an act committed in ignorance, like Oedipus's unintentional killing of his father, leads not just to his wife-mother's suicide and his own self-blinding but also to his sons' fratricidal deaths and his daughter's suicide by hanging—the same method employed by her mother. All this happened because Oedipus's parents chose to ignore a prophecy that any male child they conceived was destined to kill his father and marry his mother. Likewise, in *The Godfather*, Michael, once he chooses to play avenger, becomes the victim of his own decision, with each act of vengeance steeping him deeper in blood until revenge becomes so automatic that it supplants free will.

The Godfather had such broad appeal that it became the first R-rated family film, forcing parents to distinguish between hard and soft "R" movies (*Death Wish* [1974] being hard "R"; *Saturday Night Fever* [1977], soft as well as another family favorite). Had *The Godfather* been directed by someone like Kazan, who had been working in Hollywood since 1944 and on Broadway since the mid-1930s, it might have lacked the passion and vitality that a comparatively inexperienced director, producer, and cast brought to the film. It was the relative youth of the company in which everyone except Brando was unencumbered by a persona that allowed Coppola and Puzo to proceed as if there was no precedent for what they were doing, since other Mafia movies such as *The Black Hand* (1950) and *Pay or Die* (1960) had nothing in common with the family dynasty epic they were making. There was also nothing in the work of either Coppola or Puzo to suggest they could bring it off.

Just as Puzo's first two novels gave no indication that *The Godfather* was in the offing, neither did Coppola's first four films: *Dementia 13* (1963, horror), *You're a Big Boy Now* (1966, screwball), *Finian's Rainbow* (1968, musical fantasy), and *The Rain People* (1969, romantic melodrama). Nor was the cast especially promising—at least on paper. Although Al Pacino (Michael Corleone), age thirty-three, had worked in the theater, he had only one film credit, *Panic in Needle Park* (1971), in which he played a heroin addict. James Caan (Sonny Corleone), age thirty-four, was slightly more experienced, having been in movies since 1963. Yet most viewers would have associated him not with *Lady in a Cage* (1964) or *T.R. Baskin* (1971) but with the TV movie, *Brian's Song* (1971), in which he portrayed football player Brian Piccolo, whose death from cancer ended a promising career. Diane Keaton, age twenty-eight, who played Michael's second wife, Kay, had only done *Lovers and Other Strangers* (1970). Compared to the others, the forty–year-old Robert Duvall (lawyer Tom Hagen), who had entered the business in 1962, was a veteran with thirteen films to prove it; like Caan, Duvall was a *Rain People* alumnus. John Cazale ("Fredo" Corleone), age thirty-three, was another newcomer, with only two other films on his resumé.

If there is any further proof that Paramount originally regarded *The Godfather* as a low-budget mob movie, it was the studio's choice of producer: Albert S. Ruddy, age thirty-six, who had produced Paramount's unmemorable *Little Fauss and Big Halsy* (1970). Ruddy was hired either because he was perceived as being able to make a movie on the cheap (as he did in his debut film) or because he had also produced the successful 1960s television series *Hogan's Heroes*, inspired by the Paramount classic,

Billy Wilder's *Stalag 17* (1953). Whatever the reason, Ruddy was only a few years older than Coppola (then thirty-two) and most of the leads, with the exception of the forty-seven-year-old Marlon Brando.

Initially, Coppola was Brando's only champion, so much so that he feigned an epileptic seizure to get Stanley Jaffe to relent and at least allow the actor to test for the part of the don. Jaffe added other conditions, including working for scale. For six weeks of work and a percentage of the film, Brando did not do badly: $1.5 million.[10]

Because of his relative inexperience, Coppola needed an expert director of photography, which he found in Gordon Willis, also a relatively new arrival but soon to become one of the industry's major cinematographers. Willis's genius is even more evident in *The Godfather Part II*, which, visually, is one of the glories of the American screen. As temperamental an artist as Coppola, Willis understood that low-intensity lighting would give *The Godfather* a visual style consistent with a family that moved within two worlds: the sunlit and the crepuscular. The don's study looked as if the frames had been stained in a forbidding brown, suggesting a chamber where one of the Borgias would have held conversations never intended for the ears of others.

That *The Godfather* was Paramount's highest-grossing film of the 1970s was due to a convergence of talent, not all of which was ever intended for the project, that meshed in such a way as to produce a work of art. Conversely, *The Brotherhood* looked authentic only in the few scenes shot in Sicily, where the action begins and ends (all else being a flashback). *The Godfather* was the genuine article for all of its 175 minutes. First, there was a deliberate effort to involve as many Italians as possible in the production: director-screenwriter Francis Ford Coppola; coauthor Puzo; actors such as Al Pacino, John Cazale, Richard Castellano, Talia Shire (Coppola's sister), Richard Conte, and Al Martino; and composer Nino Rota, to cite the most important. And if it seemed odd that jazz singer Morgana King was playing Mama Corleone, she was working, as she always did, under her stage name. She was christened Maria Grazia Morgana Messina de Bernardinis.[11]

The Godfather was not cast entirely with Italian-American actors. Actually, Al Pacino was the only one in a leading role, the others being members of the supporting cast or extras. James Caan was hired to play Michael's brother, Sonny. Caan's being a Jew was irrelevant; Edward G. Robinson and Paul Muni were both Jews but gave thoroughly convincing performances in *Little Caesar* (1930) and *Scarface* (1932), respectively, as Italian gangsters modeled after Al Capone. What mattered was that Caan looked and acted as if he were a Corleone (and one whose brother could easily be Al Pacino). It was quite different in *The Brotherhood*, where viewers were expected to think of Kirk Douglas and Alex Cord as having had the same father. There were two other characters—Irish lawyer Tom Hagen and Michael's second wife, Kay, a New England WASP—that probably could have been played by nonethnic looking Italian-Americans, but none were seriously considered for the roles that went to Robert Duvall and Diane Keaton.

Jaffe's wisest decision was allowing the Omaha-born, Christian Scientist–raised Marlon Brando to play Vito Corleone, although apparently Laurence Olivier had been a candidate for the part. If Olivier's Jewish-accented Shylock in *The Merchant of Venice*, which he played on the London stage in 1970, was any indication, there would have been authenticity to spare—but the kind that comes from a voice that has mastered the character's inflections, not necessarily the character. Brando's raspy drawl and internalized speech, sounding as it were emanating from a cavern within himself, proved that the actor who played Stanley Kowalski, Napoleon Bonaparte, Mark Antony, and Emilio Zapata could now add Vito Corleone to his portrait gallery.

If it is true that the filming took place in the midst of threats, bomb scares, and general harassment,[12] with some Italian-Americans threatening a boycott because *The Godfather* glorified the Mafia ("mythologized" is the better word), the answer is the film itself. *The Godfather* is so family-centered that the only difference between the Corleones and the folks next door is their business, which extends beyond importing olive oil, and their code of honor, which requires extreme measures to be taken when it is violated. Since the Corleones never thought of themselves as belonging to the Mafia (a term used only by outsiders), "Mafia" is used only once in the film—and not by one of the Family. "Family" in either the singular or plural (e.g., The Five Families) was the expression of choice.

The Corleones had both a uniqueness and a universality that allowed viewers to distance themselves from the particulars and respond instead to what is common to all families: the ebb and flow of affection, tension, conflict, estrangement, exile, and rapprochement, with a rhythm that is never uniform but always erratic—and in the case of the Corleones, wildly so.

It is also a rhythm that is operatic. Operaphobes who saw *The Godfather* never suspected they were experiencing opera without the customary arias and ensembles but with set pieces that are now legendary (the horse's head, Michael emerging from the men's room ready for revenge, a baptism intercut with a hit, the don's death amid the tomato plants) enclosed within a libretto with which Verdi could have worked wonders. *The Godfather*, which cost $6.2 million, is a tribute to Coppola's artistic deviousness, which, by 1998, had netted Paramount $86.7 million.

When Dino De Laurentiis discovered that Paramount owned the rights to *The Godfather* even before it was published, he set his sights on another book that appeared in 1969—a nonfiction work published three months before *The Godfather*: Peter Maas's *The Valachi Papers*, based on interviews with informant Joseph Valachi.

Filmed at Dinocittà before Dino's dream evaporated in receivership, *The Valachi Papers* had an even more provocative title in Italy: *Joe Valachi: I Segreti di Cosa Nostra* ("*Joe Valachi: The Secrets of the Cosa Nostra*"). Since De Laurentiis's easy access to money occasioned rumors that the Dino De Laurentiis Corporation was a Mafia front, producing *The Valachi Papers* might have seemed a brave move; at least that is what De Laurentiis hoped the public would believe: "When I did 'The Valachi Papers,' Mafia come to me and say-a, 'Dino, no do,' but I do."[13] The only Cosa Nostra members who might have been offended by the film were those—if any existed—who were sensitive to on-screen violence. *The Valachi Papers* was on the order of the semi-documentaries of the late 1940s (e.g., *Call Northside 777* [1948], *The Naked City* [1948]), only bloodier. The "*segreti*," if any were to be divulged, were not apparent. Although real names were used in the film (Joe Valachi, Albert Anastasia, "Lucky" Luciano), these had already appeared in Maas's book and were well-known to the public. *The Valachi Papers*, released in November 1972, had only one thing in common with *The Godfather*, which had enjoyed a prestigious five-theater opening eight months earlier: an "R" rating. Since Paramount was not about to release two films on the same subject, De Laurentiis had Columbia distribute *The Valachi Papers*, as it had *Barabbas*, *Kiss the Girls and Make Them Die* (1967), *Anzio* (1968), and *A Man Called Sledge* (1971).

Knowing that *The Valachi Papers* would invite comparison with *The Godfather*, De Laurentiis prepared a six-page statement for an unspecified readership, arguing that the films were complementary, rather like a two-way mirror, each reflecting a different image of the Cosa Nostra.[14] The text was really a self-advertisement with De Laurentiis arguing that, in the past, the Mafia had never tried to suppress films that portrayed it unfavorably (as if there were that many) but had now taken offense at *The Valachi Papers* for supposedly stripping it of its mystique. The organization

(Mafia, Cosa Nostra, syndicate, or the euphemism of the month), however, never lost its mystique; no movie could accomplish such a feat. Taken together, both films may have succeeded in educating audiences about hits and payoffs, vendettas with ghoulish scenarios, favors granted and denied, hand-kissings, closed-door conferences, and a hierarchy of dons, consiglieri, and capos. Yet neither completely tore away the veil of mystery, although *The Godfather* succeeded in revealing the organization's protocols and codes without reducing them to articles in a manual. Still, the organization the world calls "Mafia" continues to live up to the name its members use among themselves: *cosa nostra,* "our thing"—not one to be shared with the public.

De Laurentiis was right on one point: *The Valachi Papers* was based on fact; *The Godfather,* on myth; the former "explodes the Mafia phenomenon *from within* … *The Godfather* … *from without.*"[15] Indirectly, De Laurentiis was suggesting that myth has greater drawing power than fact, as *The Godfather* grosses and awards (three Oscars, including Best Actor and Best Picture) proved, and *The Valachi Papers* did not.

Filming of *The Godfather* began at the end of March 1971 in and around New York City, including Queens, Staten Island, and Long Island. Perhaps it was wise for the company to be three thousand miles away from the studio, since a transaction had just been completed that would eventually amount to little but at the time augured ill for Paramount's future: the sale of half of the lot and the reconfiguration of the Marathon Street property. As it happened, there was neither a sale nor a reconfiguration. But the idea of selling even half of the lot indicated that Bluhdorn and Davis considered Paramount as nothing more than a fifty-two–acre property.

When Gulf + Western went searching for a buyer, Bluhdorn must have prepared the list of eligibles. Only he could have come up with an Italian real estate and construction company on whose board of directors sat the mysterious Michele Sindona.

In spring 1970, shortly after production had been relocated in Beverly Hills, Bluhdorn was deep in negotiations with Sindona, his Sicilian counterpart. The stock swap that would give Società Generale Immobiliare half of the Paramount lot would also give Bluhdorn a seat on Immobiliare's board of directors, where he would join his new *compare.* It was inevitable that Bluhdorn would not only meet Sindona but also do business with him. Since both men moved in a shadow world, Sindona's being darker and more ominous, their paths would eventually cross.

Exactly when Bluhdorn became aware of Sindona is uncertain, but by 1964 it would have been impossible for an acquirer of companies like Bluhdorn to be ignorant of someone so like himself. In early autumn 1964, *Time* magazine carried a piece on Sindona that linked Sindona's unswerving commitment to capitalism (and, conversely, his loathing of socialism) with his concept of history.[16] A student of Machiavelli, the subject of his thesis at the University of Messina, where he specialized in tax law, Sindona saw a connection between Machiavelli's belief that nations undergo cycles of prosperity and adversity and his own (not terribly original) theory that some countries experience economic growth while others stagnate. Thus Sindona did not limit himself to acquisitions in a single country. By 1964, he was involved as president, vice president, or director of companies in Italy, Britain, France, Switzerland, and the United States.

First, Sindona acquired a controlling interest in a company such as the Chicago-based food packager, Libby, McNeill and Libby. That was in 1963; the following year, it was Brown, the ailing New Hampshire paper and plywood company. It was Sindona's practice to invest in troubled companies and turn them around, then sell them at a profit or have them distribute another product. If none of these methods worked, he would spread a former owner's stock around in various Sindona-controlled companies, as was learned several years after Sindona's death, when Vatican stock from a Geneva-based pharmaceutical company specializing in fertility drugs found its way into the outposts of Sindona's empire.[17]

It was the Brown takeover that brought Sindona to Bluhdorn's attention. Paper and plywood, like zinc ore and batteries, were commodities Bluhdorn understood. In 1967, when Sindona's attempt to merge Brown with the Riegel Paper Corporation ran up against antitrust laws, Bluhdorn arranged for a meeting with Sindona in Rome, a city Bluhdorn loved; it was also accessible to Sindona, who lived in Milan where he practiced tax law; finally, it was the home of Dino De Laurentiis Cinematografica. Paramount had been distributing De Laurentiis's films since 1955 and continued doing so throughout the Bluhdorn years: *Barbarella* (1968), *Danger: Diabolik* (1968), *The Violent Four* (1968), *Fraulein Doktor* (1969), *Waterloo* (1971), *Serpico* (1973), *Three Tough Guys* (1974), *Mandingo* (1975), *Three Days of the Condor* (1975), *King Kong* (1986), *Face to Face* (1976), *Lipstick* (1976), *The Serpent's Egg* (1978), *Hurricane* (1979), *Ragtime* (1981), *Fighting Back* (1982), and *Dead Zone* (1983)—the last released the year of Bluhdorn's death.

De Laurentiis, however, had known Sindona earlier; around the same time as Bluhdorn's meeting with Sindona, De Laurentiis was able to prevail upon Sindona for a $1 million loan to relocate in New York. De Laurentiis's idea of relocation was a Central Park South duplex within walking distance of his office on the fifteenth floor of the Gulf + Western building on Columbus Circle.[18]

Like Bluhdorn and Sindona, De Laurentiis was a seasoned traveler in the netherworld of the deal. The Hollywood netherworld, however, was different; while there were many winding corridors, each maneuverable with varying degrees of difficulty, there was one that led to the main chamber, where a presence even darker than De Laurentiis held court: Sidney Korshak, mob lawyer and deus ex machina for friends in need. It was not surprising that De Laurentiis knew Korshak; although they were not cut from the same cloth, they seem to have had the same tailor.

To the FBI, Korshak was "the most important contact that the mob had to legitimate business, labor, Hollywood, and Las Vegas."[19] When Robert Evans, who referred to Korshak as "my *consigliere,*" wanted Al Pacino for Michael in *The Godfather,* he discovered that the actor had signed to do a film at MGM. A call to Korshak, who only required the proper spelling of Pacino's name, resolved the problem.[20] When MCA's Lew Wasserman and De Laurentiis became embroiled in a dispute over remaking *King Kong,* Korshak mediated—at a price, of course. By paying Korshak twenty-five thousand dollars or thereabouts, De Laurentiis produced *King Kong* (1976) for Paramount, although Korshak and Wasserman were known to be the best of friends.[21]

With such a formidable trio as Bluhdorn, De Laurentiis, and Korshak operating at Gulf + Western, Sindona had come to the right company. When he and Bluhdorn met in early January 1968 to discuss the sale of Brown to Gulf + Western, it was the beginning of an association that would eventually lead to Sindona's foray into Paramount real estate. By the end of February, the deal had been completed; the Brown stock, for which Sindona had paid $9.4 million, cost Gulf + Western $15.5 million.[22]

If it is true that "of all the men he came to do business with, Sindona admired none more than he did Charles Bluhdorn,"[23] it was probably because Bluhdorn was an alter ego, an entrepreneur like himself who believed in free enterprise and resisted any attempt on the part of the government to interfere with what he considered a natural consequence of capitalism. Bluhdorn would have agreed, although he could never have appreciated the amount of reading that had brought Sindona to that conclusion.

Michele Sindona was one of the few criminals ever sentenced to life imprisonment who could legitimately be called an intellectual. Even Nathan Leopold, a fellow Nietschean, lacked Sindona's breadth of knowledge. Born in a small Sicilian town in 1930, Sindona seemed destined to be a scholar. He developed an affinity for Latin, which stood him in good stead when he became a tax lawyer and used his knowledge of the language to translate arcane laws that, interpreted properly, proved enormously beneficial to his clients. But his love of Latin went beyond the mere language; it extended to such authors as Virgil and Cicero. Similarly, his Italian was not merely a vehicle of communication but a means of understanding Dante and especially Machiavelli, on whom he wrote his thesis at the University of Messina, from which he graduated in 1942. While he continued to immerse himself in other writers such as Nietzsche, Adam Smith, and Pascal, it was Machiavelli who most influenced him.

Sindona's obsession with accumulating wealth by acquiring controlling interests in companies was an outgrowth of Machiavelli's belief in the consolidation of power. Empires thrive by planting colonies, creating extensions of themselves and producing dutiful children doing the will of the mother country–parent. But Sindona, a student of Roman history as well as of Machiavelli, knew that, beginning with the Roman Empire, the *princeps*, as the so-called "emperor" chose to be called, wielded the *imperium,* or supreme command. Thus, if Sindona were to be the equivalent of a Roman *imperator*, one of the emperor's many titles, he would first have to found his empire, which he did with a Geneva-based holding company, and then colonize to provide the empire with revenues, tributes, and booty, which he did through his numerous acquisitions.

Sindona's classical education gave him access to the Vatican, which has always regarded Latin as a living language despite its so-called death. In the late 1950s, Sindona, now widely respected as a tax advisor, made it possible for the Istituto per le Opere di Religione (IOR), known (perhaps inaccurately) as "the Vatican Bank," to establish a presence in Italy's financial capital, Milan, by purchasing the stock of Banca Privata in a complex arrangement that left Sindona with a 20 percent stake.

Like Bluhdorn's, Sindona's interests were far-ranging: pharmaceuticals, textiles, publishing, metals, real estate—anything that seemed like a good investment. He would either purchase shares in a company or act as intermediary in a sale, merger, or write-off. Thus in 1970, Bluhdorn, who had seriously considered unloading Paramount a few years earlier, proposed a deal enabling him to buy into SCI through a holding company partially owned by Sindona and for Sindona to get the half of Paramount lot. The arrangement has been variously described, but one thing it was not was a sale of Paramount Studios. Bluhdorn's proposal came at the right time. Since the Italian government had decided to tax the dividends of Vatican stocks, the Vatican relinquished its controlling interest in SGI. Sindona negotiated a sale of practically all of the Vatican's shares, which went to Bluhdorn, along with a seat on the SGI board, in exchange for a 50 percent share in *Darling Lili*, for which Paramount had high hopes that were later dashed.[24]

Sindona was not the type to "go Hollywood," as Bluhdorn had done. The glamour part of the industry meant nothing to Sindona, who thought movies were lowbrow. He particularly deplored Paramount's decision to film *The Godfather*, which, he felt, betrayed the inner workings of an organization that prided itself on secrecy. If Italians, mafiosi or otherwise, were indicted as criminals, their sentences would be far more severe—which is what happened in Sindona's case. For Sindona, the lot meant real estate and perhaps hotels such as SGI's Meurice and Grand in Paris, and the Watergate complex in Washington, D.C.

By 1975, the Bluhdorn-Sindona deal had unraveled. The reasons will probably never be known. Either the alleged sale never went through (Paramount stated earlier that nothing would be finalized until a long-range study had been completed), or—more likely—Sindona's financial and legal problems had become so apparent, especially to the SEC, that Paramount used them as an excuse to bow out, particularly since the SEC was checking into Gulf + Western's affairs.

The SEC had been investigating irregularities at Gulf + Western since 1974, but it was not until 1979 that formal charges were made, among which were undisclosed profits for sugar revenues, stock transfers to make losses look like profits, and an outrageous scheme to turn Blake Edwards's *Darling Lili* (1970) into a profitable film—one that was originally budgeted at $11 million, gradually climbed to $16.5 million, and ended up costing over $20 million—a high price for a flop.[25] Given his penchant for films with European settings, Bluhdorn probably greenlighted *Darling Lili*; then, when he sensed it would be a disaster, assumed it might have greater appeal abroad, particularly in Britain, because of its star, Julie Andrews, who played a German spy masquerading as an English music hall performer during World War I.

Gulf + Western then struck a deal with Commonwealth United Entertainment (UK), in which the rights to *Darling Lili* would be exchanged in return for $31.2 million in Commonwealth United debentures and a $10 million promissory note. When Commonwealth United suffered a financial crisis, rather than acknowledge the loss, Gulf + Western substituted income from other transactions and continued to carry the debentures on the books at $31.2 million, even though their market value was only 1 percent of that amount.

Among other questionable transactions was the Immobiliare deal, in which the sale of half the lot to SGI International was listed at $15 million and recorded as gain, while it should have been applied to the loss incurred from the Commonwealth United fiasco. Gulf + Western had incorporated the Marathon lot as a subsidiary of Paramount, thereby divorcing the studio from the property on which it was located. Various assets were then transferred to Marathon Studio Facilities, with a reported gain of fifty thousand dollars.

At first, Bluhdorn denied the charges, insisting that Gulf + Western had been in compliance with SEC regulations. Although the SEC pressed on, Bluhdorn stood firm. Finally, in 1981, Gulf + Western and the SEC settled their differences, with the company neither admitting nor denying fraudulent activity. All that happened was that Gulf + Western agreed in the future to adhere to the SEC rules governing financial reporting.

Sindona was less fortunate. The 1970s were the beginning of the end for him. Shortly after Sindona finished doing business with Bluhdorn, he turned to New York's Franklin National Bank, paying Loews Corporation $40 million for a 21.6 percent stake. He had picked the wrong year: in 1972, the economy was in disarray, and Sindona's pyramid, built on an unstable foundation of financial irregularities and fraud, began to crumble, starting with Franklin National, whose collapse in 1974 set off a chain reaction: SGI stocks fell, Sindona's banks in Italy were wrested from his control, and the Vatican lost about $30 million.[26]

Machiavelli believed that success is dependent on *fortuna* and *virtù*: luck, the incalculable element in life, and the untranslatable *virtù*, best understood as a combination of ability, initiative, and hard work. Until 1974, Sindona had the winning combination; then *fortuna* failed him, perhaps because his *virtù* had been weakened, if not corrupted, by his dream of being an economic autocrat, the *princeps* of Wall Street to whom no door was ever closed.

Instead of becoming the world's premier capitalist, Sindona had now become its victim. In 1980 the sixty–year-old Sindona was sentenced to three twenty-five–year terms and one twenty-four–year term.

And this was just in the United States. In Italy, he was convicted of contracting the murder of Dr. Giorgio Ambrosoli, the Milanese lawyer appointed to investigate the bank failures in Italy. On 18 March 1986, a Milan court sentenced him to life imprisonment. Two days later, Sindona went into a coma and subsequently died; the cause of death was cyanide poisoning. Potassium cyanide—laced morning coffee is a method favored by the Mafia to silence prisoners who know too much. Or perhaps it was suicide, which Sindona had attempted in New York the previous year by slashing his wrists. One will never know.

Although Sindona prided himself on being a disciple of Machiavelli, he might have remembered that the master's examples were drawn from classical and Renaissance sources, offering only general principles for survival in the twentieth century. Machiavelli's famous comparison of the lion and the fox seems to have eluded him. While Sindona had the cunning of a fox, he ended up being bagged like a lion because of a character flaw that another sixteenth-century writer, greater than Machiavelli, had isolated earlier. Of all of Shakespeare's tragedies, the one most applicable to Sindona was *Macbeth*. Just as the witches spun a web around Macbeth that eventually entrapped him, bankers, cardinals, lawyers, counts, and mobsters lured Sindona into one with more strands that any dramatist could envision. Given the same material, Shakespeare would have reduced the number of villains and clarified the action so that the story line had linearity. But Shakespeare at least offers the best explanation of Sindona's tragic flaw, or what Sindona the classicist would have called the Achilles heel, the vulnerable spot he looked for in others, not realizing that he had his own: "I have no spur/To prick the sides of my intent, but only/Vaulting ambition" (*Macbeth* 1,8). Sindona would have agreed about the nature of his ambition, but, as he watched his empire fall, he must have realized, like Macbeth, that there was no turning back: "I am in blood/steeped in so far that, should I wade no more/Returning were as tedious as go o'er" (3,4).

Charlie Bluhdorn had fascinating business partners, but none more so than Michele Sindona (1930–86).

6

The Diller Days

Bluhdorn was obsessed with finding a surrogate son. Eventually, he found one in Barry Diller. In the meantime, Bluhdorn had to settle for Frank Yablans, who appealed to him for different reasons. There was no way Bluhdorn could wax paternalistic about Yablans. With Yablans, it was a question of background, not age. Yablans, who was born in 1935, was nine years younger than Bluhdorn; Bluhdorn was older than Robert Evans, who was born in 1930. Evans, however, inspired fatherly feelings in Bluhdorn, who was more influenced by appearance than age. Evans conformed to the surrogate son model more than did the aggressive, fiercely independent Yablans. When Bluhdorn first met Evans, the latter was an actor-on-the-verge-of-becoming-a-producer with matinee idol looks; he was also in his mid-thirties but seemed considerably younger to the forty-year-old Bluhdorn, who appeared to have bypassed youth, as if residing in a no-man's land between birth and death.

Professionally, Yablans was cut from a totally different cloth: distribution, a field he had entered in the late 1950s as a Warner Bros. salesman. Although a distribution background was never considered a prerequisite for running a studio, it was by no means a drawback; in fact, it could even be a vertical move if, within the distributor, there was a producer waiting to emerge; in that case, distribution was only a transitional phase.

There is nothing uniform about distribution; it is a diverse field embracing the various strategies used to package a film from its inception to its release. While sales falls under the distribution rubric, so does strategic marketing, which is far more specialized; for example, determining release dates by taking into consideration such factors as genre, time of year, and competing product; deciding on wide or limited release; creating tie-ins (merchandizing novelizations, T-shirts, toys, soundtracks); and creating press kits. Preparing a press kit, however, is not the same as schmoozing with the exhibitors for whom the kit has been prepared. Similarly, the sales pitch Willy Loman used on the road in his heyday—which is never dramatized in *Death of a Salesman,* even in flashback—would never have worked on the floor. A traveling salesman like Willy would never have understood the difference. To Willy, selling meant "a smile and a shoeshine."

In film, the product is often intangible; it is the difference between peddling a dream and an article of clothing like women's stockings, one of Willy's specialties. A film might not even be ready for viewing or, if it is, has yet to be screened; it exists within the glossy kit amid the stills and studio bios designed to hook the exhibitor. And what the kit cannot accomplish, the sales staff must by using the rhetoric of the pitch: reducing the film to either a label ("actioner," "erotic thriller") or a concept (a descriptive summation in no more than twenty-five words).

Historically, marketing and sales have always been distinct in the sense of publicizing the product as opposed to pitching it. Until the 1970s, marketing and sales personnel—distribution people in general—labored under a veil of anonymity: one saw the ads and, if invited to a screening, came away with a kit; but the film was the thing. Producers were even better known than directors of publicity and marketing, who were rarely quoted in the press except for movies that either needed hype or could use more. However, when Sid Ganis, who had been in distribution and marketing before joining Paramount in 1988 as president of the motion picture group (a new name for an old job), was asked about the role two often overlapping activities play in moviemaking, he was uncommonly clear without being technical: "If you think of [filmmaking] as a triangle, production is on top . . . and marketing and distribution anchor the triangle."[1]

Ganis was making a distinction that, if implemented properly, could result in a model studio, even one existing concentrically within the corporate circle. Getting fifteen hundred prints of a film into theaters is one thing; getting 15 million people to see it is another. In Hollywood, distribution, in all its aspects, was rivaling production in importance. *Close Encounters of the Third Kind* (1977) cost $18 million to shoot and $9 million to market. Increasingly, it cost about half as much to distribute a film as to make it.

This had not been the case three decades earlier. Although budget breakdowns did not include distribution categories as such, they did reveal, for example, how much publicity or stills might have cost. The Bette Davis vehicle, *Dark Victory* (1939), cost approximately eight hundred thousand dollars, which placed it within the five-hundred-thousand- to 1–million- dollar range of most Warner Bros. films—$1 million and above meaning big bucks and big budget. Of that $800,000, there was a $150,000 miscellaneous category comprising publicity, sound operations, music, properties, incidental labor, travel, and meals.[2] What "publicity" probably meant—on the West Coast, at least—was stills, posters, and the all-important trailer. Naturally, Warner Bros.' New York office, where distribution was based, had its own budget for promotional materials (such as press kits, and newspaper and magazine ads). Even so, it is inconceivable that marketing expenses for *Dark Victory* would have reached anywhere near half the budget. Of course, merchandise tie-ins had not yet come into vogue, so marketing was less complex and costly. What mattered in the case of *Dark Victory* was spending money to develop the script ($85,000), cast it ($225,000 for actors and director), and give it the right look in terms of lighting, decor, costumes, and makeup ($360,000). In 1939, marketing meant newspaper and magazine ads, press kits, posters, lobby cards, one- and two-sheets, etc. It did not mean making movie-related paraphernalia available to tourists and theme store shoppers. A studio president (or motion picture group chairman) who came out of distribution would appreciate, for example, how certain kinds of films fare better in one season than in another (science fiction in summer, epics in winter) and how some require a "platform" or staggered release policy to build an audience, while others are given the saturation treatment, reaching fifteen hundred screens on the first day.

Yablans could have fit into Bluhdorn's Paramount, where distribution was assuming an increasingly greater role. To Bluhdorn, Yablans was a welcome relief after Jaffe, whose inability to suffer fools had become legendary; it even extended to Bluhdorn himself, to whom Jaffe was often unconscionably rude. Although Jaffe later invoked his relative youth when explaining his behavior, the truth was that he was a brilliant executive whose displays of temper were sometimes natural, sometimes rehearsed. Jaffe was known to practice rage in order to program himself into an aggressive mode.

Yablans was too ingenuous to fake temperament; his came naturally. Born on New York's Lower East Side and raised in the Williamsburg section of Brooklyn, Yablans was unencumbered by Jaffe's family connections and educational baggage. His father was a taxi driver, and his mother believed that chicken soup solved most of life's problems.

Yablans was also not that different from Bluhdorn. He was a hustler who had started in sales, first as a Warner Bros. trainee in 1956. Two years later, he was Warner's regional manager for Illinois and Wisconsin. By 1969 he had moved to Paramount as assistant general sales manager. Upon becoming national sales manager the following year, he consolidated the publicity and advertising departments on the principle that they were not distinct but complementary. Bluhdorn then began to take notice of Yablans; he was amazed at how aggressively Yablans promoted the mediocre *Paint Your Wagon*.[3] When Yablans did the same for *Darling Lili,* he grew in Bluhdorn's estimation and, as he did, so did his rank: vice president, sales (April 1970); senior vice president, marketing (October 1970); executive vice president (April 1971); and then president and COO (late spring 1971).

Yablans's career was either a case of too much, too soon or too much at any given time. The pace at which he advanced is the stuff of which resumés are made; and while Yablans had every reason to feel flattered, his promotions should have culminated in head of marketing, not studio president.

Jaffe had spoiled Bluhdorn. It was not that Jaffe exuded sophistication but rather than he wore the mantle of his father; and while it was a far-from-perfect fit, it still trailed behind him. Yablans had no such legacy but, then, neither did Bluhdorn, who, despite a cultured French wife and awkward attempts at being worldly wise, was a supremely successful vulgarian.

Regardless, Yablans had to look, play, and especially sound the game. He was given diction lessons, dressed in tailor-made clothes, and ensconced in the northeast corner on the thirty-third floor of the Gulf + Western building, where he sat at a desk in a split-level office looking at least six inches taller than 5 feet, eight inches, his actual height. This was an old technique used by, among other less-than-tall moguls, Harry Cohn, who had his desk on a one-inch riser so that those entering would have to look up at Harry, who, in turn, would look down on them.

Since Yablans was a New Yorker, he remained within commuting distance of his office. A Brooklyn address, however, was as undesirable as a Brooklyn accent. Like Jaffe, Yablans commuted from Westchester County— but from the more affluent suburb of Scarsdale. But he neither drove to work nor took the train: he arrived at Gulf + Western Plaza in a chauffeured limousine. And as he became more involved in production matters, he moved to Beverly Hills.

Yablans was beginning to enjoy the perks that included lunch at restaurants like New York's "21" Club and La Grenouille. If he was behaving like a nouveau riche, it is because he had newly discovered the riches that were his for the taking. To Yablans, tailored suits and luncheons at fashionable restaurants were insignia that implied greatness without the need for any further explanation.

While Yablans had no trouble enjoying his new position, he was by no means living off the fat of Gulf + Western. As soon as he came on board, he had to confront the beast known as the budget. Here his background in sales stood him in good stead, since he obviously knew what films cost, either from sources within the industry or by inference. For 1972, he set a conservative budget of $25 million. Never expecting *The Godfather* to be the hit it was, he allocated $5 million for the film, once budgeted at $1 million; it ended up costing more—and making more—for Paramount.

Yablans happened to be at Paramount at a time that is often called Hollywood's Second Golden Age—the 1970s, when the emergence of such directors as Francis Ford Coppola, Martin Scorsese, Steven Spielberg, and Peter Bogdanovich heralded a film renascence. The 1970s was also the decade, arguably the last, when the auteur theory held sway. Any college student taking an introductory film course was exposed to auteurism, popularized by Andrew Sarris, which enshrined the director as the creative force behind a film. Thus it became fashionable to cite not only a classic like *Psycho* in the possessive case ("Alfred Hitchcock's *Psycho* [1960]") but also the works of lesser directors ("Edgar G. Ulmer's *Detour* [1946]"). Monographs and articles on the great, near-great, and never-great abounded, as did director-centered courses.

Even before Yablans replaced Jaffe in 1971, it was common knowledge that some young directors in Hollywood were revitalizing the American cinema, creating what is called both the Second Golden Age, or, less hyperbolically, the New American Wave. Three in particular interested Bluhdorn: Bogdanovich, Coppola, and William Friedkin, all of whom were the same age, having been born in 1939. By 1972, each had racked up one commercial and critical success: Friedkin's *The French Connection* won the Oscar for Best Picture of 1971; Bogdanovich's *The Last Picture Show* (1971) won in the categories of Best Supporting Actress and Actor (Cloris Leachman and Ben Johnson) and introduced audiences to Timothy Bottoms, Randy Quaid, and Jeff Bridges. Bogdanovich was also obsessed with film, having published interviews with John Ford (1967),

Howard Hawks (1962), and Alan Dwan (1971); his taste was incredibly catholic. Bogdanovich considered himself such an auteur that, when he had completed his ill-conceived movie version of Henry James's *Daisy Miller* (1974), he agonized over whether it should be advertised as "A Peter Bogdanovich Film of Henry James's *Daisy Miller;* or Henry James's Novella Directed by Peter Bogdanovich; or Henry James's *Daisy Miller,* a Film by Peter Bogdanovich; or Peter Bogdanovich's *Daisy Miller,* from Henry James's Novella."[4]

Finally, there was Coppola, whom Bluhdorn and Yablans knew better than the others because of *The Godfather,* which had not yet been released. But they also knew Coppola as a writer, one of several who contributed to the script of *Is Paris Burning?* and coauthor of the script for *Patton* (1970), which won several Oscars—one for Best Screenplay.

With the cult of the director established as an article of faith, and three such auteurs available, the Directors Company was launched at Paramount in 1972 with the understanding that Bogdanovich, Coppola, and Friedkin would be expected to make twelve pictures over a six-year period (approximately two a year) wholly financed by Paramount with a budget fixed at $31.5 million. The company would be based on the lot, and the auteurs would enjoy (relative) autonomy.

Although Yablans was once thought of being the impetus behind the company,[5] the idea was probably Bluhdorn's. However, it is difficult to imagine Bluhdorn's coming up with such a harebrained notion by himself; more likely, the resident auteurs, particularly Coppola, convinced him of its viability.[6] Yablans was too much of a pragmatist to think that a mini-studio within a studio that itself was a subsidiary could keep the stars encircling the mountain peak.

Yablans also knew a fiefdom when he saw one. Reportedly, when Bluhdorn broke the news to him, Yablans exploded: "I think it's shit. I think it's the worst, stupidest, dumbest idea I ever heard in my life. . . . Why don't you just give 'em the company, Charlie?"[7]

The inevitable failure of the Directors Company was not so much Bluhdorn's uncritical acceptance of auteurism and its elevation of the director from foreman to author as his ignorance of film history. It was one thing for a director (D.W. Griffith) and three actors (Charlie Chaplin, Mary Pickford, and Douglas Fairbanks) to team up and form United Artists in 1919; they were creating, if not a studio as such, then a company for distributing their own films.

A little more than a quarter of a century before the formation of the Directors Company, Frank Capra, Sam Briskin (who was responsible for Capra's long association with Columbia Pictures [1927–39]), George Stevens, and William Wyler formed Liberty Films with the idea that Capra (Liberty's president), Stevens, and Wyler would produce and direct one film a year, with RKO as distributor.[8] While the three directors had already made their share of classics (and Stevens and Wyler would make more after 1945), Capra was, artistically, treading water. Liberty Films had one release to its name: Capra's *It's a Wonderful Life* (1946), which, ironically, came out the same year as Wyler's *The Best Years of Our Lives,* a Samuel Goldwyn production that far outgrossed *Life,* which found an audience after becoming a holiday perennial on television.

To save face (and money), a stock transfer was arranged with Paramount in 1947, stipulating that Capra, Stevens, and Wyler would make three, four, and five films respectively for the studio. As it happened Capra made only two: *Riding High* (1950), a remake of the superior *Broadway Bill* (1934), and *Here Comes the Groom* (1951), remembered only for the Bing Crosby–Jane Wyman duet, "In the Cool, Cool, Cool of the Evening," which won an Oscar for Best Song. Neither was on a par with Capra's Columbia films, including the bloated but sporadically powerful *Mr. Smith Goes to Washington* (1939).

Wyler and Stevens were more obliging. Wyler fulfilled his five-picture commitment with *The Heiress* (1949), *Detective Story* (1951), *Carrie* (1952), *Roman Holiday* (1953), and *The Desperate Hours* (1955); Stevens came close with *A Place in the Sun* (1951), *Something to Live For* (1952), and *Shane* (1953).

One can understand a director's setting up his own production company (e.g., Leo McCarey's Rainbow Productions, John Ford and Merian C. Cooper's Argosy Pictures), but the idea of three directors going into partnership—when Wyler and Stevens, at least, could have cut multipicture deals with the studios—was a sign of Capra's fear of the uncertain future that awaited him in postwar Hollywood.

Of the three, only Capra, who felt his directing days were coming to an end (as they were), seemed to have this sense of foreboding. Choosing RKO as Liberty's distributor would have made sense ten years earlier when the studio distributed some of Disney's and Goldwyn's films. RKO was the studio where directors such as Robert Wise and Leo McCarey found a temporary home until they became successful enough to move elsewhere, working either within the system or in independent production. It was also at RKO that Stevens made twelve films between 1934 and 1940, including *Alice Adams* (1935) and *Quality Street* (1937), both with Katharine Hepburn; *Swing Time* (1936) with Fred Astaire and Ginger Rogers; and one of Cary Grant's best vehicles, *Gunga Din* (1939). Wyler's connection with RKO was more tenuous: the studio distributed *The Little Foxes* (1941), which Wyler directed for Sam Goldwyn.

Although Liberty Films was Capra's brainchild, he had only an inkling of the kind of film he wanted to make: on the assumption that audiences had had their fill of war and suffering, Capra envisioned movies that were "safely noncontroversial [and] escapist."[9] This was hardly the kind that would appeal to Wyler and Stevens, who were far more serious moviemakers than Capra.

Capra's era was over; he had not had a hit since *Mr. Smith Goes to Washington,* his last film for Columbia. Stevens and Wyler, however, had been more successful. With *The Talk of the Town* (1942) and *The More the Merrier* (1943), both Columbia releases, Stevens returned to the kind of screwball comedy that Capra had abandoned. Wyler had won an Oscar for his direction of *Mrs. Miniver* (1942), the best-loved homefront movie of the war years. Capra would no longer be a contract director; the creative vein had been mined, and there was little else for him to do but bask in the glow of elder statesmanship. Liberty was a mistake; it was the wrong combination of the wrong directors for the wrong reasons. That the creator of such populist fare as *Mr. Deeds Goes to Town* (1936) and *Mr. Smith Goes to Washington* could prescribe a diet of "escapist" movies for postwar America—and expect the directors of *Mrs. Miniver* and *The Talk of the Town* to digest it—suggests Capra understood neither the public nor his colleagues.

Since Bluhdorn was not a student of film, the Liberty venture would have meant nothing to him. What did matter was that three directors had become bankable. Since Yablans needed to generate product, Bogdanovich, Coppola, and Friedkin seemed the most likely sources. Of the three, not even two could claim to have achieved in their early thirties what Wyler and Stevens had in their sixties. Part of the fault lay in themselves; one could expose the personal lives of Bogdanovich and Friedkin, as Peter Biskind has already done in *Easy Riders, Raging Bulls,* and reveal all the deterrents that kept them from becoming great filmmakers: drugs, sex, and, worst of all, self-absorption. Yet none of these would have mattered, particularly in the emancipated seventies, if the end result had been art. In the case of Friedkin and Bogdanovich, their cinematic prime was over before they joined the Directors Company. Friedkin never surpassed *The*

French Connection, which was made for Fox. Bogdanovich might have fared better than he did at Paramount if he had not been so taken with his reputation as auteur and film authority. His only successful Paramount film was *Paper Moon* (1972), which, like *The Last Picture Show,* was shot in black and white and evoked an era (the Great Depression) that Bogdanovich knew from the movies of the 1930s. Bogdanovich never found his own style; he was so steeped in film history that Billy Wilder called him the "Frank Gorshin of filmmakers," implying that, like the popular 1970s impersonator, he could imitate but rarely originate.[10] Thus, *Picture Show*'s appeal lay in Bogdanovich's recreation of the early 1950s through the use of hit songs and TV shows, and his choice of "the last picture show," which, in Larry McMurtry's novel, is the obscure Audie Murphy movie, *The Kid from Texas* (1950). Bogdanovich substituted Hawks's *Red River* (1948), which is not only a fitting coda but also a tribute to a director who, by then, had become a friend.

During the brief period when the Directors Company was in existence (1972–74), only Coppola showed any promise, despite the unevenness of his post-1974 films. What bothered Yablans about the trio was the fact that they regarded their work as cinematic art rather than commercial film, even though they were working at a major studio. It hardly mattered to Yablans that film was gaining respect as an academic discipline or that the proliferation of film texts pointed to a recognition of the motion picture as art, not just popular culture. To think that the trio would eschew art for commercialism was ludicrous: they were too cognizant of film history (Bogdanovich), too serious (Coppola) or semi-serious (Friedkin) to consider themselves as anything other than artists. Friedkin did a commendable job filming Harold Pinter's puzzling play, *The Birthday Party* (1968), although he would never return to such blatantly noncommercial material again.

Friedkin is an interesting case. He could only have become part of the Directors Company on the basis of *The French Connection* and the endorsement of Bogdanovich and Coppola. During the Company's two-year existence, Friedkin did not make a single picture for Paramount. In fact, during that time, the only film he directed was *The Exorcist* (1973) for Warner Bros. His first Paramount film was *Sorcerer* (1977), a mediocre remake of Clouzot's masterpiece, *The Wages of Fear* (1952). *Sorcerer* was actually a Paramount/Universal coproduction, with Paramount handling foreign distribution; and Universal, domestic.

Bogdanovich gave the company one hit, *Paper Moon,* and one flop,

Daisy Miller. Yablans should have realized that Bogdanovich was erratic; he might deliver an occasional winner, but his heart was in the past. That was evident in his first film, *Targets* (1968), also a Paramount release, which not only starred Boris Karloff but also included clips from Karloff in Outside the Law (1931). Bogdanovich's outstanding achievement is not *Picture Show,* brilliant as it is, but another Columbia release, *Nickelodeon* (1975), which illustrates what Bogdanovich does best: evoke the past—in this case, that of the American film. By interweaving fiction, history, and anecdote, Bogdanovich recreated a time when movies were shown in converted storefronts; former lawyers found themselves behind the camera directing, rodeo performers in front of it acting, and literate teenagers off in a corner writing scenarios by ransacking the classics.

It was not the failure of the Directors Company that forced Yablans out of Paramount. Part of the reason was his ego, which grew out of proportion as he began to perceive himself as more of a producer than Bluhdorn's appointee. Since he knew from experience that self-promotion is not that different from film exploitation, he garnered so much publicity that he alienated Bluhdorn, who preferred someone who did not share his grandiose dreams with the press, especially about becoming United States president. Since Bluhdorn had all he could do to dispel rumors about the Mafia's buying into Paramount, he was furious when Yablans announced he would be playing a mobster in Elaine May's *Mikey and Nicky* (1976).[11] If Yablans ever appeared in the film, which was savaged by the critics, it must have been in a bit part. Since the film was released after Yablans left Paramount, it would not have made any difference.

Bluhdorn could have removed Yablans for any number of reasons, but his alleged payroll padding and other unorthodox business practices provided Bluhdorn with an excuse. Was it a case of the proverbial finger in the till? In corporate Hollywood, "a finger in the till can also get broken."[12]

While Bluhdorn's own indiscretions, financial and otherwise, were far more incriminating, the difference was the age-old distinction between the sins of the fathers and those of the surrogate sons. In short, Bluhdorn got away with it; Yablans did not. When Yablans turned into a braggadocio, he became an embarrassment. In his quest for an heir, Bluhdorn discovered he had acquired an overage prodigal; he had also failed to realize that elevating Yablans to the Paramount presidency was like drafting a minor leaguer into the majors. Within his league, Yablans was a star. However, Bluhdorn probably never appreciated the ad campaigns for *The Godfather* and *The Great Gatsby* that Yablans spearheaded. And while *The Godfather Part II* probably would have been made regardless of who was in charge of the studio, Yablans made the film a priority.

Although Yablans could not take credit for the film's artistry, he did not interfere with the true artists (except in his refusal to hire Brando in any capacity, even for a brief flashback). Coppola was again director, and both he and Puzo collaborated on the screenplay; other returnees were Gordon Willis as director of photography, Dean Tavoularis as production designer, Nino Rota as composer, and cast members Al Pacino, Diane Keaton, John Cazale, Talia Shire, and Morgana King in their original roles. But the real casting coup was Robert DeNiro as the young Vito Corleone. Yablans was right about Brando, whose presence in the sequel, even in a cameo appearance, could easily have thrown the film off base. De Niro, on the other hand, did not have a self-focusing persona, nor, at that stage in his career, did Pacino. Consequently, the lives of Vito and Michael Corleone, which kept diverging in *The Godfather*, now ran parallel to each other through a skillful mingling of present and past. Although *The Godfather* still remains a brilliant fusion of two genres (crime film and family saga) into one (crime family), the sequel is an epic, covering more than half a century and thus becoming a microcosm of American life from the early 1900s to the end of the 1950s.

In *The Godfather*, Vito Corleone, somewhere in his late fifties, is approaching the end of his life. Despite the title (which is ambiguous since it eventually refers to Michael as well), one knows more about the son than his father, the Sicilian immigrant who came to America as a nine-year-old. The sequel fills in the missing details by interweaving Vito's life in flashback (the early decades of the century) with Michael's as it unfolds in the present (the mid- to late 1950s). The flashbacks are occasioned by an image or action common to both time frames. For example, the first begins as Michael is putting his son to bed. The time is the mid-1950s. Michael's face is left of frame. The shot slowly dissolves to one of Vito, right of frame, putting his son, Fredo, to bed in New York's Little Italy in 1917.[13] Later, the news that Kay has had a miscarriage triggers a flashback to Little Italy in the early 1920s with Vito hovering over the young Michael, who has been stricken with pneumonia. When Kay confesses that her miscarriage was really an abortion, the admission occasions a flashback to a life that was terminated a quarter of a century earlier when Vito returned to Sicily to kill Don Ciccio, who was responsible for the murder of his parents. And after Vito exacts his revenge, Coppola dissolves back to

1959, fading in on the casket bearing the body of Michael's mother, Mama Corleone.

Visually, Willis and Tavoularis distinguished between the worlds of father and son (as well as turn-of-the-century and mid-century America). Vito's story had the look of faded photographs in a family album; Michael's world, on the other hand, unfolded in a series of glossies, so slickly executed that one could barely detect the rot beneath the veneer. *The Godfather Part II*, which was nominated for eleven Oscars, received six, twice as many as *The Godfather.* Best Picture, Director, Supporting Actor (DeNiro), Adapted Screenplay, Score, and Art Direction.

That was not enough to save Yablans's job. However, his association with Paramount did not end with his departure. Like so many others, Yablans withdrew into the mysterious realm of "independent production," which offered ex-presidents two alternatives: remaining at their old studio at a much lower salary but with their overhead covered, "possibly waiting years for an OK from their successor to get a film produced"; or going elsewhere, "using their own money, begging for distribution and paying their own overhead."[14] Yablans was just another independent producer with a Paramount connection; the studio released *North Dallas Forty* (1979), which Yablans coproduced and coauthored, although he had to resort to arbitration to get a writing credit; and *Mommie Dearest* (1981), which he produced and coauthored along with three other writers. Although he later went to MGM, where his tenure was even briefer than it had been at Paramount (1983–85), Yablans was never able to stage the kind of comeback that Stanley Jaffe did; after alienating Bluhdorn, Jaffe quit Paramount and moved over to Columbia in 1971, returning to Paramount ten years later—first as a producer, then as president and COO of the reconstituted Gulf + Western, called Paramount Communications, until he was ousted when Viacom bought Paramount Communications in 1994.

Yablans was a casualty of New Hollywood, where the pool of creative executives had shrunk from Olympic size to Beverly Hills backyard. The few who managed to stay afloat remained pretty much within the depth levels their talents allowed. Yablans's level was distribution, once considered a field distinct from production. But in the 1970s it seemed that production was ancillary to distribution.

The former line of demarcation between distribution and production had become a divider affording easy access to the other side. Just stoop down and slip under the velvet rope. The worst that can happen is that you will be denied admittance. For reasons ranging from a lack of self-knowledge to a feeling of invincibility (perhaps the result of having been a studio president at thirty-six), Yablans may not have appreciated the fact that his strengths did not lie in production. Once Yablans left distribution in 1971, he had little more to offer Paramount. His slipping under the rope is typical of corporate Hollywood, in which a title such as executive producer, once bestowed on Jack L. Warner and Hal B. Wallis (both of whom deserved it), was now given to hangers-on, flashes in the pan, and new M.B.A.s from New York University and Harvard. By the 1970s, opening credits had become a string of names, occasionally hyphenated. In 1976, Billy Wilder looked through his copy of the *Hollywood Reporter* and came upon the following ad for a new Twentieth Century-Fox film: "*Silver Streak* A Martin Ransohoff-Frank Yablans Production An Arthur Hiller Film A Miller-Milkis-Colin Higgis Picture." His response was not so much typical Wilder as a candid assessment of ego run riot: "This is insane. What happens is that somebody buys a property or two people buy it, so their names must appear. If the star is involved in the production, then his name appears. The director says it must read 'A Bill Friedkin Film' or 'Bill Friedkin's Film.' Then the schleppers and the hangers-on get into the act. The vanity game is enormous."[15]

It was either vanity or chutzpah that caused Yablans's reach to exceed his grasp. In his *Elegy*, Thomas Gray compared unrecognized talent to a flower "born to blush unseen." The flower image is equally applicable to the corporate world (including contemporary Hollywood), where talent often does not grow either because it has been planted in soil unconducive to growth or because it has been transplanted into an environment where it cannot possibly thrive. Yablans was a perfect example of the latter.

Yablans's successor, Barry Diller, had a knack of picking the right spot where his talents could get enough care and attention to grow. Diller was thirty-two when he succeeded Yablans in 1974. There was nothing especially impressive about Diller's background. Like Alfred Hitchcock's father, Michael Diller was an old-fashioned greengrocer in San Francisco before the Dillers moved to Los Angeles in the late 1940s when Barry was seven.[16] Barry was clearly college material, but after graduating from Beverly Hills High School in 1959 he was ambivalent about pursuing a degree. After testing the waters at UCLA, he decided against academe in favor of media. At the time Diller could not quite decide between television and film. It was impossible to be a student at Beverly Hills High, and a classmate of Marlo Thomas, without being aware that Marlo's father, Danny, was the star of the sitcom, *Make Room for Daddy* (later retitled *The Danny Thomas Show*), which first aired on ABC before moving to CBS in 1958.

The Thomases proved invaluable to Diller's career. Through Danny, Diller got a job in the mail room of the William Morris Agency, the first rung on the ladder for all aspiring movie and television executives. Through Marlo, Diller was introduced to an ABC executive, Leonard Goldberg, who was so impressed by his combativeness and refusal to back off from confrontations that he offered Diller a position at the network, where he eventually became assistant to the head of programming.

The job required Diller's relocating to New York, where his rise was swift and where he also found a way of uniting his dual interests in film and television. Even as early as 1950, it was impossible to watch television without noticing the number of feature films that were being shown. First, there were British films, most of which were obscure except for an occasional classic like Hitchcock's *The 39 Steps* (1935). Then the Poverty Row studios began unloading their libraries, knowing that it was only a matter of time before television offered the equivalent of their kind of entertainment. Republic's B westerns made their way to the tube as early as 1948. By 1950, the movies of the defunct PRC (e.g., *Lady in the Death House* [1944]), *Fog Island* [1945]) were being aired on CBS; the following year, Monogram started divesting itself of its library. Soon, the major studios would also be leasing to television.

While Diller was in high school, television—as well as film—history was being made. At the end of 1955, RKO, which ceased being a studio two years later, began leasing its films to television. A few months later, Columbia announced that a package of pre-1948 films would be released to television through its subsidiary, Screen Gems. By 1956, Warner Bros., Fox, and MGM had succumbed. In 1957, Columbia struck a deal with Universal to release Universal's pre-1948 films through Screen Gems. The following year, MCA bought the rights to license Paramount's pre-1948 films to television.

In June 1959, as Diller was about to graduate from Beverly Hills High, such films as MGM's *China Seas* (1935), Warner Bros.' *The Big Sleep* (1946), Fox's *Cry of the City* (1948), RKO's *The Locket* (1946), Universal's *Weird Woman* (1944), Fox's *Thunderhead, Son of Flicka* (1945), and Columbia's *Port Said* (1948) had been shown on television.

While Diller was trying to decide between getting a B.A. or finding a job, television history occurred with the premiere of NBC's *Saturday*

Night at the Movies on 23 September 1961. The telecast of Fox's *How to Marry a Millionaire* (1953), with Marilyn Monroe, Lauren Bacall, and Betty Grable, marked the first time a post-1948 movie from a major studio had been shown on television, thus signaling the end of the studios' reluctance to license more recent films to the networks. The response to *Millionaire* was so overwhelming that other networks followed suit.

Diller came of age at a time when film and television, which once ran parallel to each other, began to intersect. In 1968, Diller, twenty-six and vice president of prime-time programming, decided it was time ABC elbowed its way into a market that NBC seemed to have cornered. In 1966, NBC contracted with Universal to produce original two-hour movies for its new series, *World Premiere,* marking the beginning of network-studio cooperation. ABC's *Movie of the Week* was Diller's answer to *World Premiere.* Rather than use a studio like Universal, Diller decided in favor of independent producers. Actually, he had little choice. Except for Universal, the studios proved uncooperative because they feared competition with their own releases. If Universal seemed the exception, it was because the studio's new owner was MCA, which had been involved in television since 1952 when its subsidiary, Revue, had begun producing and distributing such shows as *Stars over Hollywood, Alfred Hitchcock Presents, General Electric Theatre, Wagon Train,* and *Ozzie and Harriet.*

The *ABC Movie of the Week* was conceived as a ninety–minute series (unlike the two-hour *World Premiere Movie,* which soon experimented with a ninety–minute format), aired on Tuesday evenings from eight-thirty to ten o'clock. The movies featured a mix of recognizable Hollywood and television performers (e.g., Milton Berle, Walter Brennan, Eva Gabor, Ken Berry, George Maharis, Janet Leigh, Pat Boone, Sammy Davis Jr., Sebastian Cabot, Ricardo Montalban, Eleanor Parker) in films with plots that had been time-tested for success. The series premiered on 23 September 1969 with *Seven in Darkness,* a plane crash movie with a twist: the survivors were blind. The inaugural season also included *The Immortal,* in which the main character's blood contained antibodies that made him immortal; *The Over-the-Hill Gang,* a Western spoof; *The Young Lawyers,* in which law students defended a taxi driver falsely accused of a crime; and *The Ballad of Andy Crocker,* a drama about a Vietnam vet starring Lee Majors and Joey Heatherton.

The *Movie of the Week* proved so popular that it spawned the *Wednesday Night Movie of the Week* in 1972. The Tuesday night series lasted until 1975, after which ABC played around with other time slots, resulting in the *ABC Monday Night Movie* and the *Sunday Night Movie*. Diller had not underestimated the public's interest in movies, old and new. Between 1970 and 1972, *Movie of the Week* came in fifth in the Nielsen ratings.

Inspired by the success of BBC's miniseries that reclaimed an audience eager for the television version of the nineteenth-century novel with its leisurely storytelling and intricate plotting, Diller launched ABC's first miniseries, the six-hour *QB VII* (1974), which may have lacked the cachet of *The Six Wives of Henry VIII* (1971) but proved that public television viewers were not the only ones interested in serialized drama. What miniseries fans really wanted was an ongoing narrative that, unlike the soaps, concluded after a certain number of episodes. The concept caught on, and by 1976 a series like *Rich Man, Poor Man*—a family saga about two totally dissimilar brothers—could unfold in twelve 90–minute installments on Tuesday nights. However, by that time, Diller was already at Paramount, where he had arrived in October 1974. In fact, he was at the studio five months after *QB VII*, ABC's first miniseries, was aired the previous April.

Bluhdorn was well aware of Diller's reputation at ABC in 1974 when his dissatisfaction with Yablans prompted him to seek a successor who had to meet other qualifications besides competence: youth, aggressiveness, and, of course, surrogate son potential. Although Diller believed his age had nothing to do with his appointment, he did not know the extent to which Bluhdorn was obsessed with youth. But then Diller either did not know or did not appreciate the role that age had played in the battle for Paramount in 1966. Yet why should anyone, born in 1942, care about an attempt to remove a studio from the control of men old enough to be his own father, born in 1909?

Apparently, Bluhdorn's first encounter with Diller was over the phone. Bluhdorn called to offer Diller a package of Paramount releases that he was willing to license to ABC. When Diller realized the films were not only mediocre but also overpriced, he reacted, as he often did, by slamming down the receiver.[17] Ordinarily, such rudeness would have signaled the end of any relationship, except that Bluhdorn knew he was trying to foist inferior product on ABC and was impressed that Diller was too savvy to be conned.

Since Bluhdorn was far from mild-mannered himself, he sensed that he had found his alter ego in Diller. And since Diller could tell the difference between quality and dreck, this was exactly the studio president Bluhdorn was seeking.

Diller's first job had nothing to do with moviemaking: Bluhdorn expected him to relocate production at Marathon Street now that the SGI deal had fallen through. Even if Bluhdorn had not entrusted Diller with the task, Diller would probably have insisted upon the move; since the lot would remain intact, there was no reason for the production staff to be half an hour away in Beverly Hills while the other executives were in scenically unattractive West Hollywood. Diller represented a mentality that was quite different from that of Evans or Bart: Diller may have talked film but he thought television. And at ABC, the producers were not across town on the East Side. No longer would production be treated like a first-class flyer, segregated from the rest of the company in Beverly Hills. From now on it would be economy class for the Canon Drive crew. There would be no more luncheons at The Bistro; for ambience, the dispossessed could amble over to the Nickodell, an art deco artifact where they could sink into leather-upholstered booths and be served by waitresses who looked like extras from Central Casting.

By early 1975 production was back at Marathon Street; and no sooner had the Canon Drive offices been vacated than Dino De Laurentiis moved in, providing a Paramount presence but giving the studio films such as *King Kong* (1976), *Lipstick* (1976), and *Hurricane* (1979) that in no way measured up to what Evans and Bart had produced during that brief period when they had enjoyed a quasi autonomy rare in an industry where micromanaging is standard. In 1975, however, the move from Canon Drive to Marathon Street meant little in Hollywood. What mattered was that an outsider had arrived in town. Hollywood did not throw out the welcome mat for Diller, who, after all, was from television—the medium that allegedly hastened the end of the studio system and became film's chief competitor. The big screen/small screen distinction had become the equivalent of the Hollywood/Broadway dichotomy of the studio years, when arrivals from the theater (and the East in general) were treated as visitors from another planet—talented aliens who knew how badly their services were needed but were nonetheless contemptuous of the medium that paid them more than they would ever get in New York. Although Diller was from television, he was neither a true New Yorker nor a cinemaphobe—only a media czar in the making, eager for any opportunity, whether in television or film, that would help him achieve his goal. In Hollywood, however, Barry Diller was the new kid on the block.

Diller knew that, to succeed, he would have to surround himself with his own lieutenants. Thus there was no place for the team of Bart and Evans. By the time Diller came on board, Bart was ready for an occasional production deal, such as the film version of Hemingway's *Islands in the Stream* (1977). He also knew that longevity was not the norm in corporate Hollywood. Evans saw the handwriting on the wall during a breakfast meeting with Diller at the Bel-Air Hotel when Diller, in his characteristically unsubtle way, made it quite clear that Evans worked for *him*, leaving Evans no alternative but that great face-saver, independent production.[18] Jaffe had departed, Bart was leaving, and Evans was about to resign. Diller did what any studio president would do: he insulated himself with his own.

No one could have been more different from Diller than Michael Dammann Eisner.[19] Growing up on New York's Park Avenue exposed Eisner to a world that Diller never knew—a world of housekeepers, private schools (including the seven-hundred–acre Lawrenceville Academy near Princeton), country clubs, summer homes, and Broadway plays— the first of which Eisner saw at the age of five. It was his early exposure to the theater that led to Eisner's lifelong obsession with the performing arts. He enrolled at Ohio's Denison College as a premed student but quickly switched to English with a minor in theater. After graduating in 1964, Eisner thought he might succeed as a playwright, until he discovered his plays were unproduceable. Still living in New York (although no longer on Park Avenue), Eisner was desperate to find work, preferably without resorting to family contacts.

Having worked as an NBC page for a summer, Eisner decided to try the network again. NBC responded with a job requiring Eisner to log the number of times commercials appeared within a particular show. Eager for a more challenging position, Eisner moved over to CBS, where he was entrusted with an equally tedious task: determining the placement of commercials in Saturday morning children's shows.

Eisner could not have suspected that his brief exposure to children's programming would stand him in good stead when he grew tired of doing arithmetic and, in 1966, applied to ABC. Then, Eisner knew nothing about Diller; he only knew that ABC was his last resort. Diller, however, was taken with Eisner's letter; he was also a shrewd judge of talent, although in Eisner's case it was talent in the raw. Eisner was a child of the 1960s, who looked it in dress, hair, and appearance. However, unlike the flower children of his generation, Eisner only seemed indifferent to convention. Nor was he "going with the flow," to use one of the many idioms of the Age of Aquarius. Eisner knew how to chart his course, which pointed to ABC.

By taking on Eisner, Diller was unwittingly reviving the Evans–Bart or "strange harmony" formula: the pairing of a business genius with a high school diploma (Diller) and a neophyte with a college degree and major career potential (Eisner). Just as Bart and Evans played off of each other's strengths and compensated for each other's weaknesses, so did Diller and Eisner. Born in the same year (1942), Diller and Eisner were products of television, not movies. "Movies" meant movies on television first, then movies in theaters. In 1966, however, neither Diller nor Eisner thought that within a decade they would be working together at a movie studio.

By 1969, Eisner had become director of program development at ABC. The following year, recalling that Eisner had had experience in children's shows, Diller also entrusted him with the task of revitalizing ABC's Saturday morning lineup. ABC had achieved great success on Saturday mornings with *The Beatles* (1965–69), a half-hour animated series depicting the Beatles as cartoon figures. Eisner revived the format, first with *Jackson 5IVE*, which premiered in 1971 in the 9:30 A.M. slot and featured the Motown group within a cartoon-like context with a wisp of a plot, a few songs, and a spot devoted to Michael and his brothers. The following year, *The Osmonds* joined *Jackson 5IVE*. The Osmond Brothers had achieved great popularity in the 1960s with their appearances on the *Andy Williams Show*. The brothers' wholesome image was not lost in the switch over to animation, and the plots were, as one might expect, lessons in tolerance and understanding. Soon *The Brady Kids*—another half-hour program with animated equivalents of the six children from ABC's hit series—was added to the Saturday lineup. Eisner also experimented with Saturday morning reruns of sitcoms, such as *Bewitched*, that were suitable for children. Children who could accept pop artists and sitcom characters in cartoon form would have no difficulty accepting a household in which the wife happened to be a glamorous witch.

Saturday morning programming became even more adventuresome in October 1972 with the *ABC Saturday Superstar Movie*, hour-long animated features that were either compilations of earlier cartoon programs or originals with characters derived from such familiar sitcoms as *Gidget*, *That Girl*, and *Bewitched*. That same year Eisner launched *Afternoon Specials*, one-hour animated original dramas geared especially toward children. The first, *The Last of the Curlews*, which told of the last surviving members of a bird species, was typical of the series that was generally aired at 4:30 P.M. in the East on Tuesday afternoons.

One of Eisner's coups, however short-lived, was acquiring *Bugs Bunny*, which had previously been part of the CBS Saturday lineup. *Bugs* remained at ABC for only two seasons (1973–75); it would have stayed longer except that Warner Bros. tried to foist *Road Runner* on the network as a condition for retaining the broadcast rights. Since Eisner saw no place for *Road Runner*, *Bugs Bunny* returned to CBS.

In 1970, the year that Eisner took over children's television, ABC added another Saturday morning show: *Will the Real Jerry Lewis Please Sit Down?* with an animated Lewis as a bumbling janitor. At the time, Eisner and Diller merely thought of it as a series inspired by the antics of the former Paramount star that drew on comic routines from his movies, little knowing that before long they would both be at Lewis's old studio. Nor could Eisner have suspected, when he was juggling time slots for ABC's animated programs, that his career would peak at the studio whose name is synonymous with animation.

Eisner also provided ABC with non-animated series, including some classic sitcoms, the best of which aired as he was about to leave the network. Eisner was attracted to series about people who were totally opposite of the ones he knew on Park Avenue: buddy cops (*Starsky and Hutch*), assembly line workers in a Milwaukee brewery (*Laverne and Shirley*), cab drivers who would rather act or box (*Taxi*), a high school teacher returning to his alma mater (*Welcome Back, Kotter*), and a waitress who marries a Philadelphia blueblood (*Angie*).

It was assumed that when Diller moved to Paramount in the fall of 1974, Eisner would inherit his job at ABC; instead, the network bypassed Eisner and hired the considerably more experienced head of CBS, Fred Silverman. However, Diller needed someone to function as a buffer not so much between himself and Bluhdorn, who could be managed, but between himself and Martin Davis, who, as long as Bluhdorn was in power, could be kept at bay. Eisner became the perfect buffer; since Eisner needed to save face, he gladly accepted Diller's invitation to join him at Paramount. By 1976 Eisner was serving under Diller again, as he had at ABC.

There was another position at Paramount that had to be filled. Evans's departure left a gap in production that Diller, a film novice but a quick study, planned to fill on an ad hoc basis. Diller's first selection was an eyebrow raiser: Richard Sylbert, a production designer, Oscar winner for art direction (*Who's Afraid of Virginia Woolf?* [1966]) and Oscar nominee for his extraordinary recreation of 1930s Los Angeles in *Chinatown*. Sylbert was elated, believing—and rightly so—that a production chief who had had experience shaping a film's look had an advantage over someone who had never worked with the raw materials that gave a movie its visual style. It was wishful thinking. In classic Hollywood, an art director such as MGM's William Cameron Menzies was almost like a production head. But in corporate Hollywood, an artist is no more welcome in the executive suite than an academic. Sylbert needed help. He was impressed by Don Simpson, who would never have ended up at Paramount had it not been for Sylbert. In 1975, Sylbert extended an offer to Steve Tisch— nephew of the chairman of the hotel and theater chain, Loews Corp., Laurence Tisch (who eventually became head of CBS)—to join Paramount as a production executive, title unspecified. Tisch declined but recommended Simpson, a self-mythologizer with meager film credentials (a bit of marketing at Warner Bros.) but with a brashness and self-confidence that endeared him to Sylbert. Sylbert then recommended Simpson to Diller, who apparently saw *his* mirror image in a fast-talking, idea-spouting newcomer whose age was just right: compared to Sylbert, born in 1926 (and thus *ancien régime*), Simpson, born in 1943, was Diller's contemporary. There was, however, a crucial difference: Simpson was an alcoholic and drug addict who died of an overdose at fifty-four.

Simpson's demons would surface later. Before they did, he moved rapidly up the Paramount ladder: vice president of creative affairs (Peter Bart's former title) in 1977, vice president of production in 1978, president of production in 1980, and president of worldwide production a year later. Top of the mountain, or so it seemed.

The films made during Simpson's three-year tenure were, for the most part, hugely successful, compensating in revenues for what they lacked in quality. But the emphasis was not on quality. Diller and Eisner had recreated Paramount in the image of the only medium they knew: television. As Eisner explained to Sylbert: "Sometimes we're going to win, and sometimes we're going to lose, but we're going to make a lot of movies, with a lot of laughs in the middle, and nothing too serious. And we're going to make a lot of money."[20] The "we" were Diller, Eisner, and the production head of the moment, who needed Eisner's blessing for every project slated for production. Between 1980 and 1983, Simpson was, to invert Carson McCullers's pronouns from *The Member of the Wedding*, "the me of the we." The films of the Simpson years were a mingled yarn, most of it coarsely spun. While Simpson fought valiantly to make

An Officer and a Gentleman (1982), a property that Eisner disliked, the film was merely a variation on the boys-into-men movies of the World War II era, with the boys as West Coast cadets. Still, it grossed more than any other Paramount film that year: $52.2 million.

Thanks to Simpson, the early eighties proved a windfall for Paramount. The hits far outnumbered the flops, although the hits, while popular, lacked the genius of those of the previous decade (e.g., *The Godfather* films, *Chinatown, Serpico*), which were also works of cinematic art. One could hardly say that about Paramount's Eddie Murphy films. The fact that Murphy made his name on television with *Saturday Night Live* explains his Paramount debut, *48 Hours* (1982), which might be described as "*Starsky and Hutch* Meets *I Spy*, with a Twist": the African American member of the interracial team (Murphy and Nick Nolte) is a convict on a two-day hiatus from prison. If *48 Hours* evoked memories of both television series, it might well have been that audiences were familiar with the character types. Purged of its R-rated language, *48 Hours* could have been an ABC Movie of the Week. However, if it were, it would not have enriched Paramount's coffers or Eddie Murphy's bank account. Even before *48 Hours* opened, Eisner sensed Murphy's star power, which was confirmed when the film grossed $30.3 million. Yet two months before *48 Hours* was released, Eisner, merely on the basis of the rushes, decided that Murphy had to be a Paramount regular even if it meant a dream contract allowing Murphy to develop his own properties, with the expectation that his presence at the studio would attract top writers and directors. That presence was sufficiently potent to prompt Eisner to guarantee Murphy $1 million, not just before the projected film was completed but before it even went before the cameras. Naturally, Paramount could pass on the property, but Murphy would still have the $1 million.[21]

Paramount was hoping Murphy would initiate something comparable to the Pink Panther or James Bond series, even though Murphy's talent had little in common with Peter Sellers or Sean Connery. *48 Hours* succeeded because of the delightfully incongruous pairing of Murphy and Nolte, who did more than just complement each other; they interacted as a comic team, not merely as costars. In *Trading Places* (1983), Murphy was paired with his *Saturday Night Live* colleague, Dan Aykroyd, in a comedy about a con artist (Murphy) and an Ivy Leaguer (Aykroyd) who switch classes as the result of a heredity versus environment experiment conducted by two wealthy old codgers (played brilliantly by Ralph Bellamy and Don Ameche, both pushing eighty). This was the kind of film that, in his heyday, Preston Sturges could have made into a classic, as he did with *Sullivan's Travels* (1941), in which a Hollywood director feigned poverty to see how the other half lived so that he could make a proletarian epic, forgetting that the downtrodden have no interest in seeing their condition ennobled by Hollywood. Unlike Sturges's masterpiece, *Trading Places*, which has no social conscience, is a bawdier version of a *Saturday Night Live* sketch. It also made Paramount $40.6 million.

Murphy could never be another Inspector Clouseau or James Bond. He could, however, becomes a series character, specifically one in keeping with the image he projected in his first film: an African American who had learned more from the streets than he did from school and found himself implementing that knowledge in white America.

Although *Beverly Hills Cop* (1984) had been conceived as a vehicle for Mickey Rourke or perhaps Sylvester Stallone, the decision to refashion the script for Murphy, as a Detroit cop in Los Angeles searching for his friend's murderer, was a wise one. The juxtaposition of Eddie Murphy and Lotus Land was based on the same comic premise—again, the incongruous—that made *The Beverly Hillbillies* such a successful series (1962–71), despite its unabashedly lowbrow humor. In fact, *Beverly Hills Cop* is another example of a Paramount film that could easily have been developed for television—minus the obscenities and graphic violence. But had that happened, Murphy would never have been given a new contract, now worth $15 million, nor would Paramount have enjoyed the revenues from a film that cost $14.8 million to make and grossed $244.8 million domestically and $81.6 internationally.[22] But even before the revenues were tallied, Paramount knew it had a hit when, within two weeks of its release in early December 1984, *Beverly Hills Cop* had already grossed $36.5 million.

Although *Beverly Hills Cop* was a Don Simpson–Jerry Bruckheimer production, Simpson was no longer president of production in 1984. In fact, he had not held that title since late 1982, when Eisner, who could no longer tolerate Simpson's flagrant substance abuse (which had become common knowledge) and boorish behavior at meetings, fired him. In corporate Hollywood, firing is often accompanied by a production deal. Unlike the usual scenario of vacating the office and driving off the lot (at which point, one's parking space is given to someone else), the firing-cum-production deal requires the deposed executive to relocate to a different office with a different parking space, probably one that belonged to someone less fortunate who had departed with a couple of pictures and a plant in need of watering. Simpson teamed up with Jerry Bruckheimer, who had some impressive production credits of his own (*Farewell, My Lovely* [1975], *American Gigolo* [1980]). Bruckheimer was as stable as Simpson was erratic. Together, they gave Paramount a string of hits: *Flashdance* (1983), *Beverly Hills Cop II* (1984), and *Top Gun* (1986). Then came the failure of *Days of Thunder* (1990), with Tom Cruise racing cars instead of flying planes. Audiences preferred Cruise the pilot to Cruise the stock car racer, and *Days of Thunder*, which was budgeted at $40 million (and soared to $70), grossed only $82.7 million domestically. It was the end of Simpson-Bruckheimer at Paramount. And within less than a decade, it was the end of Simpson. Drugs and obesity had taken their toll, and Don Simpson collapsed in his bathroom of a heart attack on 19 January 1996.

When Eisner fired Simpson, he did not have to look far for a replacement. He found someone who, like himself, also hailed from Park Avenue, although one would never have known it from his appearance. Jeffrey Katzenberg looked like a cartoon figure brought to life, with glasses that suggested a nerd and a smile that evoked a hayseed on his first visit to the Big Apple. Katzenberg's ingenuousness was part of his persona; the person was something else.

If a true production head like Irving Thalberg had been around in 1983, he would have found Katzenberg's appointment something of a mystery. Perhaps the best explanation is Katzenberg's ingratiating personality, which concealed the vengeance-seeking litigant that emerged later. In the 1970s, however, Katzenberg was a charmer, perpetually smiling and looking more like the administrative assistant who takes the lunch orders than a movie executive. Katzenberg, however, did not wear the motley on his brain. Never quite knowing where the next job would take him but confident one would emerge that would lead to his dream career, Katzenberg was not thinking Hollywood in the early 1960s. A Park Avenue product like Eisner, Katzenberg had an equally charmed childhood, made possible by his stockbroker father. Katzenberg's formal education ended with high school—not just any high school, but the prestigious Fieldston School in the Riverdale section of the Bronx. College was not for Katzenberg, as he learned after spending two terms at New York University.

Now in his early twenties, Katzenberg seemed to suffer from aimlessness, lacking the ability to focus on a goal and pursue it. In this respect, he was different from Eisner, whose early attraction to the performing arts led him to television and then film. With Kazenberg, first it was politics—working as an aide to New York's mayor John Lindsay in 1965. It was a job that made him aware of the various avenues to power. If, to quote *Twelfth Night* (2,5), "some are born great, some achieve greatness, and some have greatness thrust upon 'em," Katzenberg was the exception: he worked at greatness by studying it. He would never be a Lindsay; for one thing, he was neither a fashionable dresser nor a strikingly handsome man. But he could be one of Lindsay's—or anybody's—entourage. And that is how Katzenberg presented himself: as a courtier eager to do the bidding of the prince until succession time came around. Even when it did, Katzenberg would never be the successor. Like Eliot's Prufrock, he was a Polonius, not a Hamlet. But he would have a quite a career.

After eight years of working for Mayor Lindsay, Katzenberg realized that Lindsay's political career was over in 1973 with the end of the Vietnam War. The fact that the war had been lost, which was painfully apparent when Saigon fell to the North Vietnamese in 1975, did not matter. Although Katzenberg seemed to have political aspirations, his primary interest was not party politics so much as getting the candidate elected for whom he was campaigning. For Katzenberg, winning was all; the winner was not that important.

Essentially, Katzenberg was apolitical; what passed for commitment was an obsession with success, both the candidate's and his own as a member of the winning team. In the late 1960s and early seventies, Katzenberg thrived on the victories of others. When it came time to branch out on his own, he decided it would not be in politics but in another, more glamorous, form of showmanship: film. Beating the drum for a mayoral candidate is an interim job; touting a movie is full-time employment, which also pays better.

In the early 1970s, working in the mail room of a talent agency or, even better, as an agent were the two best ways to hook up with a studio. Diller chose the former; Katzenberg, the latter. A stopover at New York's International Famous Agency brought him to David Picker's independent company, Two Roads Productions, in 1974. Katzenberg could not have chosen a better access road to the Hollywood highway. In 1969, Picker, a Dartmouth graduate, became president of United Artists, with his brother Arnold as board chairman. In 1973, Picker left UA after it underwent a typical industry reconfiguration that left him as chief executive (but not chairman and CEO). Picker formed his own production company, Twin Roads, releasing through United Artists. Twin Roads' best-known release was *Smile* (1975), a charming (but commercially unsuccessful) film about teenage beauty contests, with Broadway-style choreography by Michael Kidd.

Accustomed to television's chain-of-command mentality, where jurisdiction is defined either by title or appointment, Diller thought that Picker, as a studio ex-president-turned-independent producer, might do well as president of Paramount. But the title that Picker was given in 1976 was "president of the motion picture division," a new designation for an old office. Diller had bought the notion that production and distribution should fall under the purview of one person—in this case, Picker. That mentality had become so pervasive that when Ned Tanen was president of Universal in 1976, he found himself in charge of both production and distribution after Universal's figurehead president, Henry "Hi" Martin, whose background was almost exclusively in distribution, retired in 1979. It was marketplace reasoning: selling a film is even more important than creating it, given the discrepancy between the number of films made and those that made money. Even if Diller suspected that distribution and production were distinct and should remain that way, he did not know how they should be separated, who should do the separating, and who should head each division once they were no longer joined at the hip.

Diller did know, however, that he needed Eisner, to whom he could entrust tasks he could not handle himself. Picker's tenure was, understandably, limited to a few months. Part of the problem was the title and its duties: "president of the motion picture division" could include anything and everything, even marketing. The title would be modified, but first Diller needed executives his own age. Picker, ten years older than Diller, would only qualify as "Old Hollywood" to someone born in 1942.

Meanwhile, Picker proved an invaluable contact for Katzenberg, who had now masked his aggressiveness with a sincerity that had translated into a work ethic that would have even amazed the New England Puritans. However, Katzenberg did not have to do a makeover; there was no way he could look East Coast Brooks Brothers or West Coast Armani. He was a cartoon figure come to life, with a smile that belonged in a toothpaste commercial. His would be the open-necked shirt, the bespectacled face, the nerdy look, and the frozen grin.

If it is true that when Katzenberg appeared for an interview at Paramount he behaved with an obnoxiousness that would gotten anyone else the boot, it would have been in keeping with the persona that he had now adopted and that any studio head might well desire. Being raised on

Park Avenue and educated at a top prep school is no guarantee of savoir faire. A childhood acquaintance remembered an incident that had occurred outside Katzenberg's Park Avenue apartment house where the young Katzenberg "grabbed an opponent's water gun, pinned him to the ground, then squashed the other kid's hand into a pile of dog droppings."[23] Diller did not need someone to leave an adversary's fingers in excrement; he needed a subordinate with no qualms about telling laggard directors and temperamental stars that, unless they shaped up, they would be camping on a dung heap.

Gall, masked by a toothy guilelessness, was Katzenberg's strong suit. His lack of a college degree and ignorance of the classics—which became evident when he moved to Disney and requested a synopsis of *The Scarlet Letter*—made him the ideal second banana. As production head, he was able to forge an alliance that developed into a friendship with Eisner, which later degenerated into enmity after they had both relocated at Disney.

But it was at Paramount where Katzenberg was nicknamed the "golden retriever," a label most would have found demeaning, suggesting, as it did, a dog that would come back to its master, sporting in its mouth whatever had been thrown to it. But some interpreted the moniker as a metaphor for Eisner's reliance on executives to "sniff out promising ideas."[24] Even if it were a metaphor, it evoked a canine image, which Katzenberg's demeanor only perpetuated.

What is amazing about Katzenberg's rise is its rapidity, which his lack of experience did not seem to warrant. But being an indefatigable newcomer paid off, as Katzenberg advanced from executive director of marketing (1976) to a series of production jobs, culminating in senior vice president of production (1980) and finally president of worldwide production in 1982 after Simpson was fired. It was while working under Simpson in the late 1970s that Katzenberg first displayed his knack for retrieving. He had become obsessed with the notion of turning the television series *Star Trek* into a movie despite Simpson's doubts about its commercial prospects. Although *Star Trek* has now become a cottage industry with fan clubs, conventions, and merchandise ranging from *Enterprise* miniatures to Klingon ware, it was not that way when the series premiered in September 1966. Whatever audience there was out there was either building or silent. The former was the case. The Trekkies did not declare themselves until NBC announced the show's cancellation in 1968. Soon, a barrage of letters convinced the network to grant *Star Trek* a reprieve. Since the series fared no better the following season, NBC terminated it in March 1969. *Star Trek* did not return to the air until 1987 when it appeared under a new name, *Star Trek: The Next Generation,* followed by *Deep Space Nine* (1993) and *Star Trek: Voyager* (1995).

In the intervening years, *Star Trek* had grown into a cult as well as a cottage industry, even attracting academics who found Homeric and Shakespearean parallels between the journey of the *Enterprise* and Odysseus's homeward voyage, and between the wizardry of Mr. Spock and Prospero in *The Tempest.*[25] Apparently, Patrick Stewart, who played Capt. Jean-Luc Picard in *Star Trek: The Next Generation,* thought so, too, since in 1995 he appeared as Prospero on Broadway in the most successful production of *The Tempest* that had ever been staged.

Katzenberg, who had been a Trekkie in the 1960s, felt that the time was right to turn *Star Trek* into a full-length movie. If *Star Wars* (1977) could become one of "*Variety's* All-time Rental Champs," so could *Star Trek: The Motion Picture* (1979), which grossed $150 million in revenues, in addition to spawning seven sequels. If *Star Trek: The Motion Picture* was the first Paramount release in which Katzenberg had significant input, it was both an index of his taste and a harbinger of things to come. When Katzenberg moved over to Disney, where he was frequently seen in Mickey Mouse T-shirts and Mickey Mouse ears, it was as if he had found an Eden where he could relive his childhood permanently, which may explain why, physically, he never seems to change. Had Katzenberg stayed at Paramount, he might have come to work sporting Vulcan ears.

Once he became known as *Star Trek's* champion, Katzenberg joined the Diller-Eisner team, making it a triumvirate. The team would be joined by a fourth, Dawn Steel, who never acquired enough power to make it a quadrumvirate for reasons that had as much to do with her sex as with the triumvirate's dissolution. Steel had more in common with Diller than either Eisner or Katzenberg, although she worked well with all three. Born in 1946, Steel was the right age for Diller's Paramount. Like Diller, she felt no need to pursue a college degree. She knew she had a flair for marketing, and working at Bob Guccione's *Penthouse* magazine convinced her she was right. Erotic merchandising became her specialty; she found phallic potential in amaryllises, which she promoted as "penis plants"; next, it was "cock socks" (penis warmers). Inspired by the sales for Gucci toilet paper (named after *Penthouse's* publisher), Steel formed her own company, Oh Dawn, to market her designer brand.

In 1978, when a junior executive at Paramount told her about a marketing position at the studio, Steel applied and was hired as director of merchandising, creating product tie-ins with Paramount television series and films. Steel had come to the right studio. Product merchandising at Paramount had proved to be highly lucrative, as films were exploited for their soundtrack, nostalgia, faddist, or gimmick potential. *The Great Gatsby* tie-ins went in for 1920s nostalgia, capitalizing on the film's emphasis on white: white Tupperware and white sportswear.[26] *King Kong*'s were more generic: chocolates, styrene cups, and key chains. Steel had found her metier; she also found a supporter in Eisner, who thought she had production potential and made her vice president, production, in 1980.

If there is a single Paramount film with which Steel is identified, it is *Flashdance* (1983), which, in her autobiography, she called "my first green light."[27] *Flashdance* has a complex production history that is incommensurate with the film's quality, although not with its popularity. *Flashdance* was little more than a $7 million MTV video expanded to ninety-six minutes that turned out to be box-office gold, grossing $217 million worldwide. Supposedly, twenty-seven directors turned down the story of an aspiring dancer who, to make ends meet, resorts to "flashdancing," something between interpretive dance and bump 'n' grind. Paramount was the logical studio for *Flashdance*, which was really the flip side of *Saturday Night Fever* (1977), set in Pittsburgh instead of Brooklyn, featuring a female welder instead of a male paint store employee, and sufficiently hip to appeal to the youth market that, by 1983, was ready for a dummying down of a theme that had been treated more intelligently a decade earlier.

Like most autobiographers, Steel does not tell the entire story. Certainly she championed *Flashdance* and, as vice president, production, could nurse it along, presumably with the consent of Katzenberg, now production head as well as her boss. However, the film was a Simpson-Bruckheimer production. This was the kind of project that would have intrigued Don Simpson, who was also attracted to scripts with working-class characters. More likely, Simpson and Steel both fought to make *Flashdance* because they were sympathetic to a character battling the odds to realize her dream, as they were doing also. Since Simpson was no longer production head, he could not green-light *Flashdance*, even though it came out under the Simpson-Bruckheimer production banner. Steel was the one responsible for getting *Flashdance* made, with, one suspects, some help—mostly vocal—from Simpson. Regardless, *Flashdance* was more than a movie; it was a marketing event. It was the merchandising of the film, not the film itself, that revealed Steel's true gift. *Flashdance* was made to be marketed; the MTV music videos enticed viewers into buying five million soundtrack CDs.

It was during the Diller-Eisner-Katzenberg era that "high concept" became a buzz word that soon was synonymous with New Hollywood. It was also a term that seems to have originated at Paramount, coined by either Diller or Eisner, perhaps suggested by Spielberg, and best articulated by Simpson—all four of whom were at Paramount in the early 1980s in one capacity or another.[28]

Simply (or, to its detractors, simplistically) put, "high concept" refers to a film that can be summarized in a sentence (or even a fragment) so that it can be marketed in such a way that audiences will readily infer the nature of the plot, and perhaps even the genre, from the ad. *Jaws* (1975) is a perfect example. The ad featured a young woman, swimming (it seemed) in the nude, while below her lurks a shark—its head pointed upward, its beady eyes aware of her presence, and its jaws sporting spikelike teeth ready to sink into her flesh. Pitching the film was easy—perhaps even unnecessary—since it was based on Peter Benchley's best-seller. Even so, for executives, who green-light on the basis of an "idea" (the key word in high concept) that turns their eyes into dollar signs, the plot could be summarized as "Summer resort attempts to cover up shark attacks for fear of losing tourists—a little sex, *Psycho* scares, and a PG rating."

If Diller and Eisner have been identified with "high concept," it is probably because of their television background, where TV movies, particularly the ABC movies of the week, required succinct descriptions, in fragment form, for *TV Guide* and similar publications with weekly television listings. Even if it seems hard to imagine Diller or Eisner coining "high concept" (which sounds more like marketing jargon than a type of movie), it is easy to understand how it has become synonymous with them. The success of the *Movie of the Week* was partly due to the plots, most of which were simply variations on a theme. Plane crash plots were common. Planes could crash anywhere: in the jungle, where the survivors have to worry about headhunters (*Five Came Back* [1939], remade as *Back from Eternity* [1956]); in the Pacific, where a plane runs out of fuel and disappears without a trace (*Flight for Freedom* [1943]); or in the desert (*Flight of the Phoenix* [1966]), where the survivors not only have to contend with the heat but with each other. What made *Seven in Darkness*, the *Movie of the Week*'s debut film, slightly different was the premise: the seven were sightless.

In the past, that sort of twist would have been called a "hook" or, more accurately, a gimmick. Now it is a "concept." Musical theater underwent a similar change in the late 1960s as the book musical fell into desuetude and the concept musical took its place. Theatergoers accustomed to musicals on the order of *Oklahoma!* and *South Pacific* were instead given an "experience": flower children begged them to "Let the Sun Shine In" (*Hair*), a cat ascended to heaven on a tire (*Cats*), and a falling chandelier barely missed the first row of the orchestra (*The Phantom of the Opera*). The difference, however, is that there is more plot in *Jaws* than there is in either *Cats* or *Phantom*—the latter making all the film versions of the Leroux novel seem like models of plot construction.

Like so many terms that have entered the critical vocabulary, "concept film," "high concept," and now "very high concept" (presumably meaning a two-sentence summary) cannot accurately describe films of great complexity, such as *Nashville* (1975), which interconnects the lives of twenty-four characters over a weekend culminating in tragedy and thus is classifiable neither in terms of plot or genre. Moreover, what is a concept to one executive (teenage serial killers) might be a genre to another (crime movie). That executives are forced to distinguish between generic types and one- or two-sentence summaries speaks volumes about the business. *Five Came Back*, *Flight of the Phoenix*, and *Seven in Darkness* have a common note: they are all about plane-crash survivors and their fates. Each makes its own contribution to the genre; whether a film is high, low, middle, or very high concept depends on the finished product.

"High concept" calls attention to the disparity between classic and contemporary Hollywood. In the past, studios had story editors who, in turn, had a stable of readers (now known as "story analysts") who synopsized the latest books, articles, and plays, both published and in galleys. A typical synopsis was a rather detailed one-page, single-spaced, typed summary. In the Cy Coleman–Larry Gelbart Broadway musical, *City of Angels* (1991), set in 1940s Hollywood, a movie executive is introduced to a writer whose name he recognizes: "I've read a synopsis of everything you've ever written," he gushes. Lillian Hellman, who worked as a reader at MGM in the early 1930s, remembered the "idiot-simple" synopses she wrote for Louis Mayer.[29] The difference between high concept and old synopsis is one of length. Unable to absorb a full page of text, busy executives require something between a paraphrase and a precis: the traditional synopsis reduced from a page to a sentence or two, preferably using familiar points of reference. For example, a proposed movie about a monster from the deep wreaking havoc on a luxury liner might be pitched as "*The Beast from 20,000 Fathoms* Meets *Titanic*."

There is no honor in having coined "high concept," a travesty of Northrop Frye's "high mimetic," not to mention conceptual thought. What Diller and Eisner achieved was not so much "high concept" as "high transfer." Their world was television, viewed as a concentric universe within which lay smaller circles such as news, sitcoms, talk shows, and film. "Film" then was a microcosm within a universe called television. Diller and Eisner reconfigured that universe so that the small world—and therefore the small screen—became the big world and the big screen. It was simply a matter of converting a microcosm into a macrocosm.

"Barry and I began to run Paramount like a real business," Eisner boasted.[30] But the business was television.

The Paramount releases of the Diller-Eisner era were qualitatively different from those of the previous decade. Accustomed to televison budgets, Diller and Eisner were more cost-conscious than Bart and Evans. The films produced during Diller's tenure (1974–84) included many high-grossers but nothing of the stature of *The Godfather* and its even more brilliant sequel, *Nashville, Day of the Locust,* and *Chinatown.* If *Reds* (1981) seemed an exception, the reason was Warren Beatty's obsession with directing and starring in a historical saga about the Russian Revolution and playing the American Socialist who witnessed it, John Reed. Beatty was allowed to go over budget partly because of his friendship with Diller but more likely because Diller was looking for a prestige film to justify such money-making mediocrities as *Friday the 13th* (1980) and *Airplane* (1980) and to compensate for the public's indifference to such superior fare as *S.O.B.* (1981), as incisive a study of post-studio Hollywood as had yet been seen (with the added attraction of a bare-breasted Julie Andrews); *The Warriors* (1979), inspired by Xenophon's *Anabasis,* in which gang members attempt to return from Van Cortland Park in the Bronx to Coney Island in Brooklyn via a subway system they barely understand; and *Days of Heaven* (1978), which, visually, ranks among the most painterly films ever made and, thematically, harks back to the Hollywood of the Great Depression in its compassion for migrant workers who lose their innocence in the city.

Eisner naturally had a say in the releases, and it is to his credit that he did not veto *Days of Heaven,* even though his credo was commercial hit, not artistic flop. It was not that television had affected his taste; rather, it was that televison was both his training ground and the index by which he measured success. If a series became a hit, so, too, could a film. But what was the elusive formula? It was not entirely critical raves. *Laverne and Shirley* was savaged by the critics yet reached first place in the Nielsen ratings during the 1977–78 season.

Eisner and Diller developed a formula that had proved successful in *Movie of the Week*: a mix of plots (romance, fantasy, blue-collar, domestic tragedy, thriller, sexy melodrama, alienated youth, nostalgia, and unlikely teamings). If viewers were taken with the two totally dissimilar buddy cops in *Starsky and Hutch*, they might respond favorably to a gay cop/straight cop (*Partners* [1982]) or a white cop/black con (*48 Hours* [1982]) movie. They shunned the former but embraced the latter, making a movie star out of Eddie Murphy.

As with the movies of the week, casts were composed of film and television personalities—some new, some established, some vintage, and most at salaries that would not bankrupt the studio. By hiring actors in the autumn—or in some cases, winter—of their careers (e.g., Audrey Hepburn in *Bloodline* [1979], Ralph Bellamy and Don Ameche in *Trading Places*, Lauren Bacall in *The Fan* [1981], Burt Lancaster in *Atlantic City* [1980]), Diller and Eisner were able to offer the public recognizable names without paying salaries comparable to what the actors would have received in their prime. The best films of the Diller-Eisner era were those that did not have big names in either starring or supporting roles. Even if *Ordinary People* (1980) had not grossed $76 million, its production costs would not have affected Paramount adversely. Apart from hoping for some familiarity with Judith Guest's best-seller on which the film was based, Paramount was also counting on Robert Redford's name—not as star, but as a first-time director—and Mary Tyler Moore's television following. However, *Mary Tyler Moore Show* regulars, who associated the actress with her television character, Mary Richards, saw someone quite different in *Ordinary People*, in which Moore played the glacially detached mother of a disturbed son (Timothy Hutton). When Hutton shows no interest in the meal his mother has prepared, Moore methodically scrapes the food from the plate into the waste disposal, as if it were garbage. *Ordinary People* was a small film that became a big hit.

Another such movie was *Terms of Endearment* (1983). Had it been developed for television, *Terms* would have fallen into the "disease of the week" category because of its terminal illness theme. In the 1970s, television discovered the dramatic potential of cancer in such TV movies as *Brian's Song*, an *ABC Movie of the Week* (1971) about Brian Piccolo of the

Chicago Bears; *Babe* (1975), which did not flinch from dramatizing the last days of tennis star Babe Didrikson Zacharias; and *Dark Victory* (1976), an NBC movie based on the Bette Davis classic of the same name, in which a young television executive (Elizabeth Montgomery in the Davis role) learns to accept the fact that she is dying of brain cancer. Terminal cancer was also a plot peg for reconciling estranged parents and children: *Strangers: The Story of a Mother and Daughter* (1979) and *Homeward Bound* (1980).

When director-writer James Brooks approached Eisner about making the film version of Larry McMurtry's *Terms of Endearment*, Brooks proposed a $8.5 million budget—cheap by early 1980s standards, when the average movie cost more than twice as much. Programmed to be economical from his days in television, Eisner hesitated. The commercial prospects for a movie about a terminally ill wife and mother seemed dim, even though the subject had not alienated television viewers. Eisner finally agreed to a bottom line budget of $7.5 million, assuming that Brooks would pick up his marbles and try another studio. Brooks, who had created *The Mary Tyler Moore Show,* got the extra $1 million from MTM, Moore's own company.[31] *Terms of Endearment*, which eventually grossed $147 million, may have been about terminal illness, but it was also a multiple Oscar winner: Best Picture, Best Actress (Shirley MacLaine), Best Supporting Actor (Jack Nicholson), Best Director (Brooks), and Best Adaptation (Brooks). Unfortunately, Debra Winger as the doomed wife was also nominated in the Best Actress category, putting her in competition with Shirley MacLaine, who did a star turn as Winger's mother. Winger's, however, was the more subtle performance.

Paramount could only hope to gain with a movie like *Saturday Night Fever* (1977); only the lead, John Travolta, was at all recognizable—but from television. With TV performers, there is always a gamble: audiences are either curious to see how a television star fares on the big screen or they hesitate before paying to see someone they can watch free. In the case of *Saturday Night Fever*, it was not just Travolta's association with *Welcome Back, Kotter* that made the film so popular, but its theme: a blue-collar kid who works in a paint store in the Bay Ridge section of Brooklyn trying to make it big—"big" defined as winning a disco contest. It is not difficult to see why *Saturday Night Fever* grossed $260 million: the Bee Gees soundtrack, Travolta's ingratiating performance as Tony Manero (including an authentic Brooklyn accent), his then-linear frame, and the film's insistence that all differences are reconcilable—including those between a nineteen–year-old male whose world is Bay Ridge and a slightly older female who has discovered Manhattan, self-improvement, and the New School. But *Saturday Night Fever* is so seductive that even though we know the Tony Maneros will only have their shining hour on the dance floor, we root for them while wishing they had loftier goals.

In *Grease*, his second film for Paramount, Travolta played Danny Zuko, a 1950s version of Tony Manero. Again, Paramount scored a hit, partly because *Grease* was based on the retrograde musical that was still running on Broadway when the film opened (and still enjoys periodic revivals) and partly because it was aimed at three types of audiences: the youth market, the baby boomers, and the generation that knew where it was on December 7, 1941. Audiences weaned on television went for Travolta; boomers, to relive their high school days and groove on faux fifties pop; and the Depression Babies—who remembered Pearl Harbor, gas rationing, and Betty Grable in a white bathing suit looking provocatively over her shoulder—for the supporting cast that consisted of a mix of old Hollywood (Eve Arden, Joan Blondell) and 1950s television (Edd Byrnes, Sid Caesar). If Olivia Newton-John looked too old to pass for a teenager, the eternally young Travolta more than compensated for it. Paramount had covered all bases. *Grease* had something for everybody, and the returns proved it—$350 million.

Despite Paramount's attempt to showcase television performers in movies, not everyone who tried to go big screen succeeded. History was repeating itself, although this time it was a matter of television—rather than stage—actors crossing over to film and experiencing the same fate that had befallen a number of theater greats in the 1930s and 1940s who either failed to adapt to the new medium or to win over a new kind of audience. Ethel Merman, Tallulah Bankhead, Katherine Cornell, Maurice Evans, Mary Martin, and Helen Hayes may have enchanted New York theatergoers, but they never enjoyed the dual careers of Claudette Colbert, Henry Fonda, Jessica Tandy, and Hume Cronyn, among others, who shuttled between Broadway and Hollywood depending on where the better prospects were. Similarly, there were stage actors who also worked in live television in the 1950s (e.g., Paul Newman, Joanne Woodward, James Dean, Ben Gazzara) before becoming successful film stars; on the other hand, the equally talented Kim Stanley, Lois Smith, and Barbara Baxley, who were as luminous on live TV as they were on the stage, never even became minor screen celebrities. The only plausible answer is the one given by Eric von Stroheim in *Sunset Boulevard* (1950) when he attempts to explain to William Holden the mysterious process by which someone becomes a star: "Every once in a while the camera falls in love with a face." The movie camera loves in its way; the television camera, in its. Lacking a camera, the theater requires presence; unencumbered by setups and editing choices, the stage expects actors to transcend the aspect ratio nature has given them without mechanical aid. Similarly, the television camera can capture facets of a performer's personality that elude the movie camera, and vice versa. John Travolta, Robin Williams (the alien from Ork in *Mork and Mindy*, another ABC sitcom that Eisner shepherded), and Eddie Murphy went on to become bona fide movie stars. Henry Winkler, Tony Danza, and Farrah Fawcett, who had all appeared in successful TV series (Winkler in *Happy Days*, Fawcett in *Charlie's Angels*, Danza in *Taxi* and *Who's the Boss?*) fared poorly in their Paramount debuts: Winkler in *The One and Only* (1978), Danza in *Going Ape!* (1981), and Fawcett in *Sunburn* (1979). Like many Paramount films of the 1975–85 period, these would have been better movies of the week than feature films if they were buttressed with some names from the past that might compensate for watching television performers who could have appeared to better advantage in their own series. The flaw in the Eisner-Diller philosophy was the belief that the chief differences between a TV movie and a theatrical film were image size, venue, and interchangeability of performers. TV audiences would probably have accepted any known sitcom actors in the *ABC Movie of the Week*; however, placing some of them on the big screen not only invited comparison with their television image but also with actors who have acquired a screen persona without having gone the TV route.

Television also imbued Diller and Eisner with a respect for the producer and a suspicion of directors who pose as auteurs. In television, directors are faceless. If anyone in television acquires a name besides a performer, an anchor, or a talk show host, it's a producer—and not very many of those, either: Steve Bochco (*Hill St. Blues, L.A. Law, Doogie Howser, M.D., NYPD Blue*), Norman Lear (*All in the Family, Maude, Sanford and Son*), David E. Kelley (*Ally McBeal, The Practice, Chicago Hope*). But they are known for their series, not for themselves. On the other hand, who knew, or cared about, the director of a given episode of *The Jeffersons* or *Happy Days*?

Within a few years of his coming to Paramount, Eisner issued his manifesto: the "MDE Philosophy (1982)." The fact that he used his initials as a mark of authorship suggests he had now become secure enough to formulate policy—the same policy that he would have enforced had he remained in television. The ninety–minute movies of the week inspired him to aim for films that were a little longer—not much, perhaps, but somewhere in the vicinity of a hundred minutes. Anticipating objections that he was an opportunist who had figured out that hundred–minute movies would guarantee more showings in theaters, Eisner had a ready explanation: "At 100 minutes people's minds begin to wander," Eisner maintained, implying a lack of faith in myriad moviegoers, past and present, who had no trouble sitting through *Gone with the Wind* and both parts of *The Godfather*.[32] Eisner was not one for exceptions: "Keep the movies light, keep the movies short and keep the movies coming."[33]

According to Charles Fleming, who has had access to both the "MDE Philosophy" and an earlier text written largely by Don Simpson somewhere around 1980, the Simpson manifesto was the unacknowledged basis of the "MDE Philosophy."[34] Yet Simpson was merely expanding upon an earlier theory of Spielberg's: "If a person can tell me the idea in 25 words or less, it's going to make a pretty good movie. I liked ideas, especially movie ideas, that you can hold in your hand."[35] What mattered to Simpson was not the word count but the idea, a term he emphasized in his "Paramount Corporate Philosophy": "a powerful *idea* is at the heart of any successful movie; a good idea is one that seems imaginative, original: a creative writer can ... greatly enhance an idea that would otherwise have been only mildly interesting."[36] One can only speculate on the kind of production head Simpson would have been if he could have exorcised his demons. Given his ability to articulate his "ideas" in language that did not reek of the marketplace, Simpson might have steered Paramount in a direction somewhere between Evans/Bart and Diller/Eisner.

But Diller and Eisner had never divested themselves of the television mentality. Just as ABC had to come up with movies for Tuesdays, then Wednesdays as well, and finally Sundays, too, Paramount also had to keep grinding out the product. Since Diller and Eisner shared the same background, Diller was in complete agreement with the "MDE Philopsophy." In fact, he would have agreed even before the philosophy was promulgated. Diller's main concern was to enforce it, since his contacts in Hollywood were then minimial.

The Paramount films of the Diller-Eisner-Katzenberg era (roughly from the mid-1970s to the early 1980s) were markedly different from those of the Evans-Bart years. There were hits (*Foul Play* [1978], Eddie Murphy's early films, *Heaven Can Wait* [1978], plus the aforementioned

Saturday Night Fever, Terms of Endearment, Grease, Star Trek: The Motion Picture, etc.), to be sure. But artistically there was nothing comparable to the *Godfather* films, *Chinatown, Nashville, Murder on the Orient Express,* or *The Day of the Locust,* none of which were remotely high concept. The closest approximation to *Chinatown* in terms of direction, writing, and performance was *Atlantic City,* but that was because of a perfect mesh of director (Louis Malle), writer (playwright John Guare), and stars (Burt Lancaster and Susan Sarandon). Yet *Atlantic City* was another film not easily categorized; how does one pitch a film in which a city suffering from urban decay is a metaphor for the blighted lives of the characters?

The Diller-Eisner films had something else in common: with few exceptions, they were not the work of major directors or auteurs. And the auteurs, past and present, whom Diller managed to recruit, gave Paramount inferior product: Elia Kazan's *The Last Tycoon* (1976), a lifeless version of F. Scott Fitzgerald's last (and incomplete) novel; William Friedkin's *Sorcerer,* an overproduced remake of Clouzot's classic, *The Wages of Fear.* While it was commendable of Paramount to produce the movie versions of two E.L. Doctorow novels, *Ragtime* and *The Book of Daniel,* neither captured the density of the original even though Milos Forman directed *Ragtime* (1981) and Sidney Lumet, *Daniel* (1983), as the adaptation was called. Although it seemed that *Ragtime* was impossible to dramatize, with its mix of real and invented characters and situations, Terrence McNally's book for the 1997 Tony Award–winning musical at least succeeded in reproducing the fiercely liberal and socially conscious spirit of the novel.

Even so, *Ragtime* was a Dino De Laurentiis production, for which Diller and Eisner could take no credit; other quality pickups were Blake Edwards's *S.O.B.* and *Gallipoli* (both 1981), the latter arguably the strongest futility-of-war movie since *All Quiet on the Western Front* (1930) and one that Paul Bluhdorn had brought to the studio. At the other extreme were such low-grade pickups as *Up in Smoke* (1978), *Meatballs* (1979), *Going Ape* (1981), and the notorious *Friday the 13th* (1980), which was made for a mere five hundred thousand dollars, brought in $15.7 million, and spawned eight sequels.

If Steven Spielberg ended up, however briefly, at Paramount, the reason was Eisner's determination to keep turning out hits despite cutting deals that might, on the surface, have seemed foolhardy. In 1981, Spielberg, who had experienced a real flop with *1941* (1979) but was still bankable, and George Lucas, whose *Star Wars* (1977) was then the highest-grossing film of all time, put together a proposal with the aid of their lawyer, Tom Pollock. They would offer their combined services to any studio willing to meet their terms, which required the studio to provide complete financing; pay Spielberg $1.5 million to direct and Lucas $4 million to produce the film through his production company, Lucasfilm; charge neither overhead nor a distribution fee; waive the ownership rights in favor of Lucasfilm; split the profits so that Lucas would get half once the negative cost had been recouped and the rentals reached $50 million and 40 percent when they hit $100 million, and Spielberg would get 10 percent once the $40 million mark had been reached after recoupment (but *before* Lucas got his share)—and then an additional 15 percent.[37]

Although Diller, like practically everyone else in Hollywood, dismissed the proposition as an ego trip, Eisner did not. He was fascinated by the plot of their proposed film: *Raiders of the Lost Ark* (1981), which reminded him of some of the old movie serials that had been reedited into features for television. Eisner was right: *Raiders* was a throwback to *Nyoka and the Tigermen* (1942), a fifteen–chapter serial about an expedition in search of the "lost" tablets of Hippocrates, on which were inscribed a cure for cancer. The stone tablets in *Raiders* contained the text of the Ten Commandments, preserved in an ark—a wooden chest that had once been deposited in the Temple of Jerusalem but had long disappeared. The villains in the serial were Arabs under the rule of the wicked Queen Vultura, who, for some reason (perhaps longevity), wanted the tablets for herself. In *Raiders*, set in the late 1930s, the villains were Nazis.

Eisner convinced Diller that the film could be made for $20 million and that, with a little negotiating, more favorable terms could be reached. Eventually, the terms were slightly altered: Paramount received a distribution fee (but less than usual), and the profits were split more equitably, with Paramount getting slightly more than half. Even so, no other director-producer team could have even come close to getting the deal that Spielberg and Lucas did. Not only did they bring *Raiders* in under $20 million (and were rewarded in bonuses for doing so), but they also produced a film that, at the time, was Paramount's most profitable: $363 million in rentals.

Spielberg gave Paramount two other Indiana Jones films, *Indiana Jones and the Temple of Doom* (1984) and *Indiana Jones and the Last Crusade* (1989), both successful, undemanding, but vastly inferior to his masterpiece—the Columbia release, *Close Encounters of the Third Kind* (1977).

By the time *Temple of Doom* opened, Diller had left Paramount, followed by Eisner and Katzenberg. In 1982, Bluhdorn suddenly began delegating responsibility. He put together a council of executives consisting of Gulf + Western president David Judelson; two other executive vice presidents, Lawrence E. Levinson and James I. Spiegel; and, of course, Martin Davis. The previous year he had started selling entire subsidiaries (e.g., Brown, the paper company) or parts of them (e.g., New Jersey Zinc). On the surface, neither the creation of an executive council nor divestiture seemed unusual in a conglomerate. Only a few knew that Bluhdorn was putting his house in order; he had been diagnosed with leukemia in 1978. A few years later, colleagues noticed that his hair was styled differently. Bluhdorn had not changed barbers; he was wearing a hairpiece to conceal the baldness caused by chemotherapy. His secret was so well guarded that it was never mentioned in any of the obituaries, which reported the cause of death as a heart attack on board the company jet while returning from the Dominican Republic, where he had a home and where Gulf + Western had sugar investments. Reliable sources insist that he died in his Dominican Republic home and his body was flown to New York on the Gulfstream jet to conceal the real cause of death.[38] Even in New Hollywood, the sensational takes precedence over the truth, which ironically may well have been a combination of leukemia and heart failure. But this was not what his widow, Yvette, or Gulf + Western wanted the world to know. However, anyone bothering to consult the death certificate would discover that Bluhdorn succumbed to "generalized lymphoma."

What Wall Street knew, or at least suspected, was that if Martin Davis became Bluhdorn's successor, Gulf + Western would be a different company; what Hollywood knew was that it would also be a different Paramount with no room for the tribe of Diller—or the "Killer Dillers," as they had been dubbed.

Goodbye, Charlie

B luhdorn's death immediately aroused speculation about his successor. The corporate world, which equated Gulf + Western with metals, auto parts, tobacco, real estate, sugar, and beef (but not necessarily with Paramount Pictures), favored David Judelson or John H. Duncan over Martin Davis, the loyal retainer who had stood in the Great Man's shadow, and was often ordered to leave the room when a conversation turned private. Yet Judelson and Duncan, despite their positions as Gulf + Western president and executive committee chairman, respectively, lacked Davis's knowledge of the entertainment sector, which was exhibiting real growth, as opposed to sugar manufacturing and industrial products, which seemed to have peaked.

By streamlining the company in the years before his death, Bluhdorn had really been shifting Gulf + Western's emphasis away from consumer products (e.g., clothing, bedding, home furnishings), manufacturing, and equipment—and toward media (film, television, book publishing). In 1975, the publishing house of Simon & Schuster joined the Gulf + Western family; three years later, Bluhdorn added the Madison Square Garden corporation (the Garden, the New York Knicks, and the Rangers) to the Entertainment Group.

If "life is a casting off," as Linda Loman observed in *Death of a Salesman*, Bluhdorn spent the last years of his shedding as many vestiges of the old Gulf + Western as he could in the limited time he had, while adding replacements that would form the basis of a media-driven conglomerate. The casualties included Brown's paper operations; Marquette, the cement company; Providence Capitol International Insurance; Famous Players Realty; part of New Jersey Zinc; and Gulf + Western's one-third interest in Quebec Iron & Titanium. What Bluhdorn began, Davis completed.

Although Davis was not the unanimous choice among the elders of the board, he was the only one who understood that Bluhdorn's Gulf + Western had become obsolete. The balloon that Bluhdorn had inflated as if it were unburstable had begun losing air in 1980. Even Bluhdorn knew it was deflation time. If there was anyone who could at least bring the balloon down to earth, it was Davis, who had worked behind the scenes (as the board knew) to save Bluhdorn from ignominy when, in 1975, the SEC accused Gulf + Western of withholding $38 million in profits from the Dominican Republic, where Gulf + Western had major sugar-manu-facturing operations. Davis had also performed a rescue operation, if not a miracle, two years later when Bluhdorn was placed in the most embarrassing situation of his life when investigative reporter Seymour M. Hersh revealed, in a three-part series in the *New York Times*, that the SEC had embarked upon a thorough investigation of Gulf + Western early in 1976.[1]

In November 1974, Joel A. Dolkart, Gulf + Western's general counsel, was indicted for embezzling $2.5 million from Simpson, Thatcher, and Bartlett, the law firm in which he had been a partner. To avoid a jail sentence that could have carried up to three years, Dolkart agreed to cooperate with the SEC. Dolkart testified that Bluhdorn had not told the truth about the suit that A&P had brought against him in 1973 in which Bluhdorn was accused of purchasing a million shares of A&P stock in preparation for a takeover. Bluhdorn denied that his interest was sparked by a marketing study prepared for A&P by Gulf + Western's research department, which showed that the company could be easily acquired. Dolkart's reviving the A&P affair was a moot point, since Gulf + Western had already been forced to dispose of the stock.

Dolkart's testimony was a combination of schadenfreude and fear of incarceration. In September 1974, two months before he was charged with embezzling from Simpson, Thatcher, and Bartlett, he had been dismissed from Gulf + Western for doing the same thing.

Dolkart had little to offer the SEC, which had amassed most of the evidence itself: misleading financial statements in which profits were hidden from the stockholders; unreported use of Gulf + Western money for the vacations and chauffeur-driven limos of senior executives; inflated prices for stocks and real estate, market fluctuations caused by Bluhdorn's habit of using Gulf + Western stock as collateral for personal loans in order to purchase more stock; prepayment of sugar export taxes to the Central Bank of the Dominican Republic so that Gulf + Western could take unrestricted amounts of money out of the country; and avoidance of taxes that normally result from leasing films to television by creating a Canadian subsidiary, Paramount Television Sales, with proceeds listed as "foreign income."

Hersh's first article told the true story about *Darling Lili:* how Gulf + Western, rather than write the film off as a loss, worked out an arrangement with Commonwealth United wherein it gave $12 million in cash and 50 percent of the profits in return for a $30 million package consisting of stocks, warrants, and debentures that were used to acquire 15 million SGI shares, recorded at one and one-half times their worth, so that the Italian real estate conglomerate could purchase 50 percent of the Paramount lot. All Davis ever said about the SEC investigation was, "[Bluhdorn] put his life in my hands. I was not a target but they were the toughest seven years [i.e., 1973–82] I ever had to handle."[2] Davis handled it well; the SEC's suit against Gulf + Western was dismissed in 1981.

Since Davis was credited with having spared Gulf + Western the embarrassment of a public apology, the board regarded him more favorably; if Bluhdorn's empire had to be further downsized, if not dismantled, Davis was the one to do it. Thus Martin Davis was elected vice chairman and CEO of Gulf + Western—the position of board chair having been left vacant in Bluhdorn's memory. Yet that mattered little: Davis was running the show.

In November 1983, Gulf + Western was even leaner than it had been at the time of Bludhorn's death. By then, Davis had sold off 20 percent more of the company's holdings, including Consolidated Cigar, Chicago's Arlington Race Track and Long Island's Roosevelt Raceway, and various units of the manufacturing and natural resources groups.

By the end of 1982, it had become evident that, however Gulf + Western would be reconfigured, entertainment would be much more than a thin slice of a pie graph, as it had been two years earlier when it represented a mere 13 percent of Gulf + Western's 1980 earnings, which totaled $4 billion. A different picture emerged for fiscal 1982: 22 percent of the company's $6.4 billion revenues came from entertainment; by 1988, it was 37 percent. Publishing's contribution, which averaged a paltry 2 percent in 1980, had risen to an astonishing 23 percent by 1988.[3]

Yet even in 1982, the year before Bluhdorn's death, the Paramount purchase could no longer be dismissed as "Bluhdorn's Folly" when movies and home video brought in $479 million. The future of Gulf + Western lay, if anywhere, in communications—the perfect designation for the company, if a change of name and identity were needed. And if Paramount (film, television, home video) became the company's cornerstone, "Paramount Communications" would be more accurate than the geographical anomaly, Gulf + Western.

Although Diller supported Davis in the battle of succession, probably because Diller thought Davis was the one most likely to implement Bluhdorn's reforms,[4] he must also have suspected that Davis had no intention of continuing the Bluhdorn tradition of capricious acquisitions. If Davis's goal was a media conglomerate, it was Diller's, also—and one that he would pursue throughout his career. But each would pursue his goal separately; there was no room for Barry Diller in Martin Davis's dream: the as-yet-unnamed phoenix that would rise from the ashes of Gulf + Western.

Meanwhile, Diller—and Eisner, too—wondered about Davis's plans for Gulf + Western and their role in the new company. Davis had resented the attention Bluhdorn lavished on Diller. Bluhdorn's paternalism was bad enough; worse were his feeble attempts at matchmaking, as if Diller as heir apparent needed a hand-picked consort. Bluhdorn was either naive or chose to ignore Diller's indifference to women except as friends or social embellishments. Bluhdorn could never have fathomed a man capable of sustaining a platonic relationship with a woman as glamorous as designer Diane von Furstenberg, who became his wife on 2 February 2001. Still, Bluhdorn's obsession with finding Diller a mate, so that his surrogate son could provide him with surrogate grandchildren, must have riled Davis, who may have suspected, as others later did, that whatever Diller's sexual orientation may be, he was able to convert passion into productivity without wasting energy that could be used for a deal on a relationship.

If Davis was jealous of the bond between Bluhdorn and Diller, it was because he did not understand the basis: each was impressed by the other but for the wrong reasons. Bluhdorn was taken with what he considered Diller's sophistication, which was largely a matter of style and erudite observations that came from self-education rather than a college classroom. Diller was impressed with what he regarded as Bluhdorn's entrepreneurial genius that had led to the creation of a megacorporation, even though some of the acquisitions were more spur-of-the moment inspirations than the fruit of careful research. Diller, on the other hand, was not an indiscriminate shopper; he focused on one area, mass media. Still, if Diller had a role model, it must have been Bluhdorn; for just as Bluhdorn spent a lifetime acquiring and spinning off so that it was difficult to know Gulf + Western's exact makeup at any given time, Diller also amazed and confounded those who tried to peg him as he moved from ABC to Paramount and from Paramount to Fox, never able to satisfy the restlessness that later brought him into cable television through the back door of on-air shopping. By creating USA Networks and acquiring October Films in 1999, Diller was comfortably straddling the two media, television and film, where he had first made his mark twenty years earlier.

Diller is the kind of executive a bureaucrat like Martin Davis would envy. But Davis's envy also extended to Eisner and Katzenberg, although apparently not to Dawn Steel, who had yet to get the kind of press Diller and Eisner were receiving. Diller not only made $585,000 more than Davis in 1983 ($2 million in salary and bonuses), but both he and Eisner were credited, as they should have been, with Paramount's fiscal health. Davis resented the coverage the "Killer Dillers" were getting, notably in David Blum's flattering *Vanity Fair* piece in which Eisner was termed a "genius of intuition" and "one of the five or ten most powerful people in the movie business."[5] Davis apparently failed to understand that journalists do not associate heads of conglomerates with creativity, even conglomerates with a movie studio. Bluhdorn was better known than anyone else at Gulf + Western because of his eccentricity and the oddball nature of the edifice he built on an auto parts foundation. Neither colorful nor eccentric, Davis was too much the conventional servant-turned-master to merit a profile. When he was the subject of an article, it was more about the company than about him. If Davis wanted the kind of accolades Diller and Eisner received, he would have to reconfigure Gulf + Western as a media conglomerate—as he would in 1989.

Meanwhile, the divestitures were turning what was left of the old Gulf + Western into a sleeker, sexier operation. One thing was certain: the phoenix about to emerge would not have "Gulf + Western" emblazoned on its plumage.

A year after Bluhdorn's death, Davis announced that "Paramount .. . is no longer an island to itself, but part of the corporate scene."[6] "Media scene" would have been more accurate. Although Gulf + Western already owned Simon & Schuster, the media-obsessed Davis added another book publisher, Prentice-Hall, which joined the ever-shrinking Gulf + Western family in 1984. By 1985, Gulf + Western former staples—automotive parts, sugar, tobacco, home furnishings, and metals—no longer existed even as a segment of the company's pie graph, once the consumer and industrial products group was sold to Wickes. Three units survived the purge: financial services (commercial loans), entertainment (film, television, Madison Square Garden), and publishing (Simon & Schuster, Prentice-Hall). Soon there would be two.

By 1985, Diller, Eisner, and Katzenberg were no longer at Paramount. Diller must have suspected that he would have no place in Davis's Gulf + Western (or whatever it would be called after the winnowing was over). Apart from Diller's loathing of Davis—which had grown so intense that one observer remarked (hyperbolically, one hopes) that, if he could, Diller would "rip out [Davis's] eyes and piss in his skull"[7]—there was the matter of Diller's weakened authority.

If Diller felt an erosion of power, it was not paranoia on his part. Unable to turn the "Killer Dillers" against each other by false allegations, Davis went out of his way to lessen Diller's responsibilities by putting him in charge of the newly created leisure time group (film, television, and Madison Square Garden Corporation), while Frank Mancuso was made president of the entire film division, with jurisdiction over production, distribution, and marketing. Oddly, Bluhdorn was still living (although barely) on 28 January 1983 when the announcement appeared in the press, taking many by surprise. Diller and Eisner had to go through the motions, resorting to the usual adulatory cliches: Mancuso's promotion reflected "the availability of the perfect person" who had "proven himself worthy of meeting [the] challenge of uniting production, marketing and distribution."[8]

It is hard to believe that Davis would have made such an appointment without knowing that his boss was terminally ill and could expire at any moment, which is indeed what happened three weeks later.

On 28 January 1983, the Buffalo-born Mancuso was fifty, eight years older than Diller. Unlike Diller, who could boast of Marlo Thomas as a classmate, or Eisner, who had attended his first Broadway show, Rodgers and Hammerstein's *Oklahoma!*, at age five, Frank Mancuso, son of a post office employee, had discovered the magic of the movies working part-time as an usher at Buffalo's Lafayette Theatre. While still a student at the State University of Buffalo, Mancuso was promoted to Lafayette's assistant manager. Upon graduation, Mancuso took a job in 1958 with Basil Enterprises, which owned fifty theaters in western New York and Pennsylvania. The Paramount connection occurred four years later when Mancuso was hired as a booker at the Buffalo branch office.

For the next three decades, Mancuso was a Paramount regular. His ability to deal easily with exhibitors resulted in a series of promotions: branch manager (1965), vice president and general sales manager of Paramount Canada (1970), western division manager (1976), domestic distribution vice president (1977), executive vice president of distribution and marketing (1979), and finally president of distribution in 1980, with the added responsibility for pickups.

Mancuso's elevation to president was consistent with the growing importance of distribution, which had then become the choice route to studio head. If one could come up with the right ad campaigns and divine the right release patterns, production experience did not matter. Anyone could make a movie, but few moviemakers knew how to distribute it.

For that matter, few executives could distinguish pickups with popular appeal from independent productions that catered to highly selective audiences. Being responsible for pickups was rather like being a foster parent. The child already existed; all it needed was a home. Since acquisitions were other people's movies, it made sense to place them under the purview of the president of distribution, who would see that the producers were informed of the sales strategies being devised for their films.

Paramount had become so dependent on pickups that, in 1980, Bluhdorn's son, Paul, was made director of acquisitions, reporting to Mancuso; two years later, he was promoted to vice president, production (acquisitions). The promotion was more of a reward for Bluhdorn Junior's acquiring *Atlantic City* (1980) and *Gallipoli* (1981) for the studio than a job description. Later in 1982, Henry Seggerman replaced Bluhdorn Junior as director of film acquisitions. He too reported to Mancuso—not Bluhdorn Junior, as would have been expected in the light of Bluhdorn Junior's impressive title. Since 1980, when he was made president of domestic distribution, Mancuso had been involved in choosing the films that Paramount would distribute. He was not about to delegate responsibility to Bluhdorn Junior, whose new title may only have been an honorific.

Seggerman worked well with Mancuso. Realizing that Australia was not the continent "down under" but the home of some highly talented filmmakers and actors, Seggerman convinced Mancuso that *Crocodile Dundee* (1986) would score with audiences worldwide.[9] Seggerman was right: within ten years of its release, the film had enriched the studio by

$70 million. By putting the motion picture division under Mancuso in 1983, Davis was implicitly acknowledging Mancuso's marketing ability and his (and/or Bluhdorn Junior's and Seggerman's) knack for ferreting out successful pickups such as *Friday the 13th* and *Gallipoli*. He was also—implicitly, of course—punishing Diller for becoming a media icon, who, along with Eisner, was credited with Paramount's reputation as one of Hollywood's top three moneymaking studios since 1978.

Even if Davis had not elevated Mancuso to a position of such responsibility, Diller could not have stayed at Paramount much longer. Apart from the contempt he and Davis had for each other, Diller was meant to be a media czar, who would only work for someone else until he could found his own (as yet undetermined) kingdom. By fall 1984, Diller had moved clear across town, from Marathon Street to West Pico Boulevard, home of Twentieth Century–Fox, whose owner since 1981 was Denver oil tycoon Marvin Davis.

Compared to Paramount, Fox was a foundling awaiting adoption. In 1984, Paramount had captured 21 percent of the market share in terms of domestic rentals, as opposed to Fox's paltry 10 percent. Fox was getting by on the strength of the *Star Wars* sequels, *The Empire Strikes Back* (1980), and *Return of the Jedi* (1983), and a few others such as *Porky's* (1982) and *Romancing the Stone* (1983).

The skeptics who called Paramount "Bluhdorn's Folly" would have called Fox "Marv Davis's Dementia." There was, however, a method to Davis's madness. Marvin Davis did not plan to hold on to Fox indefinitely. First, he emulated Bluhdorn by reducing the bloat that had put Fox $600 million in debt. That meant the divestiture of as many holdings as possible that were not directly related to filmed entertainment—such as real estate, Coca-Cola Bottling Midwest, theaters in Australia and New Zealand, and some music-publishing subsidiaries. The spinoffs were not an indication that Fox would return to its former autonomous self; no studio would. Rather, they represented a stopgap measure until the rescue team arrived. The first member of the team was Barry Diller, who readily accepted Davis's $3 million-a-year offer. The second was Rupert Murdoch. Within a year of Diller's arrival, Davis sold half of Fox to Murdoch for $162 million. The year after that, 1985, Rupert Murdoch became the sole owner.

If Eisner ever thought he would inherit Diller's job, he had underestimated Martin Davis's obsession with a Paramount free of the "Killer Dillers." When Diller left Paramount in September 1984, Davis had no intention of filling his position. At the same time that Mancuso's appointment was announced, so was Arthur Barron's. Barron, then executive vice president of Gulf + Western's entertainment group, had been at Paramount since 1967, chiefly as financial administrator. Like Mancuso, Barron had no production experience, but that did not deter Davis from promoting him to Gulf + Western's entertainment group president. By dividing Diller's responsibilities between Mancuso and Barron, giving each a different title and having Mancuso report to Barron, Davis had made Eisner superfluous.

When Davis announced on 12 September 1984 that Mancuso had been made chairman and CEO of Paramount Pictures, Eisner knew that, if he remained, he would be reporting to Mancuso, which he had no intention of doing. If Mancuso could be chairman of Paramount, Eisner could be chairman of Disney—and CEO as well. Unbeknown to anyone at Paramount, Eisner had already engaged in serious discussions with Disney. On the same day that Mancuso's appointment was announced, Eisner handed in his resignation. Twelve days later, Eisner arrived at the Walt Disney Company in Burbank for his first day of work. By the end of September, Katzenberg had joined Eisner as head of Disney's motion picture and television division. Davis might have thought he was rid of his triple nemesis, but the truth is that he had lost one of Hollywood's most successful teams. Paramount was only their training ground.

Diller, Eisner, and Katzenberg were not the only ones to change their address. Although it proved a less newsworthy item, Frank Mancuso pulled up stakes in the East and swapped his home in Franklin Lakes, New Jersey, for a hilltop residence in Bel Air with pink marble floors. Not having a model to follow, Mancuso adopted a paternalistic style that, while sincere, was of little avail when someone (Dawn Steel, for example) needed an intercessor. But before the onset of disillusion, there was the honeymoon period. At first, Mancuso behaved as if he were a benign patriarch, with everyone more of a family member than an employee. And "family" extended to the studio as well.

In 1987, Mancuso decided to restore a sense of history to Paramount by renaming twenty-seven buildings after stars, executives, and various other personnel who had made the studio famous: music was named after Bing Crosby, the directors' building after Ernst Lubitsch, wardrobe after Edith Head, etc. Mancuso was able to indulge in such an admirable but ultimately inconsequential activity because three years earlier Davis had brought in Ned Tanen, former president of Universal Pictures, as president of the Motion Picture Group. Davis obviously realized that, although production, distribution, and marketing fell under Mancuso's jurisdiction, Mancuso could not possibly do justice to three such disparate functions. Tanen's appointment was intended to relieve Mancuso of some of the burdens that had been imposed on him, thereby freeing him to perform his corporate duties. Davis was so desperate to fill the void left by the departures of Diller, Eisner, and Katzenberg that it did not matter that Tanen's production company, Channel, was still based at Universal. At least Tanen agreed to take the job.

Tanen made it abundantly clear to the press that Paramount (i.e., Davis) had sought him out because of his record at Universal. In addition to telling the *Los Angeles Herald Examiner* (9 October 1984) that he was "partly responsible for the outstanding decade Universal Pictures enjoyed from 1973–82," he also announced that he did not "intend to take a back seat to anyone."

Tanen gradually assumed greater control over marketing, even though that had been Mancuso's strength. In August 1985, Barry London, president of domestic distribution, was named president of distribution and marketing, reporting to Tanen. Like Mancuso, London had started out in distribution, booking films for Los Angeles theaters. Joining Paramount in 1971, he soon became district manager of the western division and ten years later was promoted to vice president and general sales manager. Marketing had assumed such importance at Paramount that, in 1986, the entire operation was transferred to Los Angeles. With the closing of the New York office, where only the publicity staff remained, Paramount lost its widely respected president of marketing, Buffy Shutt. When Shutt left in November 1986, it was supposedly to write a book (subject matter unspecified); the real reason was her refusal to pull up stakes and relocate on the West Coast. Shutt would soon learn to make peace with Los Angeles when she and her colleague, Kathy Jones, joined Universal. Ironically, in 1999 Shutt and Jones decided to enter production, joining the tribe of ex-marketers and distribution heads who had mastered the art of promoting movies and now wanted to make them.

Paramount's obsession with marketing was further evidenced when Sid Ganis replaced Shutt. The New York–born, Brooklyn College–educated Ganis had worked at Fox and Columbia primarily as a publicist before coming to Warner Bros. in the late 1960s, where he eventually became vice president of worldwide advertising and publicity, an area in which he excelled. In 1978, he had left Warner's for Paramount where, within less than a decade, he had risen to president of worldwide marketing. If the next entry on Ganis's resumé involved production (which it did), it would come as no surprise. The center obviously was not holding. What had been a functioning mechanism had lost both form and momentum.

Tanen never intended to remain at Paramount indefinitely. In fact, he left in 1988 at age fifty-seven. Rather than replace Tanen with one person, Davis divided Tanen's responsibilities between Sid Ganis and Barry London (ages forty-eight and forty-one, respectively), who were designated copresidents of the motion picture group, each with different functions: Ganis was to oversee all phases of production, while London's bailiwick would be marketing and distribution. That each came from a marketing background and had virtually no production experience did not matter.

What mattered was the gross. Paramount captured only 20 percent of the market share in 1987, as opposed to 22 percent the previous year. In 1988, it was down to 14 percent. Paramount was no longer number one at the box office; Disney now enjoyed that distinction. Paramount was still reaping the profits of its 1987 hits, *Fatal Attraction* and *Beverly Hills Cop II.* As for new releases, in 1988 moviegoers gravitated to *The Naked Gun* and *Scrooged,* the studio's only real moneymakers. These, however, were not in the same league as Disney's *Who Framed Roger Rabbit?* and *Good Morning, Vietnam.* But then, Paramount no longer had Eisner and Katzenberg; Disney did.

Strangely, corporate Hollywood had not reached the stage where chaos threatened a studio's existence. For one thing, in 1988 there were no free-standing studios except Disney, which once had to release through United Artists and RKO and now could distribute its own films through Buena Vista Distribution. The seven studios (Warners, Universal, Columbia, Fox, MGM, UA, and Paramount) that survived the transition from old to new Hollywood were now subsidiaries of conglomerates; thus, if Paramount Pictures fell behind Disney in 1988, it was hardly panic time at the radically altered Gulf + Western, which still had enough assets (e.g., Madison Square Garden, MSG network, Simon & Schuster, theater chains, cable television) to offset losses in the filmed entertainment division. Paramount, like every other "studio," was merely a conduit for independent productions and pickups.

If an agent, star, or producer could not interest a studio in a particular property, there were several alternatives: it is shopped around until there is a buyer; it immediately goes into production (the impossible dream); it goes into development and then production; it is sentenced to development hell, followed by turnaround; it finds a home elsewhere, on network or cable television; it disappears into the limbo of the might-have-beens.

In corporate Hollywood, there are many explanations for the studio logo that appears at the beginning of a movie: the movie was developed exclusively for the studio, it was created by a production company based at the studio, it originated as a project tailored to a star under contract at the studio; it was the result of an executive's successful appeal on behalf of a film in need of a distributor or an orphaned project in need of a parent, it began as a spec script that landed on the right person's desk, someone did a pitch that wasted no time in getting the plot across in a few trendy words.

Although the 1988 releases—*She's Having a Baby, Plain Clothes,* and *The Blue Iguana*—originated at Paramount, they brought no distinction to the studio; furthermore, they lost money. What Paramount was doing wrong, Disney was doing right. If *Roger Rabbit* and *Good Morning, Vietnam* were such hits for Disney, the company's recent hires had something to do with it. In 1988, Disney enjoyed the right combination of luck, creativity, imagination—and the team of Eisner and Katzenberg, formerly of Paramount and now, respectively, chairman of the board and CEO and chairman of the motion picture and television division.

While it is true that 1987 and 1988 were years of turmoil at Paramount, turmoil does not necessarily spell disaster but merely the absence of vision and policy. The only vision that Martin Davis had was to reduce Gulf + Western to a shell that would house the media conglomerate he had been creating—a task that would be completed before the end of the decade. Meanwhile, it was the usual round of lawsuits, departures, and firings.

In 1988, one of the most publicized suits in entertainment history was brought against Paramount by humorist Art Buchwald. After the Eddie Murphy movie, *Coming to America,* was released in June 1988, Buchwald noticed similarities between the film and a treatment that he had written, "King for a Day," which Paramount had optioned in 1983.[10]

In the treatment, which seems to have been more of a plot outline, an African king, learning he had been deposed while visiting the United States, is forced to stay on, living in a ghetto and working in a fast-food restaurant. Since the plot suggested a one-character version of Eddie Murphy's second and highly profitable film for Paramount, *Trading Places,*

"King for a Day" was planned as a vehicle for the popular comic actor who was quickly becoming a Paramount regular. However, in 1985, Paramount dropped its option on "King for a Day" but not Buchwald's concept for a film in which Murphy would play an African on a royal visit to America. Alain Bernheim, Buchwald's close friend who also expected to produce the film, succeeded in placing "King for a Day" at Warner's. But in January 1988, Warner's canceled production plans because the plot was too similar to a film that Paramount was about to release, one in which an African prince (played, naturally, by Murphy) comes to America (specifically, Queens, as opposed to Washington, D.C.), where he finds a wife.

Obviously, *Coming to America* was inspired by "King for a Day." However, it then took on a life—and a plot—of its own. Paramount could have gotten off the hook by acknowledging Buchwald's contribution with a simple credit (e.g., "based on a concept by Art Buchwald"). Instead, the studio claimed that *Coming to America* was based on an original idea, for which Eddie Murphy, who insisted he had never seen Buchwald's treatment, received a story credit.

Buchwald and Bernheim's $5 million suit against Paramount (the amount increased as potential net profits were factored in, since a percentage of the net had originally been part of the deal) only succeeded in making their lawyers richer. The March 1992 decision, rendered by Los Angeles Superior Court judge Harvey A. Schneider, required Paramount to pay Buchwald $150,000 and Bernheim $750,000. The $900,000 didn't even cover their legal fees, which averaged $2.5 million.

The suit made it clear that accountancy, Hollywood style, bears no resemblance to Accounting 101. Thus, a film like *Coming to America,* which grossed more than $140 million domestically, registered a net profit of approximately $15 million once distribution fees and expenses, overhead (both Paramount's and Eddie Murphy Productions'), interest on overhead, and interest on the negative cost were deducted.[11] Buchwald learned the hard way: a cut of the net is not a cut of the gross. But only the privileged get a gross percentage deal.

The years 1987–88 were also ones of executive bloodletting. By then, Hollywood was used to the rhythm of arrivals and departures as executives followed the yellow brick road from studio to studio. Dawn Steel was not—or did not plan to be—one of the industry's itinerants. Steel felt at home at Paramount, not knowing her days there were numbered. For a woman, her ascent to Paramount's equivalent of the executive suite was swift but deserved. Steel was so elated by the ease with which she had scaled the corporate ladder that she felt secure enough to marry producer Chuck Roven on 2 June 1985.

She felt no threat when Frank Mancuso, unable to juggle all the roles that his new position required, relinquished some of his authority to Ned Tanen. After all, Tanen had told the press that, as far as he was concerned, it was a temporary appointment. Besides, Steel believed she had proved her worth by turning *Flashdance* into a moneymaker and putting *The Untouchables* (1987) into production, rightly believing it would also be a high grosser.

However, by 1987 Steel began feeling pressured, partly because she was a woman surrounded by men hoping to see her fail, partly because she now saw a side of Tanen that had not been evident when he accepted the Paramount presidency: his habit of hurling sharpened pencils at members of his staff without the slightest concern about their impact.[12] Even so, Steel believed she had an ally in Mancuso, little knowing that confrontation was not his strong suit or that, when the gods of the mountain required a sacrifice, she would be the offering.

Diller and Eisner had never found Steel threatening because they considered her one of them—not "one of the boys" but one of the pros. Nor did she find it difficult working with Don Simpson, who understood her frustration. It was as if she were trying to carve her initials on a wall that was too cracked to accommodate them. Whether Steel was trying to prove herself as Paramount's first female president of production or was simply doing her job is irrelevant; the truth is, it was a job she could have performed were it not for Tanen's erratic behavior, Mancuso's inability to take sides, and the pervasive sexism that led to her being criticized for behavior that would have been tolerated, however grudgingly, in men.

And so Dawn Steel became "Steely Dawn" and the "Queen of Mean." Ironically, "Steel" was the emblematic surname that her bodybuilder father had adopted. But in 1988 names did not matter, only epithets. The December 1988 issue of *California* magazine, which featured Steel on the cover, contained an article entitled "Who Are the Worst Bosses in California?" Naturally, Steel was one of them.

When she was made president of production in 1985, David Kirkpatrick was one of several executives who were unhappy about her appointment. Kirkpatrick, a graduate of the California Institute of the Arts, had joined Paramount's story department in 1979, leaving two years later to take a job at United Artists. Kirkpatrick was the peripatetic type that regarded Hollywood as a revolving door through which the "mobile moguls," as *Variety* once dubbed the new breed, exited one studio to enter another. When UA proved unsatisfactory, Kirkpatrick was back at Paramount a year later, this time as executive director of production. Because he had a knack for picking out properties such as *Beverly Hills Cop* that had box-office potential, he was promoted to executive vice president of production, reporting to Dawn Steel. The next stop, or so he thought, was president. Although he had been bypassed in favor of Steel, Kirkpatrick stayed on until the beginning of 1987, when he abruptly left Paramount to become production head of the troubled Weintraub Entertainment Group. Since Kirkpatrick had broken his contract, Paramount sued; the matter was settled out of court, with Kirkpatrick being ordered to repay his bonuses. One would have thought Kirkpatrick had burned his bridges at Paramount, but prodigal sons have been known to return home on foot.

Meanwhile, Weintraub Entertainment Group started going under, and Dawn Steel went on maternity leave. In March 1987, two months after Kirkpatrick had left Paramount, Steel gave birth to a daughter, Rebecca. While still on leave, she picked up the latest *Variety* and read that she had been fired. Gary Lucchesi had been named executive vice president of the motion picture group, assuming many of the duties that she had performed as president. Although Mancuso assured her she had a place at the studio, he could not explain what it was. One thing was certain: Steel was no longer head of production.

Tanen took advantage of Steel's maternity leave to remove her, although it was bound to happen eventually. She paid the price for entering the men's club and discovered that the members were really boys—and petty ones at that.

Only the self-deluded could feel secure at Paramount. Even Mancuso must have wondered how long he could last, given the criticism he had been receiving from stars and agents, who accused him of indifference (which was really a manifestation of the insecurity that comes from doing a job unsuited to one's temperament and abilities). Mancuso understood distribution; he was not meant to be chairman and CEO of Paramount Pictures. Lucchesi, too, must have wondered how long he would remain in his new position as president of production, Steel's title when she was ousted.

Not long. In July 1990, Kirkpatrick—who, after the Weintraub Entertainment Group folded, had gone over to Burbank and became production president of Disney/Touchstone—returned to Paramount. He had been away for only fifteen months! It did not seem to matter that he had jumped ship in January 1987. After all, he had had to reimburse Paramount for damage fees and bonuses, which came to around five hundred thousand dollars. The irony is that the prodigal son returned in glory, while the dragon lady departed in disgrace. In terms of personality, there was not that much difference between Steel and Kirkpatrick. Each had a reputation for being difficult, yet each was astonishingly competent. Steel could kick ass with the best of them, except that she did it in heels.

Kirkpatrick's coming in as executive vice president of the motion picture group made Lucchesi's title, president of production, meaningless. History was repeating itself; just as Lucchesi's elevation to executive vice president of the motion picture group in 1987 had represented a deliberate erosion of Steel's authority, the rehiring of Kirkpatrick with that title did the same to Lucchesi's.

Kirkpatrick was rehired for three reasons: to cut production costs, generate more in-house films, and reduce the number of projects in development—tasks requiring a certain amount of ruthlessness, of which Steel was more than capable. Steel could easily have stayed on at Paramount—antagonizing chauvinistic males and green-lighting films in which she believed, but always getting the job done. Vindication was relatively swift: less than a year after the returning Kirkpatrick was feasted with a fattened calf, which then had to be trimmed, he, Mancuso, and Lucchesi lost their jobs.

The 1990s witnessed tremendous changes at Paramount as a result of Davis's systematic winnowing of Gulf + Western. On 8 April 1989, Gulf + Western passed into history when Davis announced the birth of Paramount Communications, which, to use a movie cliché, had been many years in the making—six, to be exact. With the sale of Associates Capital, all that remained of the former Gulf + Western were its entertainment and publishing divisions consisting of the following:

- Paramount Pictures
- Paramount Pictures Television (*Cheers, Mission: Impossible, Family Ties*)
- USA Network (50 percent)
- Madison Square Garden (Knicks, Rangers, MSG Network)
- Famous Players, the Canadian theater circuit with 472 screens;

the Mann, Festival, and Trans-Lux chains; and interests in European, Latin American, and Australian circuits

■ Famous Music, the music-publishing division that controlled the rights to most of the music used in Paramount films, including such classic scores as Aaron Copland's for *The Heiress* and Franz Waxman's for *Sunset Boulevard* and *A Place in the Sun;* songs by such composers and lyricists as Frank Loesser, Hoagy Carmichael, Burton Lane, Johnny Burke and Jimmy Van Heusen, Harold Arlen, and Johnny Mercer; and such Oscar-winning songs as "Thanks for the Memory" (1938), "White Christmas" (1942), "Swinging on a Star" (1944), "Buttons and Bows" (1948), "Mona Lisa" (1950), "Que Sera, Sera" (1956), "Moon River" (1961), and "I'm Easy" (1975)

■ United International Pictures (UIP), Paramount's international distribution arm, co-owned by MCA and MGM/UA

■ Trade publishing (Simon & Schuster, Pocket Books)

■ Educational publishing (Prentice-Hall, Ginn & Co.)

In the spring of 1989, there were two scenarios for Paramount Communications: it could either grow by annexation or it could be annexed itself.

8

Sumner at the Summit

O n Monday morning, 18 March 1991, Frank Mancuso was about to leave for the studio when he received a call from Martin E. Davis, informing him that henceforth he would be reporting to Stanley Jaffe, whom Davis had just named president and COO of Paramount Communications. The call came a few hours before the press release. At least Mancuso was given advance notice, unlike Dawn Steel, who had learned about her firing from *Variety*. Although Mancuso claimed he had been taken by surprise, he should have realized that Jaffe was rising not only in Davis's estimation but in the industry's as well.

When Jaffe left Paramount in 1971, it had been a different studio; it was Bluhdorn's Paramount. Twenty years later, Hollywood was suffering from such a dearth of executive talent that the myth of the eternal return had become a reality. Those who exited in act one reentered in act two; the set looked different, but the plot was the same: the moguls on the march, stopping off at the old neighborhood before proceeding to the as-yet-unwritten third act.

Actually, Jaffe had been back at Paramount since 1982, not as an executive but as part of Jaffe/Lansing Productions, which he and Sherry Lansing had formed the same year. Lansing—a Northwestern University alumna, former high school teacher of English and math, television model, bit player (*Loving, Rio Lobo*), reader, story editor, and production executive—achieved instant celebrity in 1980 when she was named president of Twentieth Century–Fox, becoming the first woman to head a major studio. Feminists hailed her appointment as a sign that one of their own had managed to break through the glass ceiling. But their elation, and

Lansing's, was short-lived. By the end of 1982, Lansing was the *former* president of Fox, after too many of the films she green-lighted languished at the box office.

Lansing and Jaffe had both been at Columbia in the late 1970s—he as executive vice president of worldwide production, she as senior vice president of production. A dinner party given by columnist Joyce Haber resulted in a longstanding business relationship. Knowing that Lansing had once taught math in Watts and East Los Angeles and that Jaffe was a Wharton alumnus, one of the guests presented them with a math problem.[1] That they solved it in record time was not as surprising as their instant rapport. Hollywood was amazed that two such bipolar opposites— the abrasive, anger-prone Jaffe and the radiant, ever-smiling Lansing— had become close friends as well as partners.

Within two weeks of Lansing's departure from Fox, Jaffe/Lansing Productions had a distribution arrangement with Paramount. By 1991, Jaffe/Lansing had given Paramount such hits as *Fatal Attraction* (1987), which grossed $345 million worldwide; *The Accused* (1988), which won a Best Actress Oscar for Jodie Foster; and *Black Rain* (1989). Their track record indicated that they were better judges of product than Mancuso, who was held responsible for such flops as the *We're No Angels* (1989) remake, *Days of Thunder, Another 48 Hours,* and *The Two Jakes* (all 1990), although it was Sid Ganis who had put all of them into production. But Ganis had moved on to Columbia, and Davis was looking for a fall guy.

The reasons given for Mancuso's removal—lack of creative leadership, nonconfrontational style, indecisiveness, yielding to Tom Cruise's demand for $8 million rather than the agreed-upon $5 million for *Days of Thunder,* negotiating only with agents favorably disposed toward Paramount, failing to settle with Buchwald at the outset of the *Coming to America* suit when it was evident that Buchwald had a case, empowering the tyrannical David Kirkpatrick to cut production expenses at the cost of alienating everybody on the lot, including Jaffe—would have amounted to little or nothing had Paramount not fallen to sixth place, garnering only 12 percent of the market share.[2] If there was a deficit, it was primarily because of Davis's misguided attempt to stop the Time-Warner merger, not Mancuso's management style.

Davis had grandiose plans for Paramount Communications. While Bluhdorn had built Gulf + Western into a diversified conglomerate that eventually included an entertainment sector, Davis preferred a media empire, with Paramount Communications as its capital. In June 1989,

Davis was in a colonizing mood. His quarry, however, was a kingdom; if he succeeded, it would have been comparable to Caesar's conquest of Gaul.

In fall 1987, Time Inc. and Warner Communications Inc. (WCI) began discussing a merger in the form of a stock swap that would result in a made-in-heaven marriage of publishing and entertainment—the latter including a movie studio (Warner Bros.), television operations (Warner Bros. Television, Warner Cable), home video (Warner Home Video), and music publishing (the Atlantic, Electra, and Asylum labels; and through Warner/Chappel Music, an unparalleled number of copyrights). Such was the synergistic goal of Steve Ross, whose bio reads like an oldtime mogul's.[3] Born in Brooklyn to immigrant parents, Ross had a childhood not unlike William J. Fox's except that, instead of hawking his father's stove polish on the lower East Side, as Fox had done, Ross hustled supermarket shoppers in Flatbush who needed help with their groceries and bought discounted cartons of cigarettes that he sold by the pack to his father at a profit of five cents per pack. An entrepreneur before he reached adolescence, Ross was the prototypical American dreamer who never knew on which side of the rainbow the dream would end but knew only that waking too soon could end the dream forever. And so Ross kept dreaming, pausing intermittently for forays into such money-making ventures as funeral parlors, car rentals (Kinney Rent-A-Car), parking lots, garages, and cleaning operations. Next stop, show business: but first a talent agency; then a movie company, Warner Bros.–Seven Arts, which he transformed into Warner Communications Inc. in 1971, becoming WCI's chairman and CEO. Ross's fondest dream was to make WCI the world's largest media conglomerate, which could only happen if a union were forged between WCI and a company with interests in magazine and book publishing as well as cable television; in short, Time Inc.

Davis also viewed Time Inc. as a nubile prospect with a sizable dowry. Since he had made $3.35 billion on the sale of Associates First Capital, Davis was confident that he could match anything Time brought to the table. Of course, he would have preferred Time *and* WCI, but he might have recalled Bette Davis's words to Paul Henreid at the end of *Now Voyager* (1942): "Oh, Jerry, why reach for the moon? We have the stars." Bette Davis at least caught a star; Martin Davis caught nothing.

Although the Sherman Antitrust Act was being feebly enforced (a far cry from the 1940s when the Justice Department was screaming "monopoly!"), Davis had not become so monomaniacal as to think the shareholders would automatically endorse the addition of a publishing giant *and* a communications conglomerate, either or both of which could dilute the value of their stock and saddle the new entity with enormous debt. Merging with Time would be less problematic. Still, Davis seems to have had a contingency plan: if he failed to get Time, he would go after WCI.[4]

Once Davis realized that acquiring or merging with WCI required the Justice Department's seal of approval (which was unlikely without some spin-offs and the consolidation of similar units), he chose the part rather than the whole. The diversification that Davis sought was not to be found in another communications empire but in the realm of publishing—Time Inc. However, Ross, not Davis, was the one to find it.

In June 1989, Davis made a $10.7 billion cash offer (later raised to $12.2 billion) for Time Inc., which included such magazines as *Time, Fortune, Money, Life, Sports Illustrated, People,* and *Entertainment Weekly;* a publishing division composed of Warner Books, Time Life Books, and Little Brown & Co.; and cable networks Home Box Office (HBO) and Cinemax. Davis's bid forced Time, which sensed that its shareholders might figure out they would do better with Paramount, to switch from a stock swap to a cash deal—the latter not requiring the shareholders' approval. The result was an acquisition: Time Inc. would be acquiring WCI.[5] Paramount argued—in vain—that, if there were to be an acquisition, the shareholders would be better served if Paramount acquired Time than if Time acquired WCI. When the Delaware Court of Chancery upheld the Time-Warner merger, culminating in the removal of the hyphen and the birth of Time Warner, Davis had no other choice but to retreat to his own turf and give up lusting after other domains.

The fiasco proved that Davis was more adept at divesting than acquiring, although his argument—that, by shifting from stock-for-stock to cash, Time was behaving defensively (and ignoring the shareholders)—was well taken. Still, Davis's hostile offer was not worth the $55 million in legal fees.

Mancuso played no role in Davis's grandiose scheme. In fact, Mancuso was never even informed of it, which should have been a sign that he was on the way out. Regardless, someone had to be held accountable for the $7.3 million deficit for the first quarter of fiscal 1991. It would not, however, be Davis, although it was he who kept sweetening the deal with Time Inc. and, when that failed, resorted to an injunction to block the Time-Warner merger. Although Davis knew Mancuso was not at fault, this was as good a time as any to bring the Mancuso era to a close, particularly since Paramount's films had been performing so indifferently. Never having learned how to compose a "bad news" letter, Davis sent Mancuso a $20 million severance check, which was promptly returned. Davis was not the only litigant at Paramount. Mancuso retaliated with a $45 million breach-of-contract suit on the grounds that his contract had three and a half years to go.[6] The case was settled out of court—a gag rule preventing Mancuso's disclosing the amount, although it seems to have been $22 million, slightly more than he would have received had he cashed Davis's check.

By the end of 1991, David Kirkpatrick and Garry Lucchesi had been relieved of their duties, which were consolidated in a supposedly new position, president of the motion picture group/production, which was just a familiar title with an added responsibility. This was another case of old wine in new bottles; the steward of the moment was John Goldwyn, grandson of the legendary producer Samuel Goldwyn who had been at Paramount as a production executive since 1990; although the press made much of Goldwyn's lineage, no one expected his appointment to be anything other than temporary. All that really happened was that Lucchesi left Paramount but Kirkpatrick did not. The perennial survivor, Kirkpatrick was given a three-year production deal—Paramount's way of avoiding another breach-of-contract suit, since Kirkpatrick's five-year contract had three years and nine months more to go. Keeping Kirkpatrick on, particularly since he produced nothing for the studio, was typical of a spiral of mistakes, which, if they had been made half a century earlier, would have brought Paramount to the brink of bankruptcy. But Paramount was no longer an autonomous company; and the advantage, however dubious, of being a subsidiary is that the divisions that are thriving make up for the ones that are not.

By 1993, Stanley Jaffe had had enough of Kirkpatrick. To his credit, Jaffe never behaved vindictively toward Kirkpatrick, even though he could never forget the time Kirkpatrick was playing hatchet man and not only slashed the budget for *School Ties* (1992), a film about prep school anti-Semitism about which Jaffe felt passionately, but also refused to let him direct it.[7] However, by November 1993, Kirkpatrick had shown himself to be a nonproducing producer, although he was getting five hundred thousand dollars a year for sitting in Ned Tanen's old office, which he had no intention of vacating. Just as Paramount had sued Kirkpatrick for defecting to Disney (which then initiated and later dropped a suit against

Kirkpatrick for deserting the Mouse House to rejoin Paramount), Kirkpatrick was now suing Paramount. The grounds were breach of contract and emotional distress—the latter, the result of learning he had been evicted from his office when he found his furniture on the lawn. Paramount, delighted to be rid of its *bête noire,* settled with him because his contract had sixteen more months to run. Jaffe would not be staying at Paramount much longer himself; four months after Kirkpatrick exited, so did he.

At least Jaffe's second go-around as Paramount's president was longer than the first, which had lasted about a year and a half. This time, the situation was more complex, since he was part of Jaffe/Lansing Productions. Once he became president, Jaffe immediately withdrew his name, and the company became Sherry Lansing Productions. This was just the beginning of Lansing's tenure at Paramount, where she would achieve a permanence that is rare in Hollywood.

It is hard to know what motivated Jaffe's return to Paramount. At first, it might have seemed that, by bringing in his twenty-six–year-old son, Robert, as vice president of production, he was emulating Mancuso, who had found a place at Paramount for his son, Frank Junior, the independent producer. Everyone at the studio was delighted that Jaffe was not so nepotistic as to hire his sister, Andrea, whose reputation for abrasiveness matched her brother's except that her tantrums did not result in nosebleeds, as was the case with Stanley. Although she was an aggressive publicist, she encountered so many problems with producers, who questioned her marketing methods, that she was forced to resign as president of domestic marketing at Fox in 1994—the same year her brother had to leave Paramount.

At fifty, Jaffe was not fired by the same enthusiasm he had when he was Paramount's president twenty years earlier. In Hollywood, knowledge corrupts, and an insider's knowledge precludes a return to innocence. One of the reasons for Jaffe's return may have been the rumor—which was all it turned out to be—that Paramount was on the verge of acquiring NBC-TV or CBS. Then, too, Jaffe was a sports fan who would not pass up the opportunity to watch the Knicks from the best seats. Jaffe, in fact, seemed more interested in basketball, theme parks, and syndication rights for Paramount's television series than he was in movies.[8]

Jaffe did not have to worry about movies. Effective 1 July 1991, the chairman of Paramount Pictures was Brandon Tartikoff, Yale '70, who, upon graduation, decided television was his metier. By 1977, Tartikoff was in charge of comedy programming at NBC; by 1980, he was president of NBC Entertainment, a position he held for more than eleven years. When Tartkioff left NBC for Paramount, he not only left a job; he left a television legacy. Tartikoff understood that prime-time television required its share of sitcoms such as *Cheers* and *Golden Girls* and also intelligent hour-length series like *Hill Street Blues, St. Elsewhere,* and *L.A. Law.* Tartikoff's imaginative brand of programming led to NBC's becoming the top-rated network in 1986 when *The Cosby Show* and *Family Ties* ranked first and second, respectively, in popularity among viewers. NBC—which until the mid-1980s had ranked third—stayed on top until 1991, which, coincidentally, was the year that Tartikoff moved from television to film.

Tartikoff's five-year contract was further proof that, in New Hollywood, a television track record is the equivalent of a visa—or, as the characters in *Casablanca* (1942) would say, a letter of transit. Television, after all, had been the training ground for Diller, Eisner, Katzenberg, and Jaffe. Yet there were those in the industry who were dubious about Tartikoff's taste in film, wondering if the movies he had approved for NBC Productions—specifically, *Elvira, Mistress of the Dark* and *Tapeheads* (both 1988)—were indicative of what he had in mind for Paramount. Others questioned his taking a new job so soon after a near-fatal auto accident near Lake Tahoe on 1 January 1991 left him with a fractured pelvis and left his nine-year-old daughter, Calla, in need of rehabilitation therapy, which, given the nature of her head injury, required treatment in New Orleans, where a nationally recognized specialist practiced and where Tartikoff and his wife, Lilly, might have to relocate temporarily.

The skeptics had posed a rhetorical question. The answer was simple: accident or not, this was an opportunity Tartikoff could not let pass. Diagnosed with Hodgkins's disease in the early 1970s, Tartikoff may have suspected longevity was not in the cards. If so, he was right: he would die of the disease twenty-three years later at the age of forty-eight. Meanwhile, he had a chance to run a movie studio.

Since television was what Tartikoff knew, he was interested in such films as *Wayne's World* (1992), which replicated the freewheeling style of NBC's *Saturday Night Live* and *The Addams Family* (1992), a more sophisticated version of *The Munsters.* While these films may have been an index of Tartikoff's taste, they did not originate under him, nor could he take credit for their success at the box office any more than he could for the popularity of *The Naked Gun 2 1/2: The Smell of Fear* (1991), which seemed more like a succession of skits than a movie. As is always the case in Hollywood, Tartikoff was held responsible for a series of well-intentioned flops, including *Frankie and Johnny* (1991) and *Bebe's Kids* (1992), which may have received his imprimatur but not his input. The only film that Tartikoff ever had time to put into development was *All I Want for Christmas* (1991), a pitiful holiday tale of children trying to reconcile their estranged parents.

Tartikoff may have been a television visionary, but he was myopic when it came to film. Except for *The Addams Family* and *Patriot Games* (1992), Paramount's releases during Tartikoff's tenure were more reminiscent of mediocre television than such NBC classics as *L.A. Law* and *Miami Vice*. Whether or not these were the kinds of films Paramount would have made if Tartikoff had stayed on will never be known. Overwhelmed by the pace of Hollywood and Jaffe's micromanaging, Tartikoff resigned on 29 October 1992, having been in the job for one year and three months. He gave as his reason the need to be near Calla in New Orleans, although that had not seemed to be so urgent when he accepted the position or even during the time that he held it. The real reason was simple: Stanley R. Jaffe.

Jaffe had to replace Tartikoff immediately. Obviously, it would be an in-house appointment, and there was only one person on the lot suited to the job: Sherry Lansing, who, within a few weeks of Tartikoff's resignation, became chairman of the motion picture group. Lansing did not contest the sexist title; after all, unlike Dawn Steel, she had been accepted as one of the boys.

Although Lansing insisted she was not actively seeking the job, it became common knowledge that her appointment was Jaffe's idea, perhaps because he needed someone who shared his taste in films and whose equanimity would compensate for his lack of it; perhaps, also, to ensure that the films that would have come out under the Jaffe/Lansing banner if neither of them had moved into the executive suite would appear under Paramount's.

Since Paramount had fallen to sixth place in 1992, garnering only 9.9 percent of the market share (even Columbia and Universal did better with 12.6 and 11.6, respectively), Lansing was desperate for some hits in 1993, her first year in the job. However, her method of rewarding those who provided them raised some eyebrows.[9] Lansing was so delighted with the success of *The Firm* (1993) that she presented the star and director, Tom Cruise and Sydney Pollack—who made $12 million and $5.5 million, respectively (plus percentages)—with Mercedes Benz convertibles worth a hundred thousand dollars. To those questioning such largesse, Lansing insisted she was only trying to make Paramount "a warmer and more human place." Besides, she added, "It's not about cars. It's about relationships."[10]

It would not be about relationships much longer. By fall 1993, Paramount Communications had a new owner. By converting Gulf + Western into a media conglomerate, Davis had made it desirable to media conglomerateurs like Sumner Redstone.

In late August 1990, Sumner Redstone began buying up large quantities of Paramount stock, but so did Herbert J. Siegel. Siegel, however, was no more interested in Redstone's Viacom, a diversified communications and entertainment company, than Redstone was in Siegel's Chris-Craft. But each might be interested in Paramount Communications.

In May 1993, Sumner Redstone, having turned seventy, was at a stage in his life when empire-building hardly seemed worth the effort. Had he been actively looking for a studio thirty years earlier when Siegel and Martin were laying their snares for Paramount, he would have represented the kind of young blood the geriatric company needed. But Redstone was no ordinary entrepreneur; if he were, he would have retired after he acquired Viacom in 1987. Retirement was not an option when there was another sale to rack up that would make the Viacom purchase look like a bauble compared to a treasure trove like Paramount Communications. The average septuagenarian would have been satisfied with Viacom as his final trophy; it was a prospering company with cable, broadcasting (television and radio stations), and entertainment (distribution rights to television shows and feature films) divisions. But it was not enough; nothing would ever be enough for Sumner Redstone.

Cut from a different cloth than Davis or Diller, the Boston-born Redstone came from a family of New England exhibitors, although exhibition was hardly the business a graduate of the Boston Latin School and a Harvard alumnus (class of '44) was expected to enter, particularly after having stayed on at Harvard for his law degree, which he had received in 1947.[11] In the past, there had been directors, producers, and writers with baccalaureates and even higher degrees, but exhibitors were a different breed. Exhibitors owned the theaters (venues, spaces, outlets) for the product the studios siphoned into them. And how much of an education was necessary for running an outlet? Exhibition required more business savvy than brains.

Sumner's father, Michael Redstone (born Max Rothstein), was more typical of the old-style entrepreneur who set his sights on entertainment and capitalized on the venue of the moment. In 1936, after having achieved some success as a Boston nightclub owner, Michael Redstone decided to throw in his lot with a new form of exhibition: the drive-in movie. Most exhibitors would have scoffed at such a venture, as they probably had three years earlier when the first drive-in opened in Camden, New Jersey. Then, the industry was in such bad shape that even MGM, the "Tiffany of Studios," was in the red. But a dreamer—and Michael Redstone was that—might have foreseen a time when families would pile into a car and see a movie for a single admission instead of waiting in line at a theater where everyone would pay separately.

Accordingly, Michael Redstone checked out locations and decided that the Bronx was the right spot for New York's first drive-in theater, the Whitestone Bridge Drive-In, which was the fourth to open in the United States. There would be many other Redstone theaters, not all of which would be outdoors.

Until he was thirty, Sumner had shown little, if any, interest in the movies. In fact, if anyone seemed to fit the image of the twentieth-century movie czar, it was Sumner's father. Michael Redstone came from Boston's North End; after working as a truck driver, he started his own trucking business. Michael discovered mass entertainment by ushering at Boston's Olympia theater; he then graduated to nightclubs after purchasing Lou Walters's Latin Quarter on Winchester Street (not to be confused with the more famous New York equivalent). Finally, he entered exhibition. A typical scenario would have had Michael heading into production, à la Louis Mayer, who ran the gamut from rag picker and scrap metal collector to theater owner, distributor, and, finally, MGM production head; or Carl Laemmle, who traversed a similar route from exhibitor to distributor to president of Universal Pictures. Michael Redstone stopped with exhibition; his son did not.

After graduating from Harvard Law School at twenty-four, Sumner Redstone embarked upon a path that could have led to a successful career in academics, politics, or law. However, an instructorship at the University of San Francisco Law School in 1947 offered neither the challenge nor the remuneration he was seeking. In 1954, after having been an assistant to Tom Clark, the United States attorney general and a partner in a Washington, D.C., law firm, Redstone decided to join his father in the family business, Redstone Management, which evolved into National Amusements. However, in 1954, Redstone Management consisted of the Northeast Drive-in Theater Corporation. Believing that drive-ins would have their day but theaters would always continue in some form and at some location, Redstone was instrumental in moving the company into mainstream exhibition and shedding its drive-in past. The Northeast Drive-in Theater Corporation, which then became the Northeast Theater Corporation, was eventually absorbed by National Amusements. By 1999, National Amusements was the seventh-largest theater chain, with 1,235 screens worldwide. Redstone was chair and president of National Amusements; his daugher, Shari, executive vice president. At the same time, he was president of Viacom, owner of Paramount Pictures.

Thirty years earlier, it had seemed that Redstone would never leave the world of exhibition. If he was emulating Carl Laemmle or Louis Mayer, he should have found himself a studio by 1960 at the latest. Exhibition also appealed to Laemmle, who began by converting a Chicago storefront into a nickelodeon; and to Louis Mayer, who, discovering that a Massachusetts burlesque house was for sale, bought it and did the same. For Laemmle and Mayer, exhibition was the first leg of the journey to studioland once they realized the power and the glory (and the money) lay in moviemaking. Yet without their apprentice years, Universal Pictures and Metro-Goldwyn-Mayer would never have become what they did. Nor, one might add, would Viacom, without Redstone's much longer sojourn in what is often considered the backwater of the industry but Redstone knew was really a tributary: exhibition.

For almost twenty years Redstone remained in exhibition, where his legal knowledge proved useful to theater owners, whose cause he championed when the studios tried to enforce percentage arrangements that were unrealistic in view of the product being offered. But Redstone was not satisfied being a legal guru and president of the ever-growing National Amusements.

Redstone's experience in exhibition convinced him that, while the era of the studio system was over, the movie business was far from dead. Redstone was not a nostalgist; having no desire to resurrect a past in which he had played no part, he concentrated on a present he knew. Exhibition made him sensitive to the industry's resurgence in the 1970s; even before film historians dubbed the 1970s Hollywood's Second Golden Age, Redstone saw the gold in the box-office receipts. It was in the 1970s that he began to study the industry as if he were back at Harvard. He started buying stock in studios that were on the threshold of transformation, as they were about to acquire new owners. First, it was Fox. His interest in Fox was not merely sparked by the phenomenal success of *Star Wars* (1977), although the year of its release happened to coincide with the one in which he began purchasing stock in the studio. He also knew that Fox was in the throes of change; when oil tycoon Marvin Davis bought the studio in 1981, Redstone sold his stock for more than seven times what he had paid for it. Next, it was Columbia. By the end of 1981, Redstone and his family owned over 9 percent of Columbia Pictures' common stock. Although he insisted it was for investment purposes only, Redstone sold the stock at a profit the following year when Columbia was purchased by Coca-Cola.

MGM/UA seemed a dubious prospect, given its troubled history in the post-studio era; proxy fights in the 1960s had culminated in a new MGM in 1970 under the ownership of Kirk Kerkorian, who seemed to be the reincarnation of Charlie Bluhdorn.[12] Instead of starting with auto replacement parts, Kerkorian, the son of Turkish immigrants, began by buying up leftover airplanes from the second world war; from these, he created Trans International Airlines, a fancy name for an airline that flew only between Los Angeles and Las Vegas. Kerkorian, on the other hand, might have commented that "Gulf + Western" was just as high-sounding. Vegas made and unmade Kerkorian. He turned into such a gambler that it made no difference what the prize was as long as it paid off in cash and glamour. After selling Trans International to Transamerica, known primarily as an insurance conglomerate with such subsidiaries as Occidental Life, Kerkorian set out on the yellow brick road that eventually brought him into studio ownership.

The money Kerkorian made from the Trans International sale enabled him to start investing in MGM and eventually gain control of it in 1970. A decade later, he merged it with United Artists; the result was MGM/UA, a dual acronym that would have given Louis Mayer and the founders of United Artists apoplexy.[13] But since corporate America practices its own form of imperialism, colonies can be both wide-ranging and diverse. If Paramount could be inventoried along with other Gulf + Western assets such as sugar and beef, MGM/UA could also be satellites orbiting the Kerkorian constellation, along with hotel casinos.

In 1985, Redstone, sensing MGM/UA's future was far from rosy, sold his shares to Kerkorian at what seems to have been a considerable profit. Again, Redstone's timing was impeccable: in 1986, Kerkorian sold MGM/UA to Ted Turner, whose interest was not so much in the studio as in its library. Never having any intention, at least in 1986, of running a studio when he was enjoying his success as king of cable, Turner sold UA back to Kerkorian, and the MGM Culver City lot to Lorimar. Knowing that there would always be an audience for vintage movies (and needing product for his cable empire, which soon included a network devoted solely to movies of the past, Turner Classic Movies [TCM]), Turner kept the MGM library, which also included the pre-1948 Warner Bros. films and most of RKO's.

A year later, Redstone felt confident enough to go big time. The prize was Viacom, a division of CBS until 1971 when the network was forced to give it up to comply with the Financial Interest and Syndication Rule (or Fin/Syn, as it is usually termed), which required the (then) big three networks—ABC, CBS, and NBC—to get out of the syndication and cable business, thereby creating a distinction between network and cable television and granting syndication rights to the movie studios that produced the programming for the networks.[14] Although Fin/Syn was considerably modified over the next two decades, it was taken so seriously in 1971 that CBS was forced to spin off Viacom, its syndication and cable division, which was immediately taken over by a group of CBS executives who bolted from the network, eager to move into the lucrative field of program packaging and pay TV. Under the leadership first of Clark B. George, former CBS radio president, and later of Ralph M. Baruch and Terrence A. Elkes, Viacom, which had begun as a distribution outlet for such syndicated series as *I Love Lucy, Family Feud,* and *The Honeymooners,* branched out into cable television (Viacom Cable, Showtime/ The Movie Channel, Lifetime); television production; and broadcasting (radio and television stations in such markets as New York, San Francisco, Chicago, Houston, and Washington, D.C.). Within fifteen years of its formation, Viacom International, as the company was now called, may not have been a media empire, but it certainly qualified as a duchy.

It was impossible for anyone in the entertainment business to be unaware of Viacom's rapid growth during the 1970s. And as the 1980s began, the spiral continued. There were more radio and television stations to purchase, new products to distribute, partnerships with Japanese media companies to form, and an acquisition to endear Viacom to the youth of America: a majority interest in MTV Networks (MTV and Nickelodeon) in 1985, followed by total ownership the following year. One of Viacom's stockholders was Sumner Redstone, who had become so impressed by its growth that he managed to acquire a 9.9 percent interest in the company.

If Redstone was ever to fulfill his destiny as a media mogul, this was the time. Viacom stock that had been selling at $39.625 a share in March 1985 was going for $58.50 in December. At some point in September 1986, Redstone discovered that a group of Viacom executives, led by Terrence Elkes, was planning a leveraged buyout. Closing in for the kill, Redstone raised his stake in the company to 19.6 percent. In February 1987, he was prepared to make an offer, which he could never have done were it not for National Amusements, which, by 1986, had more than four hundred screens. By June 1987, Redstone had acquired 83 percent of Viacom at a cost of $3.4 billion.[15] If the cost seemed excessive, it was because Viacom's value was not readily apparent from its balance sheet. More telling was the fact that, at the time of the purchase, Viacom had put *The Cosby Show* into syndication at $2.4 million per episode. Redstone knew there was gold in syndication. A successful television series has unlimited shelf life, and syndication rights meant a constantly growing backlist where titles rarely go out of print. The product is ongoing, ready to be leased to television stations looking to fill time slots. Redstone needed a foothold in the world of media, which Viacom was more than able to provide. At the time, Redstone was not thinking of a movie studio; that would come later. Yet his attraction to a company with a successful syndication division was not that different from the appeal that Columbia had for Sony when the Japanese electronics giant bought the studio two years after the Viacom purchase: a well-stocked film library where even old or worthless titles can enjoy an afterlife on television.

Redstone worked in stages but always with one goal in mind: software. What he envisioned for Viacom was exactly what he achieved: a media conduit. Redstone was not thinking solely of the electronic media; he assumed that Viacom would have a publishing division, although, in 1987, he did not know of what it would consist. But Redstone certainly knew that newspaper tycoon Rupert Murdoch had become the sole owner of Twentieth Century–Fox and that Murdoch's mansion had many rooms. All Redstone purchased was a foundation; the house, or rather mansion, was yet to come.

During the 1980s, the American motion picture industry had witnessed more convulsive changes than it had since its inception. Others were to come. There was the extraordinary expansion of Rupert Murdoch's News Corporation. As if such trophies as the *New York Post,* HarperCollins, and Basic Books were not enough, the purchase of Twentieth Century–Fox Corporation in 1985 added another satellite to a planet that was already orbiting over four continents. Nor was it a just a matter of netting a movie studio. "Twentieth Century–Fox" no longer meant movies as it had in the palmy days of Darryl F. Zanuck; it meant videocassettes, television production, a network (Fox Television), and a similarly named cable station (FX, once known as Fox Cable).

At the time of the Fox purchase, however, Murdoch was already known as a media baron. Thus the conquest of Fox was not uncharacteristic of someone who had earlier entered the world of electronic media via satellite television with Star TV in Asia and British Sky Broadcasting (B Sky B) in the United Kingdom.

In the 1980s, it seemed as if the era of the robber barons had returned, with movie studios replacing railroads. If the barons were American, or at least English-speaking like Rupert Murdoch, the public did not mind. But when Sony purchased Columbia Pictures Entertainment in 1989, hand-wringers called it the death knell for Hollywood. While Sony's purchase of Columbia Records went virtually unnoticed, its incursion into the national art form merited the cover of *Newsweek* (9 October 1989), which featured the internationally known Columbia logo of the lady-with-the-torch wearing a Japanese wig and dressed in a kimono. To some, the Sony purchase was another day of infamy: Japan's revenge for the bombing of Hiroshima and Nagasaki. According to a *Newsweek* poll, 43 percent of the public disapproved of the deal. While many of the disgruntled probably owned or had owned a Sony product, it was something else to discover that the studio that had recently been the property of Coca-Cola (than which nothing is more American) now belonged to the company whose home was the country responsible for the sneak attack on Pearl Harbor almost half a century before.

A year later, in 1990, another Japanese electronics company—the world's largest—acquired MCA, thereby becoming the proprietor of Universal Pictures and a host of other attractions, including the profitable Universal Studio tours in Los Angeles and Orlando. Unlike Sony, which made an effort to understand Hollywood, Matsushita, a far less sophisticated company, did not. Five years later, Matsushita was ready to unload it.

While an electronics company and a movie studio at least seemed to constitute a fit, a spirits and nonalcoholic beverages company and a movie studio constituted an incongruity. And so, with Seagram's purchase of MCA in 1995, Universal Pictures became part of an inventory that included Chivas Regal and Absolut Vodka.

If any two words characterized the transformation of Hollywood during the last four decades of the twentieth century, they were synergy and incongruity. Synergy was the goal; incongruity, the result. In theory, a wedding of the print and electronic media makes sense: print advertising and journalism/broadcast advertising and broadcast journalism; movie studio/television network. Filmed entertainment is filmed entertainment, the argument went. That may be true, but television produces a different breed of executive than film. CBS's Bill Paley, NBC's Fred Sarnoff, and ABC's Leonard Goldenson would have been no more at home in Hollywood than Harry Cohn, Louis Mayer, or Darryl Zanuck would have been in New York. As for the union of publishing and filmed entertainment, print journalism and book publishing attract types that are basically disdainful of the Hollywood product; their notion of film is cinema, independent or international. As for auto replacement parts and movies, even Charlie Bluhdorn would have found it difficult to work Paramount into his crazy quilt company had it not been for the creative leadership of Robert Evans and Peter Bart; and if Martin Davis had not pared Gulf + Western down to a communications conglomerate after Bluhdorn's death, Paramount would have been an orphan in the storm, prey to corporate raiders or media moguls interested only in its film library.

No one in the industry ever believed that mergers were based on synergy. They occur for reasons that are purely pragmatic: company A needs what company B has. If the price is right, the board approves, the shareholders vote "yea," and the FCC or the Justice Department blesses the union (or winks at it), the merger goes through. By the 1990s, film executives even felt uncomfortable about using the word in interviews, knowing that synergy was impossible to achieve in a marriage where all that matters is the dowry, much less in one that leaves only top management satisfied, while the rank and file, fretting over the jobs they know will be lost, glower at the *arrivistes* from an alien medium, who feel pretty much the same about them.[16]

This was very much the case in 1989 with the creation of Time Warner, the result of Time Inc.'s acquisition of Warner Communications for $14 billion. Imagine the writers and editors of such Time Inc. publications as *Time, Sports Illustrated, Money,* and *Fortune* discovering that their parent was on an adoption kick, bringing home the offspring of Warner Bros, Atlantic Records, HBO, Cinemax, DC Comics, and *Mad Magazine.* It was not synergy; it was turf, as fiefdoms arose in an attempt to preserve whatever integrity remained. At least when Disney bought ABC/Capital Cities in 1995 for $19.2 billion, the only synergy was numerical: the whole was now made up of more parts. ABC was another outlet for Disney product, of which there was a significant amount just from the movie division, which consisted of trademarks such as Walt Disney Pictures, Touchstone, and Miramax.

The acquisition, which gave rise to a new entity called the Walt Disney Company, must have amazed retired animators who could recall a time when Walt Disney Productions did not even enjoy studio status and had to distribute its animated features through RKO. Now Disney owned a leading television network, ABC-TV, as well as a number of television and radio stations. Some might also have remembered that before there was synergy, there was reciprocity. In 1953, when both NBC and CBS rebuffed Walt Disney when he asked them to underwrite a theme park in Anaheim, California, to be called Disneyland, ABC came through with the funding. Disney rewarded ABC, then a struggling new network, with a series that made it the envy of its rivals: the enormously successful *Disneyland* in 1954, followed by the equally popular *Mickey Mouse Club* the following year.

As the 1990s began, mergermania continued. "And still they gaz'd, and still the wonder grew." One wondered if there would be a freestanding *anything* (telephone service, electronics manufacturer, publishing house, newspaper, record company) left by the end of the century.

Sumner Redstone gazed but did not wonder. He knew his time had come and Martin Davis's was over. Redstone was ready for mogulhood.

In 1984, when Barry Diller came to Fox as chairman and CEO, it seemed an improvement over Martin Davis's Paramount. Barry Diller was the kind of executive who was meant either to head his own company or remake someone else's into his own image. Having not yet reached the ownership stage, Diller set about doing at Fox what he had done at Paramount: renovating and innovating—accomplishing the former by reducing debt through terminations; the latter by creating the fourth network, Fox Television. This was something he had been unable to do at Paramount under Bluhdorn, who was more concerned about cost than he was about challenging the hegemony of ABC, CBS, and NBC. Even had Diller remained at Paramount, he would have faced opposition from Martin Davis, who was similarly unmoved by the idea until 1993, when he finally agreed to the creation of the United Paramount Network (UPN) in a joint venture with Chris-Craft.

It was different at Fox under Rupert Murdoch. Learning that Metromedia was interested in unloading its seven television stations, including the flagship station known to New Yorkers as Channel 5 (now WNYW), Murdoch leaped at the opportunity to create the fourth network. He not only had the means; in Diller, he also had the man. Thus, in 1986, Diller achieved a goal he had set for himself a decade earlier. While the level of entertainment the fourth network had to offer was never meant to challenge audiences' intelligence, it became so popular—as a result of such shows as *Married with Children,* which may have been the first sitcom to tackle the subject of flatulence; *Beverly Hills 90210; Melrose Place; The Simpsons; America's Most Wanted;* and *Ally McBeal*—that, within a decade of its formation, Fox Television ranked second in popularity among viewers in the eighteen- to forty-nine–year-old age group.

Diller lasted longer at Paramount than he had at Fox—ten years compared to seven and a half. Ironically, it may have been easier working for a bully like Martin Davis, who needed Diller's brand of creativity, than for the imperialistic Murdoch, who has his own brand, known as piratical expansion. By 1990, Murdoch began wondering if Diller had overextended himself. Diller was not a filmmaker in any sense of the word; thus, his involvement in the studio detracted from his real talent, which lay in generating ideas and overseeing their implementation, a gift he had evidenced at ABC when he had launched the Movie of the Week. But how do you generate product when (1) you are a cog in Murdoch's wheel, whose revolutions make Dame Fortune's seem almost uniform; (2) you are forced to witness the gussying up of mediocre movies (which would have been better left unmade) so that they will impress television critics as being major cinema; and (3) you are continually on a quest for something that will have a name only when the quester's career has ended?

One can cohabit only so long with a mirror image, and Murdoch had become Diller's. If there is any truth in Conrad's *The Secret Sharer* about the fate of doubles, one of them has to jump ship even though it may be to an unknown destination. And that is precisely what Barry Diller did at the end of 1991.

Like any CEO, Diller expected—and received—a stake in Fox. Under Marvin Davis, Diller apparently had a 25 percent interest in what was then the Twentieth Century–Fox Corporation.[17] But Fox was now part of an intercontinental chain, of which Rupert Murdoch was the clasp; and Barry Diller, a link.

At some point in fall 1991, Diller asked Murdoch for a larger share of the company, meaning not just Fox Inc. but its parent, News Corp. In the course of their discussion, Diller used a word that made Murdoch bristle. Diller had asked to be a "principal," not merely a well-compensated employee. Murdoch's reply suggested that Diller look elsewhere: "There is only one principal in this company."[18]

Diller left Fox in February 1992 with a severance package worth over $70 million, $25 million of which went into a venture that confounded the media analysts who assumed his next conquest would be NBC. As 1992 came to an end, so, it seemed, had Barry Diller's promise. To the dismay of everyone except his muse, Diane von Furstenberg, Barry Diller entered the world of televison retailing. He became a partner in the home shopping network, QVC ("Quality, Value, Convenience"). But by the beginning of 1993, Diller was more than just the third member of a triumvirate that included QVC's majority stockholders, Tele-Communications Inc. (TCI) and Comcast—then the first- and fourth-biggest cable companies, respectively. He was now CEO of the thriving new network where Susan Lucci hawked her hair products; Joan Rivers, her costume jewelry; *Wheel of Fortune*'s Vanna White, her dolls; and Diane von Furstenberg, her own line of designer silks.

To those who wondered if Diller's relationship with von Furstenberg had put him in touch with his feminine side, the answer came in fall 1993 when it became clear that QVC was merely one rung on an extension ladder. That was the year in which Sumner Redstone and Barry Diller squared off in a contest that would leave the victor in control of Paramount Communications.

Diller looked forward to the day when he could return to the company in which he had invested ten years of his life. He wanted Paramount Communications, and if he could acquire the company it would be a triumph for himself and an exit cue for Davis. Diller may not have known it, but in spring 1993 Davis was concerned about Paramount's future. Paramount had fallen to sixth place, its gross down 10.7 percent from the previous year. Although Paramount managed to release twenty-three pictures in 1992—one more than Universal and three more than Columbia—Columbia and Universal outranked Paramount, garnering 12.6 and 11.6 percent of the market share, respectively. Had it not been for *Wayne's World* and *Patriot Games,* which grossed $121.7 million and $82.9 million, respectively, Paramount would have been in even worse straits, living off the profits from 1991's *The Addams Family* and *Star Trek VI.* Davis may not have realized it, but by transforming Bluhdorn's bulging Gulf + Western into the sleeker Paramount Communications, he had made the company an appealing merger prospect. But a merger with whom? Definitely not with Diller, who in spring 1993 let it be selectively known that he had no intention of ending his career as the king of home shopping and that if Davis is wooing media moguls like Ted Turner, Davis might also have to swallow his pride and court his old nemesis.

Davis suspected a merger was inevitable; but if there was to be one, he wanted a congenial bunkmate, a somewhat difficult prospect in an environment where the loss of a private bathroom meant a loss of face. In April 1993 Davis was well aware of Diller's designs on Paramount. Never one to panic, Davis still knew he had to come up with a buyer—and fast. Davis had less to lose with Sumner Redstone, who at least would not come to the table with a list of past grievances.

In corporate Hollywood, investment bankers are frequently the puppeteers pulling the wires, tugging away to get the stiff and wooden players to relax into a deal. Herbert Allen made a career out of choreographing *pas de deux,* even when the dancers were flatfooted. And so, while Allen was advising Diller, Robert Greenhill of Smith Barney Shearson was counseling Davis. Greenhill set up a dinner meeting with Davis and Redstone on 20 April 1993. Redstone was then sixty-nine, five weeks away from turning seventy. If he was ever to parlay Viacom into a media empire comparable to Murdoch's, this was the time. And Paramount was the only game in town. The other studios had been spoken for: Columbia was a subsidiary of Sony, Universal of Matsushita, Warner Bros. of Time Warner, and Fox of News Corporation. In 1993, it would have been foolhardy even to consider MGM, which had been on the auction block so many times that there was little left to bid for. MGM was then the ward of Europe's largest bank, Crédit Lyonnnais, which had made the mistake of loaning Italian publishing mogul Giancarlo Parretti, head of Pathé Communications, $1.1 billion to buy MGM-UA, which he promptly renamed MGM-Pathé. Parretti, who had a series of convictions ranging from passing phony checks to tax evasion, defaulted on the loan in 1991. Although MGM's name had been restored, the company was the equivalent of a handyman's special, and Redstone, approaching his three score and ten, had no time for renovations.

Paramount Communications, however, was another matter. In his heart, Redstone was always an exhibitor. Although Viacom gave him a distribution outlet, it was still exhibition in a different form: instead of being dependent on distributors for product for National Amusements' six hundred screens, Redstone now had the means of distributing it, perhaps not to movie theaters but to television stations worldwide. In spring

1993, Viacom was thriving; its net income was $66 million. Two of its most popular attractions were MTV and Nickelodeon, the latter having come a long way from its kidvid origins in 1979. With the premiere of Nick at Nite in 1985, Nickeloeon became a showcase for such vintage sitcoms as *I Love Lucy, All in the Family, The Mary Tyler Moore Show,* and *The Brady Bunch.*

Redstone clearly wanted Paramount, which would provide him with the movie studio and film library that Viacom lacked. Yet Redstone would not be rushed, and it was not until mid-July that he agreed to Davis's price of $69.14 a share in cash for 51 percent of the company, with the rest in stock, making the total price close to $8.2 billion. Davis, however, faced another obstacle in mid-July: Diller was no longer a nuisance; he had become a threat. Rather than invite Diller to dinner, which would have been too formal, Davis proposed lunch in a familiar setting: the top floor of Paramount Communications on Columbus Circle, which was hardly a neutral location.[19] Davis was not playing host; he was playing master. Davis made it clear that if he were in the selling vein, he would not be negotiating with Diller, whose allies at QVC included TCI's John Malone and Comcast's Brian Roberts. With such a trio of buyers, Davis would not even have a cubicle for himself, much less an office.

Strangely enough, Davis had once courted Malone, but that was before the triumvirate. Davis may not have known much about Roman history, but he certainly knew that when three power brokers form an alliance, it is out of expediency. That was the situation in B.C. 59 when Caesar, Pompey, and Crassus entered into a coalition, known as the first triumvirate, which came to an abrupt end after Crassus and Julia, Pompey's wife (and also Caesar's daughter), died within two years of each other. Triumvirates and ententes last as long as they serve the members' needs or until the balance of power is altered. Otherwise, they come apart, often with disastrous results, such as the Roman civil war that culminated in Caesar's defeat of Pompey.

One did not need to know the past to be skeptical of the present. If Malone, Diller, and Roberts had forged a partnership, it would last only until one of them saw something shinier in the distance.

Davis could deal with Redstone, but three's a crowd. Knowing that Diller was not above making a hostile bid, Davis wasted no time. On 12 September 1993, the company directors approved the $8.2 billion merger of Paramount Communications and Viacom International. Redstone was ecstatic, calling it an "act of destiny." It was really an act of face-saving for

Davis; for Redstone, it was one of ego-fulfillment. At seventy, Redstone was presiding over a media colossus that would ensure him a place along-side Time Warner's Gerald Levin and News Corp.'s Rupert Murdoch. Paramount's publishing division, which consisted chiefly of Simon & Schuster and Prentice Hall, may have lacked the cachet of Time Inc. with its impressive array of magazines (thirty-three, with a readership of 120 million) and of News Corp., with an equally broad print spectrum rang-ing from newspapers and magazines to trade books and school texts. However, that mattered little to Redstone, who had no intention of competing in a field that was both crowded and alien to him. To Redstone, the Harvard scholar, "media" was a plural. It did not mean print; it meant movies, television, and videocassettes. And "audiovisual" would be the thrust of Paramount Viacom, or simply Viacom, as it was finally known.

At the 13 September press conference, Redstone praised Diller as one of his "great, great friends for many decades," insisting that neither Diller nor QVC posed any threat to the merger.[20] Redstone's gushing panegyric ("We each contributed to each other's success, and we're proud of it") hinted at a subtext. A week later, there was no subtext. On 20 September, QVC made a counteroffer of eighty dollars a share, signaling the start of a bidding war. It was also the kind of war in which each side had its allies: backing Viacom were Blockbuster Entertainment and Nynex, both of which showed their support by making substantial investments in the company ($600 million and $1.2 billion, respectively); behind QVC were Cox Enterprises and Bell South.

By November, Viacom had raised its bid to eighty-five dollars a share, only to hear within less than a week that QVC had countered with ninety. When the Paramount board, apparently coached by Davis, refused to consider QVC's offer, the combatants found themselves in Delaware, where the contending companies were incorporated. The ruling that came down from the Delaware Chancery Court, later upheld by the Delaware Supreme Court, was critical of Paramount's attempt to prevent the share-holders from considering QVC's considerably higher offer. It seemed that QVC had won.

But Davis and Redstone would not go gentle into the night. Bank-ing on the appeal of a merger between Viacom and Blockbuster, Para-mount kept increasing the bid until it skyrocketed to $112 a share. That was it. By mid-February 1994, the war had ended. "They won. We lost. Next." was how Diller summed it up.[21] The truth was that the victory ended up costing Viacom $10 billion, $2 billion more than Redstone had anticipated. Yet Redstone did not seem to mind. Paramount had enough subsidiaries that spinning off one or two would not be a catastrophe. For the moment, Sumner Redstone was savoring the taste of victory.

It was a victory that left Martin Davis no share of the spoils. As one of Tennessee Williams's heroines, Alexandra del Lago, put it in *Sweet Bird of Youth,* "When one monster meets another, one monster has to give way, AND IT WILL NEVER BE ME. I'm an old hand at it." Davis was only four years younger than the septuagenarian Redstone, and Redstone not only wanted a younger CEO; he also did not want Davis in any capacity. Redstone must have shown enough horror movies in his theaters to know that monsters never die; like Frankenstein's creation, they give rise to a series. Redstone's choice for Viacom's CEO and president was a Princeton B.A. ('66) and Harvard M.B.A. ('68), Frank Biondi, who began in cable television, moving from director of entertainment programming at HBO to chairman and CEO. Forced out in 1984 when HBO's profits declined, Biondi resurfaced as executive vice president of the entertainment business sector of Coca-Cola, then the owner of Columbia Pictures. Television became Biondi's forte, and he soon was promoted to chairman of Coca-Cola TV.

Biondi did not last very long at Viacom. He was out in less than three years, presumably for not providing the kind of aggressive leadership Redstone expected. Exactly what that was, even Biondi did not know. Redstone did. He wanted someone far tougher than Biondi, someone who could, if necessary, be downright ruthless. In other words, another Sumner Redstone—or, if that were impossible, Sumner Redstone himself.

Thus Redstone decided to run the whole show: he added Biondi's title to his own, becoming both Viacom chairman and CEO. To those who thought he was emulating the Roman emperors, who took on titles as honorifics, Redstone had a ready answer. Invoking his idol, Rupert Murdoch, Redstone proclaimed: "We have to seize the day like Murdoch does," referring to Murdoch's assumption of Barry Diller's title after he virtually had forced Diller out of Fox by refusing to give him a greater stake in News Corp.[22]

Filmmakers had no need to fear; Redstone was not turning producer. Arrogance was his forte, not hubris. But he had to be in control to gird himself for the next battle, which would pit him against Edgar Bronfman Jr., chairman and CEO of Seagram, which had recently purchased MCA, the media conglomerate with a host of assets including

Universal Pictures, Universal Television, the Universal Studio Tours in Los Angeles and Orlando, MCA Records, and MCA Music.

When Redstone fired Biondi on 17 January 1996, Redstone was about to start another cable network, which, he suspected, would rile MCA. And if it came to turf warfare, Biondi would be out of his element.

MCA and Viacom were joint owners of the profitable USA Network, which consisted of USA and the Sci-Fi Channel—the latter a museum for *Twilight Zone* reruns. The partnership went back to 1987, when MCA was simply the corporate parent of a brood that included Universal Pictures and Universal Television. Viacom and MCA entered into an agreement whereby each would have a 50 percent stake in whatever network was created by the other. However, once Viacom became Paramount's owner, MCA began pressuring Viacom either to bow out of USA or sell off MTV Networks. When Viacom announced it was launching Nick at Nite's TV Land, designed as another showcase for series that had gone into syndication, Seagram went on the defensive, charging it was in violation of Viacom's agreement with its subsidiary, MCA. Worse, TV Land would compete with USA, which also featured a fair number of reruns. Viacom, on the other hand, argued that TV Land was just an extension of Nickelodeon. The truth was that both Viacom and Seagram were vying for total ownership of USA Network, which had 74 million subscribers and the kind of programming (reruns, movies, and an occasional miniseries) that any company with film and television interests would find attractive.

To complicate matters, within a week of his departure from Viacom, Biondi was being pursued by Bronfman, even though his Viacom contract ran through the end of 1996. But that April, Redstone decided to release Biondi from his contract, with a $15 million severance package to boot, thereby enabling him to join MCA as chairman and CEO. Such largesse was uncharacteristic of Redstone, who, under ordinary circumstances, would have made Bronfman wait until Biondi was free to come on board. Apparently, Redstone and Bronfman reached an understanding (which must have been verbal) that if Redstone let Biondi out of his contract, which included a noncompete clause, Seagram would not oppose the premiere of TV Land, scheduled for 28 April. Significantly, TV Land debuted a week after Biondi's arrival at MCA.

On 29 April, Seagram did an about-face, charging Viacom with violating the 1987 agreement. Naturally, the case ended up in the Delaware Chancery Court, which seems to have become the Areopagus for litigious conglomerateurs.

What occurred in Delaware was a series of charges, denials, and contradictions, with Bronfman accusing Redstone of jeopardizing their partnership in USA, and Redstone accusing Bronfman of reneging on their agreement that there would be no opposition to TV Land if Biondi were released from his contract.

To Bronfman, TV Land was only part of the problem. The real issue was money and the debt incurred by Seagram's $5.7 billion purchase of MCA from Matsushita in 1995. In order to buy MCA, Seagram had sold most of its shares in DuPont, which accounted for 70 percent of Seagram's profits, the rest coming from its beverage operations. Having been denied a share in MTV Networks, Seagram coveted USA, which would guarantee an outlet for Universal's films and television shows. Yet Seagram could also use the cash (around $1.45 billion) it would get from selling out to Viacom; hence, Bronfman's inconsistent behavior—demanding that Viacom sell its share of USA to Seagram while at the same time exploring the possibility of exchanging MCA's 50 percent of USA for 100 percent of the Sci-Fi Channel.[23] In late October, just as resolution time seemed near—with Viacom becoming the sole owner of USA and MCA of the Sci-Fi Channel—the two sides stopped talking. The principal reason seems to have been money, once Seagram realized the capital gains tax it would have to pay on the $1.7 billion sale.

As a lawyer, Redstone surmised that Delaware Court judge Myron T. Steele would favor MCA, if, for no other reason, Viacom's creation of TV Land, which was more than an extension of Nickeloedon. TV Land was another rerun channel, to which MCA had no access. Even Bronfman began wondering if USA was worth the trouble, not to mention the legal fees. As an occasional songwriter, Bronfman was more attracted to the labels that made up the MCA Music Group than he was to MCA's other operations. Redstone also knew that USA's recent attempts at original programming (e.g., movies and series), in the hope of being taken seriously, could alienate viewers who associated the network with reruns and wrestling.

As expected, Barry Diller was following the battle for USA as if it were a television soap, which, in a sense, it was, with each episode bringing fresh disclosures. But there was no third act yet, only an interminable second, which came to an end in mid-May 1997 when Judge Steele decided he had had enough and ruled in favor of Seagram, charging Viacom with violating the noncompete clause in its contract with MCA, not only by creating a new cable network but also by owning others from which MCA had been excluded. Steele gave MCA and Viacom a month to settle; otherwise, he would play Solomon.

The one month stretched to four; finally, in September, Viacom and MCA wrote the third act themselves: as of 22 September 1997, MCA was the sole owner of USA Network, having bought out Viacom for $1.7 billion. Thus, instead of acquiring just the Sci-Fi Channel, MCA got USA as well.

Within a month, USA had a new owner.

While Redstone and Bronfman were feuding in Delaware, Barry Diller was in West Chester, Pennsylvania, contemplating his next move. Unable to merge QVC with CBS (thanks mainly to QVC triumvir Brian Roberts, who preferred that QVC stay cable), Diller looked elsewhere. He was committed to home shopping but not as the epicenter of his ever-expanding world. In 1995, Diller lost QVC to Comcast, then the country's fourth-leading cable company, whose president, Brian Roberts, had no intention of letting a business relationship, as distinct from a friendship, stand in the way of a sale. Diller, however, had no intention of relinquishing his dream. His immediate goal was a company with television outlets. Diller did not have to look beyond St. Petersburg, Florida, where Silver King Communications, with its twelve independent television stations, was waiting to be purchased.

That was just 1995. The following year, Diller, who had anticipated the future with on-air shopping, gained control of the Home Shopping Network (HSN) and merged it with Silver King, providing more exposure for HSN. If it seemed odd that around the same time Diller also bought Savoy Pictures Entertainment, it was not for the company's abominable movies (which included the 1995 flops, *Tales from the Hood* and *Dr. Jekyll and Ms. Hyde*) but for its four television stations, all of which were Fox affiliates. Then in May 1997, just as the Redstone-Bronfman show was winding down, Diller took advantage of America's increasing reliance on 800 numbers to purchase tickets for live entertainment events and bought a controlling interest in Ticketmaster. HSN Inc. was now a miniconglomerate. Having created the fourth network, Diller was looking for one of his own.

The press was so intent on covering the blood feud between Viacom and MCA and speculating on which would end up with USA that there seemed to be no other scenario. Hardly anyone seemed to recall that Barry Diller and Edgar Bronfman Jr. were close friends—so close that, when Seagram bought MCA, Diller encouraged Bronfman make a push for CBS as well.[24] The reason was that, while Redstone and Bronfman were battling it out, Diller had gone on such a buying spree that he seemed to be part of another drama.

Seagram's decision to become sole master of USA, after having gone into debt to buy MCA two years earlier, made sense only if it were planning something bigger—perhaps a sale that would bring in more than the $1.7 billion it had laid out for the network. To Bronfman and Redstone, USA ownership was never the real issue. The issue was who could flex more muscle, who had the higher testosterone level, and, ultimately, who would be crowned victor. In Hollywood, only the moment matters; historians take care of the future.

And so, within a month, Seagram bought USA Network and proceeded to sell it to Barry Diller. Obviously, Bronfman had been negotiating with his friend while the Viacom buyout was going on. The timing tells the story: on 22 September 1997, Seagram gets USA; on 20 October, Seagram sells it.

For $4.1 billion, Diller purchased a package: the USA Network, along with Universal's domestic distribution and production operations—the latter providing a source of product for USA, the Sci-Fi Channel, and HSN's television stations. "USA Network" was no longer accurate; the corporate name needed an "s," the plural implying further expansion, which turned out to be the case.

So much for Bronfman's complaint about MCA's getting locked out of the lucrative cable market because of Viacom's selfishness. After paying for what, in effect, were two cable stations, Bronfman proceeded to sell them to Diller, along with most of Universal Television's assets. Even though Bronfman insisted that television was not MCA's strong suit (translation: it was not a medium in which he was interested), the truth was that Bronfman was so eager to do business with Diller that he was willing to make Seagram the only media conglomerate without a strong television component.

The sale also marked the end of Kay Koplovitz's association with USA, the network which, in a sense, she had created. While working in franchise development at UA/Columbia Cablevision, Koplovitz had become convinced of the need for a sports network. The result was Madison Square Garden Sports, rechristened USA in 1980. USA, despite its patriotic-sounding name, really stood for UA/Columbia Satellite Services of America. It was Koplovitz who broadened USA's programming to include reruns of hit series like *Alfred Hitchcock Presents, Miami Vice,* and

Murder, She Wrote, as well as theatrical films, original movies, and an occasional series.

Redstone paid scant attention to Diller's USA Networks, which was obviously no match for Viacom, now ready for a comeback with the release of *Titanic* in December 1997. Paramount's past few years looked like a fever chart, as the studio had moved from second place in 1994 to fifth the following year. Yet even the fluctuating market share was deceptive, based, as it was, on one or two films that grossed heavily, compensating for those that sank from view after they opened. If Paramount came in second in 1994, it was largely because of *Forrest Gump,* which had brought in $298 million. No other release came near that. If Paramount fell to fifth place (or 9 percent of the market share) in 1995, it was because there was no *Forrest Gump,* only *Congo* ($81 million) and *Braveheart* ($75 million). Since Frank Yablans coproduced *Congo,* he at least had the satisfaction of knowing that "his" movie—which is no doubt how he perceived it—was his old studio's top grosser.

It is easy to say that none of Paramount's films of the 1990s—hits or flops—rank artistically with anything from Paramount's classical past. But the same could be said of any studio. Like Latin and Greek, the past had become a dead language in Hollywood; its shelf life existed in video stores with a "Classics" aisle. What mattered was the present. Paramount's return to third place in 1996 was due to two films, *The First Wives Club* and *Mission Impossible,* which were, historically, as unimportant as the previous year's *Congo* and *Braveheart. Forrest Gump* will find its way into film history not for its art, which it lacks, but for its computerized skewing of history, with the fictitious Gump juxtaposed with the decidedly real John F. Kennedy and Lyndon B. Johnson.

That Paramount was even involved in *Titanic* was the result of a coproduction arrangement with Fox, which actually put up most of the money for what became the most expensive movie ever made. The total cost, like that of Charles Foster Kane's Xanadu, will never be completely known (Hollywood accounting being what it is), but it is safe to say it was at least around $200 million. *Titanic* originated at Fox, where it was greenlighted by Peter Chernin, News Corp. president. It was only after Chernin had signed off on the project that Paramount became involved. Sherry Lansing and her boss, Viacom Entertainment Group chairman Jonathan Dolgen, were concerned about the public's interest in a movie that would probably run at least three hours and depicted an event that had occurred in 1912. *Reds* (1981) never made the money Paramount hoped it would, even though it was a thoughtful (although politically safe) portrayal of American radicalism. Movie epics had become hit or miss: Oliver Stone's *JFK* (1991) was astonishingly successful, while Spike Lee's impressive *Malcolm X* (1992) was not.

Dolgen wisely limited Paramount's investment to somewhere between $60 and $65 million, with Fox putting up more than twice that amount: approximately $135 million.[25] Because the deal called for Paramount to distribute *Titanic* domestically and Fox to distribute internationally, Paramount was perceived as the releasing studio.

While *Titanic* has had its share of detractors despite its eleven Oscars, it nonetheless remains an outstanding example of shrewd commercial moviemaking—becoming, within a year of its release, the most profitable film in motion picture history: $1.8 billion worldwide. Like *Gone with the Wind* (1939), *Titanic* is a middlebrow epic that hasn't the slightest interest in being taken seriously as film art. The true star is the production, which proudly calls attention to its opulence on the assumption that viewers will be so mesmerized by it that they won't mind being manipulated by a plot with enough twists to make them forget they already know the outcome. Revolving around a steerage-meets-first-class romance that ends in the death of the proletarian hero, *Titanic* is populated by so many familiar character types (overbearing mother, rebellious daughter, villainous suitor, and an assortment of snobs, bullies, and a salt-of-the-earth underclass) that it became a true family film with a discreet sex scene and one "fuck" to remain within PG-13 limits. *Titanic* was so successful in cutting across generational lines that, despite its 194–minute running time, it attracted repeaters: 63 percent of those who had seen *Titanic* at least twice were under twenty-four, while 37 percent were twenty-five or older.[26]

Although *Titanic* had grossed $600 million domestically by spring 1998, enabling Paramount to move up to second place, its success did not offset losses in other divisions. Viacom's merger with Blockbuster Entertainment in 1994 was another of Redstone's attempts to extend the boundaries of exhibition by acquiring the world's largest home video retailer. Redstone wanted to cash in on the video rental market, which, to him, meant movies—first-runs and also-rans—in a different venue. The assumption was that there were enough disaffected moviegoers tired of multiplexes, where the sound from one theater infiltrates another, and enough cost-conscious homebodies in search of a night out without going out, to keep Blockbuster stores in business indefinitely. However, an ill-advised expansion into music (Blockbuster Music), the competition of satellite television, and a proliferation of stores with inadequate selections and limited numbers of the latest releases forced Redstone to bring in someone who may never have worked in media but knew retailing: John Antioco, formerly CEO of Taco Bell. As a result of Antioco's improvements, customers were offered a wide choice of videos and an ample supply of new titles at lower prices—the latter as the result of revenue-sharing arrangements with some studios.[27] Thus, Blockbuster experienced a slight turnaround. But its fortunes would continue to fluctuate, and by the end of the 1990s there were frequent rumors of a spinoff.

In corporate Hollywood, nothing is sacred because everything, and everyone, is expendable. Once a communications company becomes a media conglomerate, the distinction between the print and electronic media is purely divisional. Of the two, the former is the first to be downsized or spun off, since print is no longer the medium of choice. The situation was slightly different at Time Warner, where, prior to the merger, a substantial print operation was already in place. Yet even when there was just Time Inc. back in the 1980s, Steve Ross was thinking ahead; hence Time Inc.'s investment in HBO and Cinemax. The moral is simple: to remain unengulfed and undevoured, a publishing house should either be a university press, which would have no appeal to a conglomerate, or an independent trade press that brings out works that are scholarly, substantial, and defiantly unsexy.

In spring 1998, Redstone decided to streamline Simon & Schuster. The education and publishing division (specifically, Allyn and Bacon and part of Prentice Hall) was sold to Pearson, the British outfit that already owned Scott Foresman and Addison Wesley Longman, along with the Penguin Group (Penguin, Viking, and Putnam); professional and reference (Macmillan and what was left of Prentice Hall) went to the incredibly diversified investment firm of Hicks, Muse, Tate & Furst, whose assets ranged from radio and television stations to movie theaters and consumer goods. Thus the same company that owned International Home Foods would now have, courtesy of Macmillan, the Betty Crocker cookbooks.

What remained at Viacom was the only part of Simon & Schuster that mattered to Redstone: the trade division, which included Pocket Books and the Free Press and accounted for one-fifth of Viacom's 1997 profits. Undoubtedly, Pearson was a better home for Simon & Schuster's educational arm than Viacom, where it was merely an additional source of income; and if selling it brought in more income, $3.6 billion to be exact, all the better. If Educational Publishing had to go, why not Professional and Reference? The inventory may not have been that extensive, but it was at least worth a cool million, which is what Hicks Muse paid for the package.

As the century was about to end, Redstone, now seventy-six, could sit in his office at the top of the Viacom building at 1515 Broadway and luxuriate in the enveloping sunset of a career that had seemed doomed twenty years earlier when he suffered burns over almost half of his body during a fire at Boston's Copley Plaza Hotel. Redstone not only survived an incident that would have prompted others in their mid-fifties to seek early retirement; he also profited financially from it by successfully suing the hotel. What others would regard as a tragedy, he considered a challenge. At seventy-six, he was ready for one more challenge.

In fall 1999, Redstone may have been content with his view from the fifty-second floor of the Viacom building, but Mel Karmazin was not satisfied with his on the thirty-fifth floor of CBS. Karmazin, then CBS president and CEO, decided he preferred Redstone's quarters, which at least afforded a view of the Hudson. He also decided that Viacom needed to expand. And what better way than to buy CBS?

At first Redstone was not interested, not so much because he doubted the wisdom of such a merger as his fear of being displaced by someone twenty years younger than himself. But Karmazin was so insistent that Redstone began to wonder if, perhaps, CBS might supply the missing jewel in a crown adorned with lesser gems. Granted that CBS was then the country's highest-ranked network, and Viacom, whose cash flow had increased to $2 billion, could afford it, there was something else that appealed to Redstone: the double irony, first, of Viacom's reclaiming the company that had discarded it in 1971 and, second, of buying the network that Barry Diller could not. There was also the satisfaction of acquiring a network far more venerable than Murdoch's Fox TV. Redstone could now be spared the embarrassment of co-owning UPN, christened the sixth network after Warner Bros. Television, which premiered around the same time in 1995, had become the fifth.

A merger with CBS would solve the problem of UPN, jointly owned by Viacom and Chris-Craft. To satisfy FCC regulations prohibiting a company's owning two television stations (even though UPN was hardly in the same league with CBS), Viacom would finally be forced to sell its share to Chris-Craft, unless, of course, the FCC relented and allowed Viacom to buy out Chris-Craft and have UPN to itself.

If Karmazin was so anxious for the deal to come off, it would have to be on Redstone's terms. Redstone wanted a guarantee that he would have a place, as well as a role, in the new company—something General Electric had been unwilling to offer him when GE was trying to unload NBC early in 1999. Redstone was interested, but not in an NBC owned by Viacom but controlled by General Electric.[28] Once it was understood that Redstone would be president and CEO, and Karmazin, president and COO of the new company, with each receiving the same salary ($1 million a year plus bonuses and stock options), Redstone was satisfied.

With a Viacom-CBS merger, there would finally be some kind of synergy, not merely the diversification that passes for it in corporate Hollywood. Viacom had syndication interests (Nick at Nite, TV Land); CBS would also have them after acquiring King World Productions, the leading syndicator of such shows as *Oprah, Wheel of Fortune,* and *Jeopardy.* Each owned television stations (Viacom, nineteen; CBS, fifteen) as well as cable networks. In cable, Viacom had the edge with Nickelodeon, MTV, VH1, and Showtime, and had half interests in UPN and Comedy Central. All CBS could claim were The Nashville Network (TNN) and Country Music Television (CMT). But that was precisely why Karmazin staked out Viacom. Although both companies had certain divisions in common, such as cable and syndication, Viacom had more of them. There were also areas (film and television production, book publishing, home video) in which CBS had nothing. On the other hand, CBS had 166 radio stations through Infinity Broadcasting; more important, Viacom lacked a network comparable in both popularity and historical importance to CBS.

A synergistic union, however, is not one of equals, but of assets, which are never equal but only similar. All one can hope for is a fit, a marriage in which a powerful alliance compensates for a less-than-desirable dowry. Viacom and CBS were undoubtedly a fit. Apart from their mutual interests, there was the all-important matter of product, which Paramount could funnel into CBS in the form of movies and television shows. In fact, Paramount and CBS had already entered the courtship stage. In 1999, three Paramount-produced shows, *Becker, JAG,* and *Nash Bridges,* were already running on CBS; and two coproductions between CBS and Paramount, *Now and Again* and *Love and Money,* premiered in September 1999.

While Viacom was the buyer, Karmazin was the victor. Even Redstone had to admit that Karmazin was a "master salesman [who] seduced us."[29] In an effort to convince the press that he and Karmazin were kindred spirits, as if that constitutes another form of synergy, Redstone emphasized their similar backgrounds. Nothing could have been further from the truth.

One might make a case for a "lowly origins" scenario: Mel Karmazin from the borough of Queens, whose father drove a cab; Sumner Redstone from Boston's West End, whose father ran a trucking business until he discovered nightclubs and drive-ins. But here the similarities end. While Redstone went to the Boston Latin School and then to Harvard, Karmazin attended Haaren High School in New York and Pace University, where he pursued a business degree at night while working for an ad agency during the day. Radio, not exhibition, was Karmazin's first and perhaps only love. After graduating from Pace in 1967, he moved into broadcast advertising. Although Karmazin held other jobs, becoming sales manager at WCBS-AM the same year he graduated from Pace was the one that convinced him he was meant for media. At the time he thought it was radio. Thinking that he could develop into another William Paley, Karmazin seized the opportunity to move on to Metromedia, eventually becoming general manager of WNEW, the radio station still remembered as the home of Martin Block's *Make-Believe Ballroom*.

After leaving WNEW in 1981, Karmazin joined Infinity Broadcasting as CEO. At last he had a position of authority in addition to working in the medium he loved. However, Karmazin knew that radio was not what it was when *Make-Believe Ballroom* had debuted on WNEW, which, in the 1990s, had become the home of controversial announcer Howard Stern. CBS was the network to which Karmazin wished to return—but in style. In 1995, he had the chance when he managed to convince CBS to buy Infinity in exchange for running CBS's radio and television operations. That was only the beginning. Within four years Karmazin was the network's CEO.

If it seems strange that someone with such limited experience in network television, and none in film, would have sought a merger with Viacom, the answer partly lies in Karmazin's obsession with ascending the ladder of success several rungs at a time because the top, like Jack's beanstalk, always seems to be getting higher. Karmazin had adopted the mantra of the new moguls: anyone can generate product, but not everyone can run the show. If the product is weak, the producer is replaced. When divisions fail to turn a profit, costs are cut, jobs are eliminated, and positions are consolidated or left unfilled. The creative end of the business means nothing to the Karmazins and Redstones, or even the Dillers and

Bronfmans. The "C" in CEO stands for "chief," not "creative." Production chiefs, or however they are designated, are perceived as the enemy, not in the sense of being a threat but a nuisance. It is the perennial we/them agon: those who want to make movies that end up on "ten best" lists or produce television series that receive retrospectives at the Museum of Television and Radio versus those who, had they then been born a century earlier, would have headed oil cartels or railroad syndicates. Then, as now, the power is in the purse and the hand that hold the strings. Thus it makes no difference if, in the future, Viacom is absorbed by another Wagnerian giant eager for its gold, which he will then fashion into a ring to fit his pinkie. All that can be hoped for is that the giant will forget his size and leave the moviemaking to puny mortals, who may be ringless but make up for it in talent.

In Mel Karmazin, Sumner Redstone has met his match. Technically, according to the terms of the merger, Redstone could fire Karmazin at any time until 2003, yet that hardly seems probable.[30] By then Redstone would be eighty. At that age, Adolph Zukor published his autobiography, *The Public Is Never Wrong: My Fifty Years in Motion Pictures* (1953). And at eighty, Zukor was content with the honorific of board chairman, which left him free to play elder statesman and enjoy the obeisance that comes at the end of a distinguished career.

There remained the unfinished business of Chris-Craft's 50 percent interest in UPN, after which Viacom was lusting. Although it would seem that Viacom had scored enough victories, the idea of total ownership of the sixth network meant perhaps not another jewel in the crown but at least a rhinestone. The only possible resolution was for Chris-Craft to sell its half to Viacom or buy Viacom's half, although no one expected Chris-Craft to buy out Viacom. On 21 March 2000, one of the most suspenseless plots in media history had reached its anticlimax. Viacom bought Chris-Craft's half for a mere $5 million. However, in light of the impending Viacom-CBS merger, it seemed questionable that the FCC would allow the new megaconglomerate to own two networks.[31]

Although race had never been an issue in the merger, it was definitely one in the battle for UPN, whose faithful viewers associated it primarily with wrestling programs. However, Viacom argued that UPN, which admittedly had lost money ($800 million, to be exact), had more to offer than *Smackdown*. The network had become especially popular with African Americans on the basis of such shows as *Moesha* and *The Parkers*. Viacom played the race card and won. And for those interested only in winning, the prize does not matter as long as another trophy is added to the collection.

Herbert J. Siegel, however, was not exactly a loser. Viacom might have UPN, but Chris-Craft owned eight UPN-affiliated stations. Chris-Craft should have been Viacom's next trophy. However, when Viacom could not meet Siegel's price, Siegel sold the company to Rupert Murdoch's News Corp. for $5.4 billion, thereby casting doubt on UPN's future in the major markets. Exactly what three septuagenarians could hope to gain by such machinations, except satisfaction, is hard to say. Even if (worst case scenario) Fox Network dropped UPN programs, there would still be other outlets, although, admittedly, none as attractive as Fox's. Act one: Siegel lost, Redstone won. Act two: Siegel won, Redstone lost, Murdoch scored. Act three: TBA.

Redstone may claim he will go on indefinitely, but Karmazin is regarded as the anointed, ready to ascend the throne when Redstone abdicates. Karmazin may be more knowledgeable about radio than film, but he must have seen two 1950 masterpieces, Joseph L. Mankiewicz's *All about Eve* and Billy Wilder's *Sunset Boulevard*. *All about Eve* purports to be about the theater, but it is really about Hollywood, where one star rises at another's expense; if the older star is reluctant to leave the firmament, the younger might have to do a bit of dislodging. In *All about Eve*. Eve Harrington rises out of Margo Channing's shadow and then is shadowed by a wannabe determined to eclipse her. *All about Eve* was a Twentieth Century–Fox release, but *Sunset Boulevard* was one of Paramount's glories. *Sunset Boulevard* is less about the inability of silent star Norma Desmond to acknowledge the advent of sound than it is about a Hollywood in which new messiahs feel compelled to consign the old believers to oblivion, if not to the flames. Corporate Hollywood is an amalgam of *All about Eve* and *Sunset Boulevard*—*Eve at Sunset,* in which Eve Harrington, after usurping Margo Channing in New York, takes off for Hollywood where she encounters Norma Desmond, who represents an even greater threat: the past. Margo was merely Broadway, but Norma is old Hollywood—and knows it. The Eves of corporate Hollywood do not live in the past; they may applaud film preservation, but they also know that many of the golden age films that will never be restored are superior to most of the current product from mainstream Hollywood.

As the current wearer of the ring, Karmazin must wonder how long it will be before some Eve—or Evan—in media land grows restless and starts thinking synergistically. While the Margo Channings and Norma

Desmonds of the industry experienced the fears and anxieties known to all artists, the screen at least afforded them an outlet. The Karmazins have even greater anxieties but lack a screen on which to project them. Such is the price for possessing the ring. All Margo and Norma possessed was their art.

Epilogue

In June 2000, Hollywood was shaken by the news that another studio had changed hands: Seagram, Universal's parent, had been purchased for $30 billion by a French company called Vivendi. The knowledgeable probably shrugged and muttered, "So Seagram finally found a buyer," recalling how Seagram had been trying to interest Sony and Disney into taking it over. Others reacted the way readers often do when hearing the name of the latest recipient of the Nobel Prize for Literature: "Vivendi *who?*" It had been quite different six months earlier when AOL made a bid for Time Warner; no one bothered to ask "AOL *what?*"

Although "Vivendi" sounds like a pop singer, it is actually the name of the world's leading water distributor and a major supplier of electric power. Like Gulf + Western, Vivendi expanded into areas that had little or nothing to do with utilities: construction, real estate, mass transit, and publishing—and those just for starters. Like Charles Bluhdorn, Jean-Marie Messier, a former investment banker and Vivendi chairman, heard the siren song of media, which, in 2000, reverberated beyond the publishing-film-televison model of the mid-1960s. Messier saw a place for the written word, although it was no more a priority with him than it had been with Bluhdorn.

To Messier, parking lots and water filters were singularly unsexy, and print was no longer the medium of choice. Thus he steered Vivendi in the direction of satellite broadcasting, the Internet, and wireless communications. Messier seemed no more interested in abandoning utilities than Bluhdorn had been in giving up the nuts and bolts of Gulf + Western to concentrate exclusively on movies. On the other hand, should

Messier decide to go the communications route as Martin Davis did, utilities would make a good spinoff. For the time being, however, Messier was going hyphenate: Vivendi would be a media-utilities conglomerate.

Naturally, Messier leaped at the opportunity to acquire Seagram, whose divisions would augment Vivendi's, resulting in diversity that would have awed even Bluhdorn, the great diversifier, himself. Although one would have thought that Seagram's appeal was Universal's film library, it was Universal Music's impressive catalog of popular and classical titles that attracted Messier, who was thinking ahead to a time when digital phones would give users Internet access to the company's musical offerings.

That the corporate name would be Vivendi Universal, with head-quarters in Paris, may have ruffled some feathers but not enough to send them flying through space. Either Hollywood's thinking had become more global since 1989 when Sony had bought Columbia, or, more likely, it was a matter of *déjà vu*. Since the studios had already known Japanese, Australian, Italian, and Canadian owners, the Vivendi purchase meant that Universal executives might have to brush up on their French, even though Messier spoke flawless English.

The Vivendi purchase rang the death knell for the sacrosanct pro-duction-distribution-exhibition model that had once been holy writ. Actually, the bell had been tolling for years, but now there was no mistak-ing the message: exhibition is all. Since the early 1970s, the studios have been functioning as distributors, releasing the product of others—the independent producers, the names of whose companies appear in the ads and often at the beginning of a movie. No longer do projects originate at a studio; they come from production companies to which the studio plays host, financing their films in whole or in part.[1] Having moved from production to finance and distribution, the studios now either release or present: *The Perfect Storm* (2000) is a "Warner Bros. release of a Baltimore Spring Creek Pictures production in association with Radio Produc-tions"; the opening credits for *Shaft* (2000) are somewhat different but amount to the same thing: "Paramount Pictures Presents A Scott Rudin/ NewDeal Production." When Paramount released *Sunset Boulevard* fifty years earlier, the studio was releasing its own film, made on its own lot. In 1950, there were only two independent production companies at Para-mount: Hal Wallis Productions and Pine-Thomas. In 2000, there were more than ten, including Alphaville, Howard Koch's Aries Films, Tom Cruise and Paula Wagner's C/W, Jodie Foster's Egg Pictures, and Robert Evans's Evans Entertainment Group.

The end result of distribution—after the ads have been placed, the press kits handed out, the junkets written off—is exhibition: loading the film onto the conveyor belt that will take it to its destination, which, in the past, would have been theaters. Now a film's destination can range from theatrical release to cyberspace, with stopovers on network and cable TV and an indefinite stay at the video store. No longer does film have to be threaded through a projector. Just press "Play," hit "Enter," or click the mouse. Movies can be seen wherever the technology exists for showing them. Exhibition is all that matters.

Zukor knew that. Hence, he created the country's largest theater chain. Yet even he would have smiled at the production-distribution-exhibition triad, dismissing it as an academic way of looking at a process that only those in the business really understand. One could easily imagine Zukor or Bluhdorn being unfazed by the Vivendi purchase. If media can find a niche amid beef, fruit, and zinc, it can also find one in the interstices between water and waste management.

What matters is the integrity of film. If a conglomerateur can respect film as an art—at least to the extent of not preventing a studio from aspiring to that goal, difficult as it is to achieve—the studio's place within the organizational chart is irrelevant. Subsidiary status is preferable to extinction. The end may not justify the means, but the means may redeem the end.

End Titles

MARTIN DAVIS left Paramount to become a partner in Wellspring Associates, a private investment firm in New York. He died of a heart attack on 4 October 1999.

After acquiring USA Network and Universal Television from Seagram in 1997, BARRY DILLER formed USA Networks Inc., whose two main divisions were television broadcasting and on-line shopping. Two years later, the purchase of October Films (e.g., *Cookie's Fortune* and *Hilary and Jackie,* both 1998) and Gramercy Pictures (e.g., *Elizabeth* [1998]) enabled him to create USA Films, whose releases include the critically acclaimed *Being John Malkovich* and *Topsy-Turvy* (both 1999). On 2 February 2001 Diller and Diane von Furstenberg were married in a civil ceremony at City Hall in New York. It was his fifty-ninth birthday.

ROBERT EVANS, four times divorced, married actress Catherine Oxenberg, some thirty years his junior, on 12 July 1998. The marriage was annulled on 27 July.

JEFFREY KATZENBERG, irked at not being made Disney president, left the studio and became a member of DreamWorks along with David Geffen and Steven Spielberg. He thereupon filed a $250 million suit against Disney, claiming he was owed 2 percent of the profits from the films he had put into production. In 1999, the suit was settled. A *Variety* headline told the outcome: "KATZ GETS MOUSE."

Like so many former studio executives, DAVID KIRKPATRICK started his own production company, Original Voices, whose first release was the well-reviewed *Opposite of Sex* (1998).

On 4 May 2000, the day the Viacom-CBS merger was approved,

SHERRY LANSING's contract was extended for six years. If she remains at the studio until 2006, she will have spent almost a quarter of a century at Paramount.

FRANK MANCUSO relocated at MGM as chairman and CEO. In 1999, Kirk Kerkorian replaced him with the younger Alex Yemenidijian, president of the MGM Grand in Las Vegas, one of the studio's prize possessions. Mancuso was then sixty-eight.

In September 1999, SUMNER REDSTONE's wife of fifty-two years, Phyllis, filed for divorce on the grounds of adultery and cruelty. This was the third time Mrs. Redstone had initiated divorce proceedings, having chosen to drop each of the previous suits.

DAWN STEEL, after being fired from Paramount, moved over to Columbia, becoming the studio's first female president until the Sony purchase left her without a job. Sexism and an inoperable brain tumor, diagnosed in spring 1996, prevented her from becoming the producer she aspired to be. She died, at fifty-one, on 20 December 1997.

FRANK YABLANS found a temporary haven at MGM/UA as vice chairman and COO. When MGM and UA were uncoupled in 1985, Yablans resigned after Alan "Laddie" Ladd Jr. was named head of both studios. It was replay time, recalling Yablans's earlier resignation from Paramount when Bluhdorn had brought in Diller as chairman. Next stop: independent production. Most recent credit: *Congo* (1995).

On the afternoon of 10 June 1976, ADOLF ZUKOR took a nap from which he never awakened. He was 103.

Notes

Chapter 1

1. Sources for Zukor's life include his own autobiography, written with Dale Kramer, *The Public Is Never Wrong* (New York: Putnam's, 1953), which totally ignores the subject's dark side, for which there is ample evidence; Will Irwin, *The House That Shadows Built* (Garden City, N.Y.: Doubleday, Doran, 1928), which is more objective but incomplete; Neal Gabler, *An Empire of Their Own: How the Jews Invented Hollywood* (New York: Crown, 1988), which offers the best overview of his career; the CMPS Zukor file, which includes, in addition to other valuable material, Chip Cleary's "Adolph Zukor: The A to Z of Paramount." No publication source is given for this article, stamped 4 Oct. 1940.

2. Terry Ramsaye, *A Thousand and One Nights: A History of the Motion Picture through 1925* (New York: Simon & Schuster/Touchstone, 1986), 85.

3. Charles Musser, *The Emergence of Cinema: The American Screen to 1907* (Berkeley: Univ. of California Press, 1994), 371–72.

4. Musser, *Emergence*, 420.

5. Kenneth MacGowan, *Behind the Screen: The History and Techniques of the Motion Picture* (New York: Delta, 1965), 155.

6. MPPCo has been the subject of various studies, the most balanced of which are Janet Staiger, "Combination and Litigation: Structures of US Film Distribution 1891–1917," *Cinema Journal* 23 (Winter 1984): 41–72; and Robert Anderson, "The Motion Picture Patents Company: A Reevaluation," in *The American Film Industry*, rev. ed., ed. Tino Balio (Madison: Univ. of Wisconsin Press: 1985), 133–52.

7. I.G. Edmonds and Reiko Minura, *Paramount Pictures and the People Who Made Them* (San Diego: A.S. Barnes, 1980), 30.

8. For the definitive Pickford biography and complete filmography, see Eileen Whitfield, *Pickford: The Woman Who Conquered Hollywood* (Lexington: Univ. Press of Kentucky, 1997).

9. Like Zukor, Lasky also has written his autobiography with a collaborator: *I Blow My Own Horn*, with Don Weldon (Garden City: Doubleday, Doran, 1957).

10. Scott Berg, *Goldwyn: A Biography* (New York: Ballantine, 1989), 27.

11. Lasky, *Horn*, 72.

12. "Paramount: Still the Best Show in Town," *Boxoffice* (July 1987): 22.

13. These are Hodkinson's own words on the first page of "Ruthless Zukor," a typescript in the CMPS Hodkinson file. Dated 2 Feb. 1962, nine years before he died, it seems to have been part of an unpublished memoir.

14. Although there have been various explanations for "Paramount," I am following the one in "Ruthless Zukor" (p. 6).

15. Lasky, *Horn*, 121.

16. Hodkinson, "Ruthless Zukor," 4.

17. Ibid., 7.

18. *Paramount Convention News*, 4 Sept. 1914, 1.

19. Irwin, *House That Shadows Built*, 218–19.

20. *History of the Development of Famous Players Corporation, with Special Reference to the Complaint of the Federal Trade Commission*, 17 Dec. 1921, 15–16. No publisher is given.

21. Hodkinson, "Ruthless Zukor," 7.

22. Ibid.

23. *History Famous Players–Lasky*, 35.

24. Richard Koszarski, *An Evening's Entertainment: The Age of the Silent Feature Picture, 1915–28* (Berkeley: Univ. of California Press, 1994), 73.

25. *The Story of the Famous Players–Lasky Corporation, Paramount-Artcraft Motion Pictures* (New York: n.p. 1919), 35.

26. For a detailed discussion of Paramount-Publix, see Douglas Gomery, *Shared Pleasures: A History of Movie Presentation in the United States* (Madison: Univ. of Wisconsin Press, 1992), 57–61.

27. "Paramount Players to Be Schooled in Their Work," *Morning Telegraph*, 25 June 1922, 1+.

28. Tino Balio, *United Artists: The Company Built by the Stars* (Madison: Univ. of Wisconsin Press, 1976), 25–26.

29. Zukor, *Public*, 78.

30. Selznick's other Paramount films are *Forgotten Face* (1928); *Betrayal* (1929); *The Dance of Life* (1929), based on the Broadway hit, *Burlesque*, which Paramount remade as *Swing High, Swing Low* (1937); *For the Defense; Honey; Sarah and Son*; and *The Texan* (all 1930).

31. On the Astoria studio, see Richard Koszarski, *The Astoria Studio and Its*

Fabulous Films (New York: Dover, 1983).

32. Koszarski, *Evening's Entertainment*, 103–4.

33. Gomery, *Shared Pleasures*, 61.

34. Jesse L. Lasky Jr., *Whatever Happened to Hollywood?* (New York: Funk & Wagnalls, 1975), 72–73.

35. On Paramount's turnaround and those involved in it, see "Paramount," *Fortune* (March 1937): 94+. Douglas Gomery, *The Hollywood Studio System* (New York: St. Martin's, 1986), 30–33.

36. Leon Barasq, *Caligari's Cabinet and Other Grand Illusions: A History of Film Design*, ed. and rev. by Eliot Stein (Boston: New York Graphic Society, 1976), 205–6. On Dreier's Paramount years as supervising art director (1932–50), see Beverly Heisner, *Hollywood Art: Art Direction in the Days of the Great Studios* (Jefferson, N.C.: McFarland, 1990), 165–83.

37. According to her daughter, Maria Riva, Dietrich "hated" the character of Erika von Schleutow but assumed Wilder would imply that Erika was not a Nazi during the war; see Kevin Lally, *Wilder Times: The Life of Billy Wilder* (New York: Holt, 1996), 174.

38. "Paramount: Oscar for Profits," *Fortune* (June 1947): 90.

39. *Palm Beach Times,* 8 Dec. 1972, C8.

40. Hal Wallis and Charles Higham, *Starmaker: The Autobiography of Hal Wallis* (New York: Macmillan, 1980), 95.

41. Shawn Levy, *King of Comedy: The Life and Art of Jerry Lewis* (New York: St. Martin's/Griffin, 1997), 99–100.

42. Wallis, *Starmaker*, 142. *See also* 145.

43. Ibid., 146.

44. Alanna Nash, with Billy Smith, Marty Lacker, and Lamar Fike, *Elvis Aaron Presley: Revelations from the Memphis Mafia* (New York: HarperCollins, 1995), 73.

45. Peter Whiemer, *The Inner Elvis: A Psychological Biography of Elvis Aaron Presley* (New York: Hyperion, 1996), 244–45.

46. Bernard F. Dick, *Radical Innocence: A Critical Study of the Hollywood Ten* (Lexington: Univ. Press of Kentucky, 1989), 223.

47. On the history of the Justice Department's investigation of Hollywood and its aftermath, see Ernest Borneman, "United States versus Hollywood: The Case Study of an Antitrust Suit," in *American Film Industry*, 449–62; Michael Conant, "The Paramount Decrees Reconsidered," ibid., 537–73.

48. Borneman, "United States," 453.

49. *Daily Variety,* 28 Feb. 1949, 1.

50. On the history of Paramount's involvement in television, see Bruce Bebb, "Paramount Television Yesterday," *Hollywood Reporter*, Collector's Issue, 10 July 1987, S94–S100.

51 Gomery, *Shared Pleasures*, 233.

Chapter 2

1. Correspondence between Weltner and others cited in this chapter comes from Box 1 (Correspondence Files, 1929–1971) of the George Weltner Collection in the University of Wyoming's American Heritage Center in Laramie.

2. Gomery, *Shared Pleasures*, 91.

3. Weltner to Balaban, 20 June 1955.

4. Rosalind Russell and Chris Chase, *Life Is a Banquet* (New York: Random House, 1977), 11.

5. Weltner to Balaban, 20 June 1955.

6. John W. Cones, *Film Finance and Distribution: A Dictionary of Terms* (Los Angeles: Silman James Press, 1992), 329–30.

7. John E. Squire, *The Movie Business Book* (Englewood Cliffs, N.J.: Prentice Hall, 1983), 245–46.

8. Weltner to Balaban, 15 Feb. 1956.

9. Weltner to Balaban, 14 Dec. 1956.

10. Weltner to Balaban, 4 Dec. 1957.

11. Weltner to Balaban, 12 Dec. 1958.

12. Weltner to Balaban, 13 Nov. 1962.

13. Weltner to Balaban, 13 Aug. 1962.

14. Weltner to Balaban, 30 July 1962.

15. Weltner to Balaban, 29 Apr. 1964.

16. Weltner to Balaban, 28 Apr. 1964.

17. Weltner to Balaban and Y. Frank Freeman, 31 Dec. 1958.

18. Weltner to Balaban, 6 Feb. 1961

19. Weltner to Balaban, 25 Aug. 1960.

20. Ibid.

21. Weltner to Balaban, 6 Mar. 1961.

22. Ibid.

23. Weltner to Balaban, 17 Mar. 1961.

24. Barry R. Litman, *The Motion Picture Mega-Industry* (Boston: Allyn and Bacon, 1998), 165.

25. Weltner to Balaban and Jack Karp, 5 June 1963.

26. Ibid.

27. Reed Abelson, "The Shell Game of Hollywood's 'Net Profits,'" *New York Times*, 4 Mar. 1996, D1+.

28. Weltner to Balaban, 27 June 1960.

29. Weltner to Balaban, 5 Nov. 1962, 2.

30. Richard Schickel, *D. W. Griffith: An American Life* (New York: Simon & Schuster/Touchstone, 1984), 497–98, 508–28.

31. Weltner to Balaban, 5 Nov. 1962, 7.

32. *Variety,* 10 Feb. 1958, 1+; approximately 750 films were involved.

33. Weltner to Balaban, 16 Nov. 1961.

34. Hitchcock owned the rights to all of them except *To Catch a Thief;* see Donald Spoto, *The Dark Side of Genius: The Life of Alfred Hitchcock* (Boston: Little, Brown, 1983), 344.

35. Weltner to Balaban, 9 Nov. 1961.

36. Weltner to Balaban, 16 Nov. 1961.

37. On the filming of *Psycho* at Universal, see Stephen Rebello, *Alfred Hitchcock and the Making of Psycho* (New York: Dembner Books, 1990).

38. Karp to Balaban, 20 Nov. 1962.

39. Weltner to Balaban, 28 Dec. 1961.

40. Weltner to Karp, 28 June 1961.

41. Weltner to Balaban, 31 Aug. 1961.

42. For a summary of Levine's career, see Mary Kalfatovic, "Joseph Levine," in *The Scribner Encyclopedia of American Lives*, vol. 2 (New York: Scribner's, 1999), 530–31.

43. Katherine Hamill, "The Supercolossal—Well, Pretty Good—World of Joe Levine," *Fortune* (Mar. 1964): 132.

44. Weltner to Balaban, 20 Feb. 1963.

45. *Daily Variety*, 15 Dec. 1986, 2.

Chapter 3

1. On the transformation of Universal from studio to subsidiary, see Bernard F. Dick, *City of Dreams: The Making and Remaking of Universal Pictures* (Lexington: Univ. Press of Kentucky, 1997), 135–222.

2. Ibid., 157–58.

3. On the Levy brothers and the events leading to the creation of CBS, see Robert Metz, *CBS: Reflections in a Bloodshot Eye* (Chicago: Playboy Press, 1975, 9–27.

4. On Feuer and Martin, see "The Hit's the Thing," *New Yorker*, 14 Jan. 1956, 33+.

5. Metz, *CBS*, 118–23.

6. Spoto, *Dark Side*, 417.

7. Weltner to Balaban and Weisl, 7 May 1965.

8. "Paramount," *Fortune* (March 1937): 212.

9. *Daily Variety*, 13 Dec. 1965, 15.

10. The best accounts of the takeover attempt are in *Variety*, 18 Aug. 1965, 1+, and 22 Dec. 1965, 3+; *Wall Street Journal*, 1 Oct. 1965, 32, and 13 Dec. 1965, 10; and *Daily Variety*, 13 Dec. 1965, 1+.

11. *Daily Variety*, 13 Dec. 1965, 15.

12. Michael Korda, "The Last Business Eccentric," *New Yorker*, 16 Dec. 1996, 82.

13. Charles Bluhdorn, *The Gulf + Western Story* (New York: Newcomen Publication 970, 1973), 22–23.

14. On Chris-Craft as a boat manufacturer, see Jeffrey L. Rodengen, *The Legend of Chris-Craft*, 2nd ed. (Fort Lauderdale: Write Stuff Syndicate, 1993).

15. Geraldine Fabrikant, "As Chris-Craft Idles, Deals Are Elusive," *New York Times*, 4 Aug. 1997, D8.

16. Chris-Craft sold its stake in UPN to Viacom in March 2000.

Chapter 4

1. Evans has chronicled his variegated career in *The Kid Stays in the Picture* (New York: Hyperion, 1994; rpt. Dove, 1995).

2. Peter Bart, "'I Like It. I Want It. Let's Sew It Up,'" *New York Times,* 7 Aug. 1966, Sec. 2, 11.

3. Evans, *Kid*, 111.

4. Ibid., 119.

5. On Leo Jaffe, see Bernard F. Dick, *The Merchant Prince of Poverty Row: Harry Cohn of Columbia Pictures* (Lexington: Univ. Press of Kentucky, 1993), 61–62.

6. The most reliable source for Spiegel's life is Andrew Sinclair, *Spiegel: The Man Behind the Pictures* (Boston: Little, Brown, 1987).

7. Elia Kazan, *A Life* (New York: Anchor-Doubleday, 1989), 514–17.

8. Sinclair, *Spiegel*, 70.

9. Paul Rosenfield, "Stanley Jaffe: How to Become a Director," *Los Angeles Times*, 6 Feb. 1993, Calendar, 21.

10. *Wall Street Journal*, 26 July 1967, 27. Ironically, the buyer, Perfect Film and Chemical Corp., decided to unload the property two years later.

11. "The Day the Dream Factory Woke Up," *Life*, 27 Feb. 1970, 40.

12. Ibid., 46.

13. Personal interview, 28 May 1998.

14. Nancy Collins, "Stanley Jaffe—With Respect to His Job," *Women's Wear Daily*, 7 Apr. 1976, 34.

15. Wayne Warga, "Stanley Jaffe: Paramount Risk Jockey," *Los Angeles Times*, 2 Jan. 1971, 20.

16. Evans, *Kid*, 239.

17. Personal interview, 23 Apr. 1998.

18. *Wall Street Journal*, 25 June 1970, 23.

19. It was probably the same in 1990 after the release of *The Godfather Part III*, in which SGI (Immobiliare) is the name of the company that Michael Corleone (Al Pacino) wants to take over. One doubts that many moviegoers or studio executives made the connection between "Immobiliare" and the company that was supposed to buy half of the Paramount lot twenty years earlier, although the screenwriters, Mario Puzo and Francis Coppola, must have hoped some would.

Chapter 5

1. David N. Eldridge, "'Dear Owen': The CIA, Luigi Luraschi, and Hollywood, 1953," *Historical Journal of Film, Radio, and Television* 20, 2 (June 2000): 149–96.

2. *Hollywood Reporter*, 19 Oct. 1961, 4.

3. *Daily Variety*, 12 May 1965, 84–85.

4. Marie Brenner, "Dino De Laurentiis Conquers America," *New York Magazine*, 21 Oct. 1974, 52.

5. Peter Bart, "The Mob, the Movies and Me," *GQ* (June 1997): 78.

6. Evans, *Kid*, 224.

7. Peter Biskind, *The Godfather Companion: Everything You Always Wanted to Know about All Three Godfather Movies* (New York: Harper Perennial, 1990), 9.

8. Michael Sragow, "Godfatherhood," *New Yorker*, 24 Mar. 1997, 45.

9. According to Harlan Lebo, *The Godfather Legacy* (New York: Simon & Schuster/Fireside, 1997), 216, Coppola envisioned a film "about a classic noble family . . . that could be about kings in ancient Greece."

10. Biskind, *Godfather Companion,* 69. Brando was also to get a percentage of the gross, which he may never have received; see Jon Lewis, "If History Has Taught Us Anything . . . Francis Coppola, Paramount Studios, and *The Godfather* Parts I, II, and III" in *Francis Ford Coppola's The Godfather Trilogy* (New York: Cambridge Univ. Press, 2000), 53, n. 20.

11. Ibid., 19. For an insightful study of Italianicity in the film, see Vera Dika, "The Representation of Ethnicity in *The Godfather*," *Godfather Trilogy*, 78–108.

12. Ibid., 52–53.

13. Mary Murphy, "The King Kong Papers: Ten Days in Dino's Palm," *New West*, 20 Dec. 1976, 32.

14. The untitled Oct. 1972 statement, stamped "From the Collection of Charles Champlin [former *Los Angeles Times* critic]," is in the Dino De Laurentiis file, CMPS.

15. Ibid., 5.

16. *Time*, 25 Sept. 1964, 92.

17. Nina Munk, "The Sindona Connection," *Forbes*, 16 Aug. 1993, 92.

18. Nick Tosches, *Power on Earth* (New York: Arbor House, 1986), 178.

19. Nick Tosches, "The Man Who Kept the Secrets," *Vanity Fair* (Apr. 1997): 178.

20. Evans, *Kid*, 228–30.

21. Dan Moldea, *Dark Victory: Ronald Reagan, MCA and the Mob* (New York: Viking, 1986), 286.

22. Tosches, *Power*, 80.

23. Ibid., 79.

24. Ibid., 113.

25. *Variety*, 28 Nov. 1979, 1+. This article summarizes the other irregularities discussed previously.

26. Tosches, *Power*, 2.

Chapter 6

1. *Screen International*, 13 Nov. 1991, 14.

2. Bernard F. Dick, ed., *Dark Victory*, Wisconsin/Warner Bros. Screenplay Series (Madison: Univ. of Wisconsin Press, 1981), 18.

3. Peter Bart, *Fade Out: The Calamitous Final Days of MGM* (New York: William Morrow, 1990), 18–19.

4. Peter Biskind, *Easy Riders, Raging Bulls: How the Sex-Drugs-and Rock 'n' Roll Generation Saved Hollywood* (New York: Simon & Schuster, 1998), 212.

5. Jon Lewis, *Whom God Wishes to Destroy: Francis Coppola and the New Hollywood* (Durham, N.C.: Duke Univ. Press, 1997), 16.

6. Biskind, *Easy Riders*, 208.

7. Ibid., 207. Yablans spoke differently to the press, calling the Company "a familial relationship"; see Jon Lewis, "If History Has Taught Us Anything," *Godfather Trilogy*, 37.

8. On the formation of Liberty, see Joseph McBride, *Frank Capra: The Catastrophe of Success* (New York: Simon & Schuster, 1992), 504–34.

9. Ibid., 508.

10. Personal Interview with Billy Wilder, 11 June 1976.

11. Bart, *Fade Out*, 20.

12. Bart interview, 28 May 1998. See also Bart, *Fade Out*, 20.

13. For the film's chronology, see Biskind, *Godfather Companion*, 98–99.

14. Bill Higgins, "Is There a Hex on Prexies?" *Variety*, 5–11 Apr. 1999, 9.

15. Wilder interview.

16. George Mair, *The Barry Diller Story: The Life and Times of America's Greatest Entertainment Mogul* (New York: John Wiley, 1997), 12–13.

17. Ibid., 47.

18. Evans, *Kid*, 177.

19. Although Eisner has written his own autobiography, *Work in Progress*, in collaboration with Tony Schwartz (New York: Random House, 1998), Kim Masters, *The Keys to the Kingdom: How Michael Eisner Lost His Grip* (New York: William Morrow, 2000), is far more informative and revealing.

20. Charles Fleming, *High Concept: Don Simpson and the Hollywood Culture of Excess* (New York: Doubleday, 1998), 30.

21. Steven Ginsberg, "Murphy-Par Deal 'Unlike Any Made by Studio in 10 Years,'" *Variety*, 10 Dec. 1982, 1.

22. "Jerry Bruckheimer: Producer of the Year Issue," *Hollywood Reporter* (Mar. 1999): 62.

23. Julie Salamon, "Jeffrey Katzenberg: Disney's New Mogul," *Wall Street Journal*, 12 May 1987, 32.

24. Peter Bayer, "Katzenberg's Seven-Year Itch," *Vanity Fair* (Nov. 1991): 146.

25. For the history and influence of *Star Trek*, see Herbert F. Solow and Robert H. Justman, *Inside Star Trek: The Real Story* (New York: Pocket Books, 1996); and, for succinctness, Richard Zoglin, "Trekking Onward," *Time*, 28 Nov. 1994, 72–79.

26. Justin Wyatt, *High Concept: Movies and Marketing in Hollywood* (Austin: Univ. of Texas Press, 1994), 149–51.

27. Dawn Steel, *They Can Kill You ... But They Can't Eat You: Lessons from the Front* (New York: Pocket Books, 1993), 145.

28. Fleming, *High Concept*, 14, 29.

29. Lillian Hellman, *An Unfinished Woman: A Memoir* (New York: Bantam, 1970), 48.

30. Eisner, *Work in Progress*, 91.

31. "How Paramount Keeps Churning Out Winners," *Business Week*, 11 June 1984, 51.

32. Fleming, *High Concept,* 30.

33. Ibid.

34. Ibid., 192–93.

35. Wyatt, *High Concept*, 13.

36. Fleming, *High Concept*, 192.

37. Ben Stein, "A Deal to Remember," *New West* (Aug. 1981): 107–8; Joseph McBride, *Steven Spielberg: A Biography* (New York: Simon & Schuster, 1997), 310–11.

38. Bart interview.

Chapter 7

1. *New York Times*, 24 July 1977, 1+; 25 July, 1+; 26 July, 1+.

2. Richard Lenzer, "Par's Davis: Maverick Who Bucks the Status Quo," *Hollywood Reporter*, 12 June 1989, 21.

3. Figures come from Paul Richter, "Thinking Big," *Los Angeles Times*, 6 June 1989, business sec., 1, and *A Comparative Analysis of Selected Entertainment and Media Companies* (New York: Columbia Pictures Industries Financial Services, 1985), s.v. "Paramount."

4. Mair, *Barry Diller Story*, 93.

5. David Blum, "Odd Man In," *Vanity Fair* (July 1983): 76.

6. Hy Hollinger, "Davis' Course for G & W," *Variety*, 6 June 1984, 32.

7. Mair, *Barry Diller Story,* 96.

8. *Hollywood Reporter*, 28 Jan. 1983, 44.

9. Personal interview, 26 May 1998.

10. The history of the lawsuit is recounted at inordinate length in Pierce O'Donnell and Dennis McDougal, *Fatal Subtraction: The Inside Story of Buchwald vs. Paramount* (New York: Doubleday, 1992).

11. For the breakdown, see *Hollywood Reporter,* 24 Aug. 1992, 18.

12. Steel, *They Can Kill You,* 205; on Steel's stormy relationship with Tanen, see Rachel Abramowitz, *Is That a Gun in Your Pocket? Women's Experience of Power in Hollywood* (New York: Random House, 2000), 315–19.

Chapter 8

1. *Vogue* (July 1984): 234.

2. Joshua Hammer, "The Fall of Frank Mancuso," *Newsweek,* 6 May 1991, 66–68.

3. On Steve Ross's extraordinary life, see Connie Bruck, *The Master of the Game* (New York: Simon & Schuster, 1994).

4. L.J. Davis, "The Office Boy," *Buzz* (Oct. 1993): 77.

5. For the details, see Bruck, *Master,* 272–76.

6. *Variety,* 22 May 1991, 1.

7. Hammer, "Fall," 68.

8. Rod Lurie, "Are They Killing Paramount?" *Los Angeles Magazine* (July 1993): 58.

9. Bernard Weinraub, "Good Job! Here's Your Mercedes," *New York Times,* 12 July 1993, B1.

10. Ibid., B2.

11. On Redstone's life and career, see Ken Auletta, "Redstone's Secret Weapon," *New Yorker,* 16 Jan. 1995, 47–63; Judith Newman, "Fort Sumner," *Vanity Fair* (Nov. 1999): 248+.

12. Kerkorian's role in the rape of MGM is vividly told by Peter Bart in *Fade Out,* especially pp. 99–107.

13. John Cassidy, "Kirk's Enterprise," *New Yorker,* 11 Dec. 1995, 44–53, contains a good summary of the MGM-UA merger and its later uncoupling; see also Stephen Prince, *A New Pot of Gold: Hollywood under the Electronic Rainbow* (New York: Scribner's, 2000), 71–74.

14. Wayne Overbeck, *Major Principles of Media Law* (New York: Harcourt, 1999), 467–68.

15. Auletta, "Redstone's Secret Weapon," 46.

16. Calvin Sims, "'Synergy': The Unspoken Word," *New York Times,* 5 Oct. 1993, D1.

17. "In Hollywood, A Nouveau Royalty Made by Mergers," *New York Times,* 1 Mar. 1991, F5.

18. Ken Auletta, "Barry Diller's Search for the Future," *New Yorker,* 22 Feb. 1993, 49.

19. Mair, *Barry Diller Story*, 247.

20. *Hollywood Reporter*, 14 Sept. 1993, 65.

21. *Time*, 28 Feb. 1994, 50.

22. *Variety*, 22–28 Jan. 1996, 1.

23. *Variety*, 28 Oct.–2 Nov. 1996, 6.

24. *Hollywood Reporter*, 21–27 Oct. 1997, 85.

25. *New Yorker*, 23 Mar. 1998, 31–32; *Hollywood Reporter*, 23–25 Oct. 1998, 53.

26. *Hollywood Reporter*, 22 Jan. 1998, 45.

27. *Time*, 3 Aug. 1998, 48–49.

28. *Variety*, 13–19 Sept. 1999, 5.

29. *The Record*, 8 Sept. 1999, B2.

30. *New York Times*, 14 Nov. 1999, sec. 3, 12.

31. In April 2001 the FCC amended its joint ownership policy to allow Viacom to own both UPN and CBS.

Epilogue

1. David Cook, *Lost Illusions: American Cinema in the Shadow of Watergate and Vietnam, 1970–1979* (New York: Scribner's, 2000), 20; Prince, *New Pot of Gold*, 61.

Index